Lecture Notes in Computer Scie

Commenced Publication in 1973
Founding and Former Series Editors:
Gerhard Goos, Juris Hartmanis, and Jan van Leeuwen

Reinhard Gotzhein   Rick Reed (Eds.)

System Analysis
and Modeling:
Language Profiles

5th International Workshop, SAM 2006
Kaiserslautern, Germany, May 31 - June 2, 2006
Revised Selected Papers

 Springer

Volume Editors

Reinhard Gotzhein
University of Kaiserslautern
D-67653 Kaiserslautern, Germany
E-mail: gotzhein@informatik.uni-kl.de

Rick Reed
Telecommunications Software Engineering Limited
Cumbria LA23 2DL, United Kingdom
E-mail: rickreed@tseng.co.uk

After the 4th SAM Workshop, SAM 2004: System Analysis and Modeling, it was
agreed to change the series title and acronym SAM from "SDL and MSC."
Other LNCS volumes for the SAM workshop series are:
LNCS 3319 Systems Analysis and Modeling, SAM 2004
LNCS 2599 Telecommunications and beyond: The Broader Applicability of SDL
and MSC, SAM 2002

Library of Congress Control Number: 2006938015

CR Subject Classification (1998): C.2, D.2, D.3, F.3, C.3, H.4

LNCS Sublibrary: SL 5 – Computer Communication Networks and Telecommunications

ISSN   0302-9743
ISBN-10   3-540-68371-2 Springer Berlin Heidelberg New York
ISBN-13   978-3-540-68371-1 Springer Berlin Heidelberg New York

Springer is a part of Springer Science+Business Media

springer.com

© Springer-Verlag Berlin Heidelberg 2006

Typesetting: Camera-ready by author, data conversion by Scientific Publishing Services, Chennai, India
Printed on acid-free paper   SPIN: 11951148   06/3142   5 4 3 2 1 0

Preface

The workshop on System Analysis and Modeling (SAM), held every two years, provides an open arena for participants from academia and industry to present and discuss the most recent innovations, trends, experiences, and concerns in the field of the ITU Specification and Description Language (SDL-2000), Message Sequence Charts (MSC-2000), and related languages such as UML, ASN.1, eODL, TTCN, and URN. It addresses modeling, specification, and analysis of distributed systems, communication systems, and real-time systems.

The 2006 SAM workshop (SAM 2006) was held at the University of Kaiserslautern, Germany, from May 31 to June 2, 2006 (`http://sam06.informatik.uni-kl.de/`). It was co-organized by the University of Kaiserslautern, the SDL Forum Society, and the International Telecommunication Union (ITU-T). Avaya Labs and Telelogic AB sponsored SAM 2006. The workshop was attended by 42 participants from 8 countries in Europe, North America, and Asia, from academia and industry.

The program consisted of ten sessions, and featured exhibits and posters. The Program Committee selected 17 papers based on a formal review for presentation and (subject to review) possible post-event publication. To emphasize the workshop character, an explicit discussion round prepared and moderated by the session chair was included in each session. After post-workshop revisions of the papers under the guidance of experienced shepherds taking into account workshop feedback, a second reviewing round took place, which led to the selection of 14 papers for publication in this volume of *Lecture Notes in Computer Science.*

A special focus of SAM 2006 was on *language profiles*, as reflected in the title of this volume. While design languages are getting richer, there is a strong interest of tool providers and users of keeping them lean, and even of tailoring them to a particular application domain. In standardization, this trend is reflected by increasing the flexibility of language definitions, and by the concept of *language profile*. In UML, for instance, it is possible to reduce and constrain the metamodel defining the UML syntax, and to specialize language constructs. In this volume, there are four papers on language profiles:

- The paper by Constantin Werner, Sebastian Kraatz, and Dieter Hogrefe presents an approach to define a domain-specific UML language profile for communicating systems. They start with a subset of UML, add static semantic constraints, and then provide a mapping to SDL-2000. This way, a formal semantics is given to the profile. The paper contributes to Z.109, which defines a UML profile for SDL.
- The paper by Joachim Fischer, Andreas Prinz, Markus Scheidgen, and Merete Tveit defines a UML profile for eODL, the extended Object Definition Language of the ITU. This again is an example of how semantics can be given to a subset of UML. Furthermore, the UML profile gives a graphical notation to eODL.

- The paper by Abdelouahed Gherbi and Ferhat Khendek proposes an extension of a UML language profile for schedulability, performance, and time published by the OMG. The extension captures multicast communication.
- The paper by Rüdiger Grammes introduces SDL language profiles as well-defined subsets of SDL that have a formal syntax and semantics. Based on the existing semantics of SDL, which is defined using Abstract State Machines, a formalized approach to automatically derive the semantics for given SDL profiles is devised. This lays important foundations for a rigorous treatment of language profiles.

Although most of the ITU languages (ASN.1, MSC, SDL, TTCN) have existed for more than a decade, the languages and their use are still evolving as the application domains are changing. For telecommunications, there is currently activity in the services layers of the network, so that service layering and the uses of XML in service descriptions are of interest. The papers in the workshop treating subjects such as scenario merging, timed sequence charts and service role composition may therefore see application in the development of future products. Of course, effective development requires good tool support, and here the trend is towards basing tools on MOF meta-models and merging UML and support for languages like MSC and SDL, as seen in the papers in this volume. In the case of MSC, there is very little to differentiate MSC from the sequence diagrams of UML, and it is possible to foresee a single joint OMG/ITU profile for the charts/diagrams in the future. In the case of SDL, to build executable models, many of the issues left open in UML (semantic variation points) for behavior descriptions have to be closed to get a well-defined behavior. There is a trend (at least for real-time applications) to use the SDL semantics for state machine diagrams, and there is renewed interest in SDL. At the time of writing, proposals are being considered for revising the SDL language to reflect some of these trends including the use of UML object modeling with implementation in SDL.

The 2006 SAM workshop was a success, thanks to the dedicated work of many people involved in the event: the local organization team, the Program Committee, the reviewers, speakers, session chairs, exhibitors, and participants. A volume such as this could not, of course, exist without the contributions of the authors who are thanked for their work. We are especially grateful for the sponsorship of Avaya Labs and Telelogic AB, and the support of the University of Kaiserslautern. Finally, we hope you will enjoy reading our selection of papers in this book and would like to see you at a future SDL Forum Society event (see www.sdl-forum.org).

October 2006   Reinhard Gotzhein
                                                                  Rick Reed

Organization

Organization Committee

Workshop Chair

Reinhard Gotzhein (University of Kaiserslautern, Germany)

SDL Forum Society

Chairman: Rick Reed (TSE Ltd., UK)
Treasurer: Martin von Löwis (Hasso-Plattner-Institut Potsdam, Germany)
Secretary: Andreas Prinz (Agder University College, Norway)

ITU-T

B. Georges Sebek (TSB Counsellor to Study Group 17, Switzerland)

Local Organization

Barbara Erlewein (University of Kaiserslautern, Germany)
Ingmar Fliege (University of Kaiserslautern, Germany)
Alexander Geraldy (University of Kaiserslautern, Germany)
Rüdiger Grammes (University of Kaiserslautern, Germany)
Christian Webel (University of Kaiserslautern, Germany)

Program Committee

Daniel Amyot (University of Ottawa, Canada)
Rolv Bræk (Norwegian University of Science and Technology, Norway)
Olivier Dubuisson (France Telecom R&D, France)
Anders Ek (Telelogic AB, Sweden)
Joachim Fischer (Humboldt-Universität zu Berlin, Germany)
Emmanuel Gaudin (PragmaDev, France)
Birgit Geppert (Avaya Labs, USA)
Uwe Glässer (Simon Fraser University, Canada)
Reinhard Gotzhein (University of Kaiserslautern, Germany)
Jens Grabowski (University of Göttingen, Germany)
Susanne Graf (Verimag, France)
Øystein Haugen (University of Oslo, Norway)
Loïc Hélouët (INRIA Rennes, France)
Dieter Hogrefe (University of Göttingen, Germany)
Eckhardt Holz (University of Potsdam, Germany)

Ferhat Khendek (Concordia University, Canada)
Martin von Löwis (Hasso-Plattner Institute, Germany)
Arve Meisingset (Telenor, Norway)
Birger Møller-Pedersen (University of Oslo, Norway)
Ostap Monkewich (NCIT, Canada)
Anders Olsen (Cinderella, Denmark)
Andreas Prinz (Agder University College, Norway)
Rick Reed (TSE Ltd. UK)
Richard Sanders (SINTEF, Norway)
Amardeo Sarma (NEC, Germany)
Ina Schieferdecker (Fraunhofer FOKUS, Germany)
Edel Sherratt (University of Wales at Aberystwyth, UK)
William Skelton (SOLINET, Germany)
Thomas Weigert (Motorola, USA)
Milan Zoric (ETSI, France)

SDL Forum Society

The SDL Forum Society is a not-for-profit organization that in addition to running the SAM Workshop:

- Runs the SDL Forum every two years between SAM Workshop years
- Is a body recognized by ITU-T as co-developing the Z.100 to Z.109 and Z.120 to Z.129 standards
- Promotes the ITU-T System Design Languages

For more information on the SDL Forum Society, see www.sdl-forum.org.

Sponsors

The organization was greatly assisted through the following sponsors:

- Avaya Labs Research, Basking Ridge, USA
- Telelogic AB, Malmö, Sweden
- University of Kaiserslautern, Kaiserslautern, Germany

Table of Contents

Language Profiles

Evolution of Development Languages

Model-Driven Development

Language Implementation

A UML Profile for Communicating Systems

Constantin Werner, Sebastian Kraatz, and Dieter Hogrefe

Telematics Group, University of Göttingen, Lotzestrasse 16-18,
37083 Göttingen, Germany
{werner, hogrefe}@cs.uni-goettingen.de, sebastian@kraatz.name

Abstract. This paper presents a UML 2 profile for communicating systems. It is driven by the experience of SDL and uses formal constraints for profile definition and mapping rules by means of OCL. It features language elements for high-level specification and description of Internet communication and signaling protocols where SDL is not optimally suited. Due to its support of several concrete notations, this profile is aligned to work with several UML 2 compliant modeling tools. In addition, an implementation by an XSLT-based mapping from UML to behavioral and structural SDL specifications is available. The intention of the paper is to present the main work done which is defining an actual profile and mapping this to SDL.

1 Introduction

The Specification and Description Language (SDL) [1] is a formal language developed and maintained by International Telecommunication Union, Telecommunication Standardization Sector (ITU-T). It is targeted at the unambiguous specification and description of the behavior of reactive and distributed systems and focusing on the object and state machine view of systems. SDL is mainly used in the design phase, where an SDL specification consists of the system architecture and the behaviors of the different processes in the system. SDL specifications can range from abstract and possibly incomplete to concrete descriptions that can be simulated and validated automatically.

Presently, the Unified Modeling Language (UML) [2] is a collection of several semi-formal standard notations and concepts for modeling software systems at different stages and views of the same system. In practice, UML is made more formal by binding semantic variations in the UML language and providing a more precise behavior either in a tool or a language profile. The lack of strong formality in non-profiled UML is beneficial at the early stages of development. In later stages of simulation, validation and implementation, UML is too imprecise to fulfill this task, for which SDL is well suited.

The goal of this work is to bridge the gap between the requirement and analysis phase, and the design phase by combining the strengths of UML and SDL. While UML features multiple viewpoints on the same system, informal object models and property model views, SDL offers detailed formalized object models with respect to execution semantics. It is argued that both languages can be combined so that the advantages of both languages could be used. This paper describes an approach for

R. Gotzhein and R. Reed (Eds.): SAM 2006, LNCS 4320, pp. 1–18, 2006.

generating full (behavioral and structural) SDL design specifications from a behavioral specification and architecture of the target system from a given UML 2[1] model. For this purpose, a light-weight extension to the metamodel of the UML is defined – a *UML profile*. This *UML Profile for Communicating Systems* (UML CS) incorporates many features from SDL. However, this profile does not simply provide a one-to-one mapping: It provides an additional set of high-level modeling concepts especially for the Internet communication protocols. Some of them are not directly supported by SDL.

In addition, a mapping implementation from a given UML model to a corresponding SDL system specification has been developed by an eXtensible Stylesheet Language Transformation (XSLT) to show feasibility and soundness of the profile's concept. The profile coupled with the XSLT mapping enables the use of a number of UML modeling tools to specify system architectures and their behavior.

The remainder of this paper is structured as follows: The following Section 2 provides an overview of the related work. Section 3 outlines the new language features which have been identified for high-level Internet communication protocol engineering where SDL is cumbersome. In Section 4, the profile design is presented with the semantic description by means of the Object Constraint Language (OCL). Section 5 briefly describes the XSLT-based mapping of a UML system specification using this profile to SDL. Section 6 provides a summary and an outlook for future work.

2 Related Work

The combined use of UML and SDL is not new. Proposals exist in other work to use UML and SDL together where the weaknesses of UML are overcome by the strengths of SDL. The current Z.109 recommendation [3] in force at the time of writing (mid-2006) imports SDL into UML by making use of the extension mechanisms available in UML. The Z.109 standard maps several UML elements to a corresponding element in SDL. Thus, the UML profile for SDL that is described in Z.109 is a specialized subset of UML. However, the current Z.109 standard is referring to the previous UML 1.3 standard. A *UML profile for SDL* [4] is being developed as a revised version of Z.109 that is based on the UML 2 standard [2]. In addition, the European Telecommunications Standards Institute (ETSI) had a work item for a *UML Profile for Communicating Systems* [5] until 2005. It became a significant contribution to the ITU-T work and is now a joint work between both organizations. The ITU-T profile describes the semantics by means of informal mapping rules which is the main difference between the ITU-T work and the profile described in this paper. Furthermore, this profile comes with an XSLT-based implementation of the mapping rules which allow to check the validity of the mapping. In [6], an approach is presented for the syntactic and semantic alignment of SDL and UML for the upcoming harmonization of both languages. But it does not present a formal, complete mapping. A mapping from UML combined with Message Sequence Charts (MSC) to SDL is presented in [7]. A mapping from standard UML elements is used to

---

[1] The profile has been developed based on the final adopted UML 2.0 Superstructure document. It is currently being updated to the new draft release of UML 2.1 [14], published in April 2006.

generate the SDL architecture and by adding the MSCs, it results in a complete SDL specification of a system. ObjecTime has introduced a methodology for describing real time systems using UML. In this approach, concepts from ROOM are introduced into UML via stereotypes. There is no attempt to map UML into SDL, but it is straightforward to map the ROOM UML elements into SDL. The approach of extending UML by stereotypes is also used for mapping SDL into UML. The Integrated Method (TIMe) uses UML for object modeling and MSC for showing the interactions between objects [12]. SDL is used to fully specify the system in terms of architecture and behavior. The TIMe method has loose mapping rules for going from UML to SDL which are based on the Z.109 recommendation. As such, the TIMe method requires designers to do the translation manually. This may lead to errors and inconsistencies.

However, the above-mentioned approaches (except for the Z.109 revision) are based on previous versions of the UML and do not use the full potentials introduced with the UML 2. Tau[2] G2 is a modeling tool which binds UML 2 semantic variation points so that UML 2 can be mapped to an execution model based on SDL. But this mapping is proprietary and based on an early metamodel of the UML 2.

3   UML Profile for Communicating Systems

SDL is the first language for specification, design and development of real time systems and in particular for telecommunication applications. The UML CS profile is mainly based on SDL. Many concepts have been re-used for this purpose: The agent concept for structuring a system design, behavioral specification using communicating extended finite state machines, data types and several object-oriented mechanisms like inheritance and encapsulation. However, it is argued that SDL is not optimally suited for current and upcoming communication protocol engineering for packet switched networks. Packet switched networks like the Internet or mobile wireless access networks demand new methodologies when modeling protocols. This includes modeling of communication path route change, robustness to message losses, roaming with handover as well as the specification of communication protocols for multi-hop overlay networks and multi-hop signaling.

3.1   Profile Features

Current developments towards all-IP networks underline the expectations that IP network communication protocol modeling will gain much more attention in the coming years. Therefore, it is necessary to add new features to the language to ease the development of IP based networks and communication protocol models. With the recent experience gained in modeling multi-hop Internet signaling protocols, some shortcomings in SDL are identified below which render some features of the Internet hard to formalize. This especially applies to robustness testing of communication protocols and to the specification and validation of multi-hop signaling protocols. By a thorough analysis of an Internet signaling protocol specification in [8], the following features have been identified to be necessary and useful to be added to UML CS

---

[2] http://www.telelogic.com/products/tau/

profile to allow exhaustive IP-based communication protocol specification and analysis while abstracting from nonrelevant details:

Randomness: For robustness analysis of communication protocols it is important to examine a communication protocol's ability to deal with occasional packet losses. It is cumbersome to model packet loss probability in the Internet by the nondeterminism features of SDL, but it can be approximately modeled using certain specific distribution functions. Unfortunately, SDL does not offer direct random functionality – except for the *none* spontaneous transition and the *any* nondeterministic decision. Some SDL tools offer a proprietary support for randomly generated values by including several libraries to SDL. Therefore, a random function is introduced to the UML CS profile which allows receiving pseudo-randomized values. Random operation calls are currently mapped to SDL by using tool specific library functions.

Input from/via: While SDL provides explicit addressing of signals for output, there is no corresponding construct for the reception of a signal available in SDL. The reception of a signal via a specific gate cannot be constrained. The reception of a signal from a specific process is possible if the SDL state machine variable *sender* is evaluated. This variable is updated when signal has been consumed with the process id of the process which has sent the signal. A modified signal receive event trigger is introduced into this profile with the optional attributes *from* and *via*. A signal can only trigger a transition if the *process identification* matches the sender or the signal is received on a specific port. Notice that the sender's address or port is evaluated before the signal is consumed while evaluating the sender variable is only possible after consumption of the signal. This is helpful if only ports (network interfaces) are relevant for message passing or addressing. One might think of a network bridge where it is only necessary to know on which side the message has been received from. The *input from/via* cannot be mapped to SDL while preserving the semantics. However, as an imperfect work-around, it is currently mapped to a signal input with a following decision that may discard the signal and return to the previous state if the consumed signal does not originate from the specified agent or gate.

Dynamic ports: Recent studies in the modeling and robustness analysis of multi-hop Internet signaling protocols have shown that SDL is not well suited to create certain network topologies, e.g. [8,9]. IP network topologies require the free placement and interconnection of router nodes in-between the signaling path. Multiple routes from the network initiator downstream to the network recipient are necessary for the study of the robustness of signaling protocols. Such a model has already been developed in [8] where considerable efforts have been undertaken to circumvent the shortcomings of SDL. To create multiple hop network topologies, a typed intermediate node (e.g. a router) is required. In SDL, a typed agent has predefined gates which enforce matching connections to other agents. This limits the amount of network topologies which can be created without creating dummy instances of agents. Dynamic ports allow agents to specify their amount varying from instance to instance. The mapping to SDL creates a new agent type for each new amount of attached dynamic ports to an agent instance. Each dynamic port instance (addressed by an index) is substituted by an arbitrary gate name. In particular, multiple dynamic ports connected to the same agent can lead to a considerable high amount of different agent types with different number of defined gates.

Soft States: During the last decade, a group of protocols have been designed using soft state for state maintenance. In contrast to hard state, a soft state itself expires if no periodical refreshes are received. Soft state protocols are expected to have lower protocol complexity in state maintenance operations especially with extreme network situations. Examples of soft state based Internet protocols are the Resource Reservation Protocol (RSVP), Next Steps in Signaling (NSIS) suite, and Session Initiation Protocol (SIP). Because researchers argue that soft state protocols are a highly attractive concept for Internet communication and signaling protocols, it has been decided to add soft state management concepts to this profile. Soft states can be defined using timers or state types with context parameters in SDL-2000. Nevertheless, a more native and intuitive integration with a sufficient high-level view which abstracts from unnecessary details will increase the acceptance of this profile for Internet communication protocol modeling. Instead, this allows a direct mapping from UML CS to SDL using equivalent constructs with states and timers. Soft states are mapped to states in SDL with an implicitly defined and initialized timer. If the state is re-entered, all defined timers for this state are re-started. As soft states may depend on multiple concurrent timers, the appropriate amount of required timers is determined beforehand.

Besides of the new features discussed, several complex language features of SDL-2000 are deliberately not supported by the profile (currently). In particular, this includes exceptions, templates (context parameters), state aggregation, state types and virtual types. One reason for this is one of the profile's design goals. That is – in spite that it is based on clarity and formal semantics of SDL – to enable mappings to other formal description techniques. As it is not sure whether these languages support exceptions, state types and other SDL constructs, these complex language features are currently left out. It is argued that they can also be substituted by core language features, for instance the replacement of exceptions by special dedicated signals.

3.2 Concept of the Profile

The profile provides structural modeling elements similar to SDL: package, system, block and process agents. System design decomposition is supported by defining nested agents within another agent. A block or process can be contained within another system or block. A process can only be contained within another process. Each of the agents may define constants, signals and operation while agent variables and timers may only be defined in a process. UML visibility modifiers (public, package, protected, private) are available and are checked by constraints prior to a mapping to SDL. Virtuality of types is currently not supported; that is, object entities (such as operations) cannot be overwritten or overloaded. The composite structure instantiates the agents including multiplicities and specifies the communication paths by means of connectors (channels) and interfaces for signals and remote procedure calls. For each agent, a composite structure is defined that specifies the interaction points (ports) between all nested agents and their environment. Single generalization is supported for all types, however, redefinition is not allowed. It is only allowed to define new, additional properties for a type.

Processes are agents modeled by active classes which execute a defined behavior after instantiation. The behavior of processes is described by means of state machines.

All other behavior, such as methods and transition effects, can either be defined by state machines or activities. As an exception, data type operators can only be defined by activities because in UML CS, an activity must not wait for triggers. As the concrete representation can vary in modeling tools, the profile supports describing behavior via stereotyped activities, textual notation, referenced state machines or nested activities associated to a state machine transition.

Figure 1 shows a simple UML CS process *ppong*. The behavior of the process (the classifierBehavior) is defined by the state machine *pingpong*. The state machine is associated with the activity *sendSig1* through the *effect* of the first transition. The signal *sig1* is defined in the class diagram of the process *ppong*. When the state machine initializes, it calls the activity *sendSig1*. This activity sends the signal *sig1* to an unspecified target, finishes its execution and returns to its caller. The state machine enters the state *waitResp*. Then it waits for the trigger *sig1*, which is raised by a signal reception event of sig1 (sent from another process not shown here). If this trigger is raised, the state machine terminates. This process can be successfully mapped to an equivalent SDL description. Notice that the control flow within a state machine is defined by a *transition*, while in an activity there is a *controlFlow* stereotype.

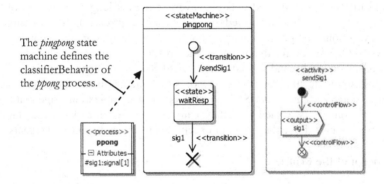

Fig. 1. Simple UML CS Process (left), its behavior definition by a state machine (center) and the invoked activity (right)

The *controlFlow* stereotype is explicitly required to constrain any attempts to define concurrency which is a capability of UML activities. However, concurrency within a UML CS state machine (and its invoked activities) is not supported.

Besides the provision of elements for specifying and describing structure and behavior of a system, the profile also contains stereotypes for defining data types with their signature, implementation (semantics) and inheritance for both value and object types. Predefined SDL data types like *Natural* and *Character* are provided as well as the composite types *struct* and *union* (the SDL choice).

3.3   Applying the UML Profiling Mechanism

The primary design goal of this profile is to include many features from SDL-2000 but to omit language elements that are rarely used or very complex to use. This profile intends to be applicable to several UML tools that support the UML 2 with compliance level 3 and diagram storage in XMI 2.1 [13]. This is not an easy task as UML only specifies the abstract syntax and only gives recommendations for concrete notational style. As most tools deviate in the implementation of the concrete syntax, this profile proposes several alternative graphical, textual and architectural notations. In summary, this profile features a combination of SDL, some extension points for enabling a mapping to other formal description techniques and high-level language concepts for communication protocol engineering for the Internet with UML 2 modeling tools.

The profile comprises about 50 stereotypes and is available for download at [10]. A stereotype extends a metaclass of the UML metamodel. It defines a name, possibly attributes (*tag definition*), constraints and concretizes the syntax and semantics.

The following Table 1 gives an example of a stereotype definition extending the UML metaclass *Signal*.

Table 1. Stereotype Definition of a «signal»

UML NODE TYPE	*UML NOTATION*	*REFERENCE*
Signal	<<signal>> **sampleSignal**	13.3.23 Signal

UML CS STEREOTYPE	*UML METACLASS*	*TAGGED VALUES*
«signal»	Signal (from Communications)	priority: Integer = 0 sender: Pid

OCL CONSTRAINTS	*INFORMAL CONSTRAINTS*

context Signal
 inv: self.general->size()<=1
 inv: self.extension_signal.priority>=0 and
        self.extension_signal.priority<256
 inv: self.ownedOperation->isEmpty()
 inv: self.extension_signal.
        sender.isReadOnly
	The optional *priority* attribute defines a possible precedence of this signal. A higher value specifies a higher priority.
	 The tagged value *sender* represents the sender process identification that has executed the output action sending this signal.

This stereotype *signal* recommends a concrete notation for this model element, which is shown in the cell labeled *UML Notation*. It adds some tag definition and tagged values shown in the cell labeled *Tagged Values*: *priority* which is of type Integer and a *sender* which is of type *Pid* (this data type is defined within the profile). In addition, constraints are defined that give some semantic restrictions on this model element, shown in the cell *OCL Constraints*. Multiple inheritance is not supported for a *signal*. The specified *priority* value must be specified within the (arbitrarily) chosen range of 0 to 255. The tag definition *sender* is set as being read only and can be evaluated in the receiving process. In addition, some *Informal Constraints* are given that explain some of the constraints in English language for clarity. In summary, the development process of the profile comprises the following steps:

- Analysis of SDL with respect to shortcomings for communication protocol engineering in packet switched networks,
- Definition of a UML profile the unambiguous specification and description of Internet protocols,
- Providing a semantics by specifying a mapping to SDL-2000 by means of OCL,
- Providing a proof-of-concept implementation mapping to SDL.

4 Defining the Semantics of UML CS

The semantics of the UML CS profile is specified by means of the Object Constraint Language (OCL) [11]. The OCL is a side-effect free, formal specification language built on simple set theory and predicate logic especially designed to specify constraint expressions easily. The stereotypes of the UML profile define invariant constraints that add static semantics to the metamodel. Furthermore, a translational semantics is given by the specification of a translational mapping to SDL-2000: OCL constraints are used to validate that the mapping from UML CS models to SDL-2000 has been done so that it conforms to the semantics. This formalism is very beneficial for the tool-supported validation of a correct mapping. In the following, the concept of OCL-based mapping is explained. Due to limited space, not all details of the mapping and type conversion can be described.

During the SDL-2000 compilation process, a SDL specification is successively transformed into an abstract syntax tree, namely AS1 defined in Z.100 main body. This AS1 is the result of parsing and checking by well-formed conditions of the SDL program. AS1 abstracts away from additional but non-essential expressions like delimiters, keywords, graphical elements, spaces and so on, focusing only on the relevant information. Furthermore, complex language constructs are decomposed into core concepts.

4.1 Overview

The assumption is that a UML model is actually mapped to SDL. The compilation of this SDL model results in an (internal) abstract syntax tree according to the definition in Z.100. To validate that the mapping from UML to SDL is correct, the model defined in the UML repository and the system defined in the AS1 of SDL are compared and cross-checked if they fulfill and match specific properties. This comparison must always evaluate that the given constraints are fulfilled. Otherwise, the mapping is considered invalid. There are two prerequisites for such a comparison: First, for the comparison of values, both data types must be type compatible. Therefore, before constraints can be applied between both models, the types have to be aligned first. Second, each composite object in both the UML repository and the AS1 tree must be uniquely addressable – in other words, repository and syntax tree must be navigable. For a specification language, the obvious choice for UML-based models is OCL as it is part of the UML standard. OCL supports navigation of the UML metamodel. Therefore, the abstract grammar has to be mapped to a MOF-compliant metamodel.

The following Figure 2 pictorially outlines the mapping concept: As above-mentioned, it is assumed that there exists an actual mapping function *Mapping* from UML to AS1 and a type conversion from AS1 to MOF data types. After the mapping of an UML element, the correct mapping is verified by post-constraints specified in OCL. Therefore, the function *Mapping* maps a UML model (e.g. given in XMI representation) to a SDL system. It is not defined how this is achieved concretely. The post-constraints only check whether both composite objects (the object in the UML repository and the object in the AS1) are equivalent after the mapping or not. OCL is a declarative language and cannot alter the system state.

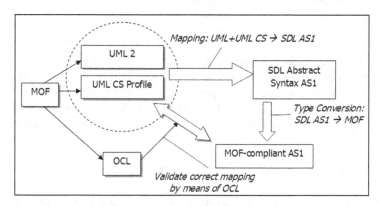

Fig. 2. Mapping Specification by OCL

There are OCL expressions specified that constrain the invariant variables or associations of the UML elements that apply to the stereotyped classes.

To specify the mapping by the function *Mapping*, only the post-operation conditions of the mapping are shown. For clarity, the SDL mapping constraints relate to the abstract syntax (abstract grammar) definition of SDL and the UML stereotypes attributes and associations. In addition, the OCL constraints only apply if a UML model is mapped that has the required stereotype applied. All constraints given must be preceded by an implication expression as the constraint is always in the context of the *Mapping* function. For example, the correct OCL constraint expression for the name attribute mapping for the state class stereotyped with «state» is the following

> *context Mapping(sdl: SDL-specification, uml: Classifier, co: NamedElement, e: NamedElement)*
> *post: isStereotypedBy(e, state) implies co.name=e.name*

where *sdl* is the root object of the SDL specification, *uml* is the system or package class object, *co* is the composite object of the SDL AS1 tree that is to be validated against the Element *e* defined within the *uml* Classifier. The definition of the operation *isStereotypedBy* is

> *isStereotypedBy(e: Element, s: Stereotype) : Boolean;*
> *post: result = e.extension->exists(e | e.type=s)*

As this applies to all following mapping rules, the context and post-constraint part has been omitted in all constraints. The abstract syntax of SDL can be regarded as a named composite object or tree defining a set of sub-components.

4.2 Type Mapping from SDL AS1 to MOF

For each core concept of SDL, the SDL AS1 defines a composite object. For example, the abstract syntax for *Channel-path* is:

> *Channel-path   ::   Originating-gate*
> *Destination-gate*
> *Signal-identifier-set*

This defines the domain for the composite object (a tree) named *Channel-path*. This object consists of three sub components, which address two gates and a set of signal identifiers. This defines the signals that can be conveyed between the two gates. These components in turn might be trees. An object might also be of some elementary (non-composite) domains: non-negative Integers (Nat), quotations, and tokens:

> *Number-of-instances   ::   Nat [Nat]*

Number-of-instances denotes a composite domain containing one mandatory natural (Nat) value and one optional natural ([Nat]) denoting respectively the initial number and the optional maximum number of instances. A Nat is mapped to a non-negative Integer value.

> *convert: Nat -> Integer*
> *context convert(nat: Nat) : Integer*
> *post: result >=0*

Quotation objects are represented as any bold face sequence of uppercase letters and digits.

> *Channel-definition   ::   Channel-name*
> *[NODELAY]*
> *Channel-path-set*

A channel may be delaying or not. This is denoted by an optional quotation NODELAY. This quotation is mapped to a String that is associated with the respective compound object. If no composite object is defined in the AS, the name of the String is constructed with the first name of its containing composite object name with suffix *-kind*. For example, the name of the String containing the Quotation object *NODELAY* for a *Channel-definition* would be *Channel-kind*.

> *convert: Quotation -> String*

Token denotes the domain of tokens. This domain can be considered to consist of a potentially infinite set of distinct atomic objects for which no representation is required.

> *Name   ::   Token*

A name consists of an atomic object such that any Name can be distinguished from any other name. A Token is mapped to a String.

> *convert: Token -> String*

The abstract syntax uses the postfix operator *-set* yielding a set (unordered collection of distinct objects).

> *Agent-graph   ::   Agent-start-node State-node-set*

In this example, an Agent-graph consists of an Agent-start-node and a set of State-nodes. A *–set* of the abstract syntax is mapped to a Set.

> *convert: -set -> Set*

UML Constraints are specified by means of a ValueSpecification. The ValueSpecification of a constraint is mapped to a String.

> *convert: Constraint -> String*
> *context convert(c: Constraint): String*
> *post: result = c.specification.stringValue()*

During translation from the concrete SDL syntax to an executable system, there are several transformation steps applied (the concrete steps are not described here; it is referred to the appendices of Z.100 [1]). As noted, the abstract syntax AS1 is a composite object tree and defines an *SDL-specification* as root. From this, the tree is traversed by means of the defined objects within the system description.

It is assumed that each object within this tree can be constrained by means of OCL. This is pictorially presented in Figure 3. Dotted lines mean (implicit) type conversion. Underlined expressions denote OCL constraint specifications applied to the object tree. The given constraints in Figure 3 are only exemplary. The type mapping specification has been described in the previous section, which provides a mapping to OCL compliant types. However, a concrete mapping is not provided; instead, it is assumed that such a mapping is already available so that all constraint qualifiers are valid (if the type compliance would fail, none of the constraint qualifiers is satisfied and the mapping is considered invalid).

The type mapping is not only being provided on leaf, elementary objects. Objects defining a set are implicitly mapped to an OCL Set, which is shown at the *Package-definition-set* object in Figure 3. The Set itself contains the set of *Package-definitions*, which itself decomposes into several objects.

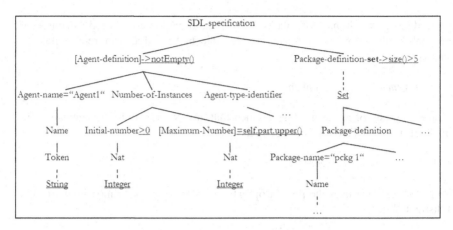

Fig. 3. OCL Constraints on AS1 Composite Object Tree

If the resolution path down to the tree leaf is unambiguous, it is assumed that derived attributes with appropriate types are available. For instance, although the *Agent-name* is resolved into a *Token*, it is assumed that this is also done implicitly at parent objects. Therefore, the correct navigation through such a composite tree would be *Agent-name.Name.Token="Agent1"*. However, the shorthand notation *Agent-name="Agent1"* is also allowed. Nevertheless, OCL constraints require some navigation on the composite objects. This is briefly illustrated in the following.

4.3   Example - Mapping the SDL AS1 for Channel Definition to MOF

The abstract grammar of a channel definition in Z.100 main body is

Channel-definition	::	*Channel-name*
		[NODELAY]
		Channel-path-set
Channel-path	::	*Originating-gate*
		Destination-gate
		Signal-identifier-set
Originating-gate	=	*Gate-identifier*
Destination-gate	=	*Gate-identifier*
Gate-identifier	=	*Identifier*
Channel-name	=	*Name*

The mapping should map the following excerpt of the composite object tree of the AS1 to a metamodel that is type compatible and navigable. This abstract grammar is mapped to a metamodel shown in Figure 4.

Note that this is only an excerpt, as the associations of the metaclass *Qualifier* are not shown. In this example, *-set* is mapped to multiplicities 1..2 as specified by the constraints written in the associated abstract grammar text. If a *-set* is unconstrained, its multiplicities are 0..*. Optional components are mapped to multiplicities 0..1.

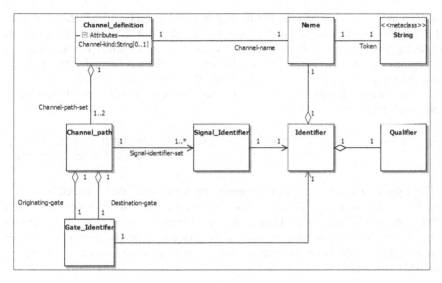

Fig. 4. Abstract Grammar mapped to Metamodel

However, quotation objects like *NODELAY* are currently mapped to a *quotation* enumeration array with 0..* multiplicity. It is assumed that all quotations are part of this array. If the quotation does not apply (e.g. a channel that does not have the quotation NODELAY), the quotation attribute is empty.

Additionally, it is presumed that derived attributes are available in each class object, e.g. the excerpted abstract syntax for the channel name is

Channel-definition	*::*	*Channel-name*
Channel-name	*=*	*Name*
Name	*::*	*Token*

To verify if the Channel-name is given, the correct navigation would be *Channel-definition::Channel-name.Name.Token<>""*. However, as the composite object tree resolution path is unique and unambiguous, the expression *Channel-definition::Channel-name<>""* is also considered valid.

4.4 Adding Mapping and Constraints to SDL AS1

Each UML CS element that does not have a concrete textual representation has a mapping described. That is, when a UML CS stereotyped modeling element is to be mapped, a set of qualifiers is specified to assert which values are assigned to the corresponding SDL abstract syntax of an element. Therefore, the semantics and definitions of the various modeling elements are derived from the SDL construct. AS1 mapping rules, which are not constrained by an OCL expression, may have an optional assigned value. For instance, the state start node of a state machine may have a name assigned or not. To improve clarity, the OCL constraints, UML metaclasses and stereotyped attributes are <u>underlined</u>. UML CS model elements with a concrete textual notation are not included in this mapping as the syntax is derived from SDL [1]. Note that within the diagram in Figure 3, an operation with the navigation such as *self.part.upper()* shown in Figure 3, is only valid when a context is specified. For clarity, the context is denoted by the stereotype name which is labeled as the heading. Thus, the navigation is always originating from the specified stereotype.

As the model repository of the UML tool is non-navigable, the following is expressed informally.

SDL-specification   :: *[Agent-definition]* = *"Agent of kind system in model repository"*
                                 Package-definition-set = *"All packages in the model repository"*

The following is an exemplary mapping specification of the extended metaclass Package by the stereotype *package*. The following constraints provide information which attributes of the model element map to the appropriate objects in the AS1 of SDL. This reads as follows: If a model element extended with the stereotype *package* is found, there shall be a *Package-definition* with its inner objects fulfilling the specified constraints.

package
Package-definition   ::   *Package-name* = *package.name*
                                 Package-definition-set = *package.nestedPackage*
                                 Data-type-definition-set =
                                        package.packagedElement->select(e |
                                        isStereotypedBy(e,dataType)
                                 Syntype-definition-set = *package.packagedElement->*
                                        select(e | isStereotypedBy(e,constant))
                                 Signal-definition-set =
                                        package.packagedElement->select(e |
                                        isStereotypedBy(e,signal))
                                 Exception-definition-set *-> isEmpty()*
                                 Agent-type-definition-set =
                                        package.base_Package.packagedElement->
                                        select(a | isStereotypedBy(a,block)->
                                        union(package.base_Package.packagedElement ->
                                        select(a | isStereotypedBy(a,process))->
                                        union(package.base_Package.packagedElement ->
                                        select(a | isStereotypedBy(a,system))
                                 Composite-state-type-definition-set =
                                        package.packagedElement ->select(s |
                                        isStereotypedBy(s, state))->select(s | s.isComposite)
                                 Procedure-definition-set =
                                        package.packagedElement ->
                                        select(s | isStereotypedBy(s, operation))

Another example of mapping specification of a system agent is shown. There are some stereotypes referenced which are out of the scope of this paper. The following example reads as follows: If a model element extended with the stereotype *system* is found, there shall be an *Agent-type-definition* with its inner objects satisfying the specified constraints:

system

Agent-type-definition   ::   *Agent-type-name = system base_Class.name*
                                       Agent-kind = "SYSTEM"
                                       [Agent-type-identifier] =
                                            system.base_Class.superClass[0].qualifiedName
                                       Agent-formal-parameter-> isEmpty()*
                                       Data-type-definition-set =
                                            system.base_Class.nestedClassifiers->
                                            select(d | d.isStereotypedBy(d,value))->
                                            union(system.base_Class.nestedClassifiers ->
                                            select(d | d.isStereotypedBy(d,object))
                                       Syntype-definition-set = system. base_Class.ownedAttribute
                                            -> select(d | d.isStereotypedBy(d,constant))
                                       Signal-definition-set = system. base_Class.nestedClassifier
                                            ->select(s | isStereotypedBy(s,signal))
                                       Timer-definition-set = system.base_Class.nestedClassifier->
                                            select(t | isStereotypedBy(t,timer))
                                       Exception-definition-set -> isEmpty()
                                       Variable-definition-set =
                                            system.base_Class.ownedAttribute->
                                            select(d | d.isStereotypedBy(d,value))->
                                            union(system.base_Class.ownedAttribute->
                                            select(d | d.isStereotypedBy(d,object))
                                       Agent-type-definition-set =
                                            system.base_Class. nestedClassifier->
                                            select(a | isStereotypedBy(a,block)->
                                            union(system.base_Class. nestedClassifier->
                                            select(a | isStereotypedBy(a,process))
                                       Composite-state-type-definition-set -> isEmpty()
                                       Procedure-definition-set =
                                            system.base_Class.ownedOperation
                                       Agent-definition-set = system.base_Class.part
                                       Gate-definition-set = system.base.Class.ownedPort
                                       Channel-definition-set =
                                            system.base_Class.ownedConnector
                                       [State-machine-definition] -> isEmpty()

5   Example of an Implementation: An XSLT-Based Approach

Besides of the informal semantics description and the OCL constraints, an XSLT stylesheet is available as a concrete example of an implementation. This XSLT stylesheet maps a UML CS model to a textual SDL system specification. This XSLT stylesheet based mapping relies on the specification of the OCL constraints described in the previous Section 4.4.

Currently, there is no UML tool on the market which is compliant to the UML 2 compliance level 3. Therefore, the XSLT requires a slightly adapted profile definition which adds lacking tagged values (attributes) and constructs to the UML tool's metaclasses.

The XSLT stylesheet parses an XML document containing an UML 2 diagram structure described in an XML Metadata Interchange format (XMI). The output of the parsed stylesheet is a valid SDL/PR which can be used for prototyping purposes in any SDL modeling application. By using XSLT, the original XML document tree is browsed and translated into its equivalent SDL representation.

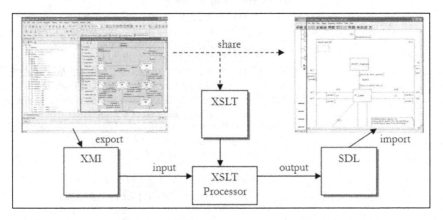

Fig. 5. Using XSLT principle

The XSLT stylesheet contains of a declarative collection of templates. A template is called when a matching tree item is found, adding the specified content within the template to the result output. XSLT uses the XPath language to browse the source tree, while providing additional functions to add flexibility to XSLT. Several XSLT processors like Xalan[3] or Saxon[4] are available for the mapping process. Figure 5 provides an overview on the transformation process.

XPath and XSLT belong to the eXtensible Stylesheet Language (XSL) family of languages that describe how files encoded in the XML standard can be transformed.

After a general source tree compatibility check, the document is parsed starting from the initial node. The path of the process is followed by resolving the appropriate transitions. Activities are converted to procedures, high-level model elements are converted to a predefined set of SDL statements. Parts of the stylesheet are included from additional files to retain clearness and flexibility of the mapper.

6 Conclusions and Future Work

This paper describes a UML Profile for Communicating Systems [10] for generating full behavioral and structural SDL design specification from a behavioral specification and architecture of the target system by means of a UML 2 model. The profile is driven by the concept and expressiveness of SDL-2000. Moreover, it features new high-level elements for communicating protocol engineering for packet switched networks.

---

[3] http://xalan.apache.org/
[4] http://saxon.sourceforge.net/

The model uses the OCL as a formal language for providing constraints on the stereotypes. It also gives mapping rules by means of OCL which are used to bind a mapping from extended UML model elements to corresponding SDL elements in their abstract syntax notation.

As a proof-of-concept, an XMI based mapping by means of an XSLT stylesheet is available. This allows specification and description by means of (many) UML 2 compliant modeling tools. The modeling tool used is MagicDraw 11[5]. It allows direct access to the model repository as well as XMI 2.1 support. However, it also lacks some packages and concrete representations of the final UML 2 Superstructure required by this profile which requires some minor tool specific adaptations of the profile's stereotypes.

While the XSLT approach has shown the soundness of the profile's concept, it is cumbersome for complex mappings. In the future, it is intended to replace this approach by Java-Document Object Model. In addition, future work includes a mapping from UML models with this profile applied to another formal description technique.

References

1. International Telecommunication Union: Specification and Description Language (SDL), ITU-T Recommendation Z.100, August 2002
2. Object Management Group: Unified Modeling Language: Superstructure version 2.0, formal/05-07-04, August 2005
3. International Telecommunication Union: SDL combined with UML, ITU-T Recommendation Z.109, November 1999
4. International Telecommunication Union: UML Profile for SDL (Input for Z.109 revision) TDV09r10, Temporary Document TD 3171R1, restricted availability, April 2006
5. European Telecommunications Standards Institute: UML Profile for Communicating Systems, ETSI Specification, June 2005
6. R. Grammes, R. Gotzhein: Towards the Harmonization of UML and SDL, Syntactic and Semantic Alignment, Technical Report 327/03, Computer Science Department, Technical University of Kaiserslautern, Germany, 2003
7. S. Bourduas, F. Khendek, D. Vincent: From MSC and UML to SDL, Proceedings of the 26th Annual International Computer Software and Applications Conference (COMPSAC '02), 0730-3157/2, IEEE Computer Society, 2002
8. C. Werner, X. Fu, D. Hogrefe: Modeling Route Change in Soft State Signaling Protocols Using SDL: a Case of RSVP, in: Proceedings of the 12th SDL Forum (SDL 2005), LNCS Volume 3530, pp. 174-186, Springer Verlag, June 2005
9. T. Melia, R. Aguiar, A. Sarma, D. Hogrefe: Case study on the use of SDL for Specifying an IETF micro mobility, COMSWARE 2006 International Conference on Communication Systems, IEEE Communications Society, January 2006
10. C. Werner, D. Hogrefe: UML Profile for Communicating Systems, Technical Report, Institute for Informatics, University of Göttingen, ISSN 1611-1044, IFI-TB-2006-03 Germany, March 2006 http://user.informatik.uni-goettingen.de/~werner/umlcs
11. Object Management Group: OCL 2.0 Specification, Version 2.0, ptc/2005-06-06, June 2005. http://www.omg.org/cgi-bin/doc?ptc/2005-06-06

---

[5] http://www.magicdraw.com/

12. R. Braek et al.: TIMe – The integrated method, Sintef Report, 1999 http://www.sintef.no/time/timecomplete.htm
13. Object Management Group: Meta Object Facility (MOF) 2.0 XMI Mapping Specification, v2.1, formal/05-09-01, September 2005. http://www.omg.org/cgi-bin/apps/doc?formal/05-09-01.pdf
14. Object Management Group: Unified Modeling Language: Superstructure version 2.1, ptc/06-04-02, April 2006. http://www.omg.org/cgi-bin/apps/doc?ptc/06-04-02.pdf

Implementing the eODL Graphical Representation

Joachim Fischer[1], Andreas Prinz[2], Markus Scheidgen[1], and Merete S. Tveit[2]

[1] Department of Computer Science, Humboldt Universität zu Berlin
Unter den Linden 6, 10099 Berlin, Germany
{fischer, scheidge}@informatik.hu-berlin.de
[2] Faculty of Engineering, Agder University College
Grooseveien 36, N-4876 Grimstad, Norway
{andreas.prinz, merete.s.tveit}@hia.no

Abstract. eODL is the ITU component description language. Its current status is that it is defined textually and there are several transformations into other languages. There are also ideas about a graphical representation for eODL. In this article we present a graphical representation for some of the eODL language elements and discuss how such a graphical representation can be implemented using a high-level formal description language in comparison with a UML profile.

1 Introduction

The advantages of graphically described models of structure and behaviour opposed to textual representations are undisputed in many application domains. Nevertheless graphical modelling languages will only gain broad user acceptance if appropriate tools become available. Besides presenting the models, these tools should allow easy processing and transformation of the models. Because of the significant expenditure for the development of such editors, the search for efficient production methods is relevant in practice. Starting from a meta-model-based definition of a modelling language, support of the construction of such editors appears to be possible even if the concrete syntax form varies.

This contribution presents two possibilities for the construction of graphical editors for a special meta-model-based language, whose graphic syntax is not specified yet and must therefore be specified first. We consider the ITU-T language eODL [1], whose standard specifies a meta-model together with a textual syntax. The starting point of the graphical syntax proposed here is a set of not-standardized graphic symbols for eODL model elements, which were introduced informally in an eODL tutorial [2]. Further suggestions have been taken from SDL [3] and UML [4,5].

The two mentioned possibilities of editor construction are mainly suitable for languages based on MOF [6] or similar meta-models (see figure 1). eODL is defined by such a meta-model. The first approach (section 3) uses an XMF case tool, for which the existing MOF based meta-model has initially to be transformed into an XCORE based model. This is not a difficult task because the

R. Gotzhein and R. Reed (Eds.): SAM 2006, LNCS 4320, pp. 19–33, 2006.
© Springer-Verlag Berlin Heidelberg 2006

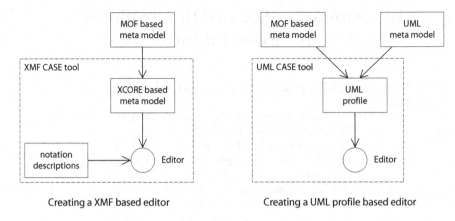

Fig. 1. Approaches of Graphical Editor Constructions

source and target models are almost identical. The concrete notation can be chosen freely with this approach. The procedure for doing so will be demonstrated for eODL based on some sample model elements.

The second approach (section 4) uses an UML CASE tool with UML profile support as the editor. By definition of a UML profile for eODL, the UML CASE tool gets restricted to the syntax of a reduced UML. This approach would be general, if the case tool had permitted the definition of specific icons. Since available UML tools do not (yet) offer such a functionality, the syntax remains restricted to the utilization of build-in UML stereotypes.

Both approaches will be explained using the well known dining philosophers example. An eODL model for the dining philosophers example in a concrete textual syntax can be found in the eODL tutorial [2].

2   The eODL Language

2.1   eODL Basics

The language eODL has its origin in the TINA-C work [7], where a description for supporting the management of distributed objects in their whole lifecycle was required. To do so, concepts and interfaces were proposed whose operations have to be provided on each node of the respective distributed computing platform. These object lifecycle operations which have to be offered to local and remote applications are essential for compliance and interoperability.

By the standardisation work of ITU-T the TINA concepts were expanded to support the lifecycle of software components from the perspectives of four different but related views: the computational, implementation, deployment, and target environment view. Each view is connected with a specific modelling goal expressed by dedicated abstraction concepts. Computational object types with (operational, stream, signal) interfaces and ports (taken from TINA and ODP [8]) are the main computational view concepts used to model distributed software components abstractly in terms of their potential interfaces. Artefacts as abstractions of concrete programming language contexts and their relations to interfaces form the implementation view. The deployment view describes software entities (software components) in binary representation and the computational entities realized by them. The target environment view provides modelling concepts of a physical network onto which the deployment of the software components shall be made. The important advantage of eODL is the technological independence of the component description from the component platform finally used. Public domain tools are made available for mapping (platform independent) eODL models to their corresponding technology units of CCM [9] and netCCM ([10], [11]).

2.2   eODL Meta-model

It is common to say that a language has three types of features: the structure, a concrete representation and semantics.

- The **structure** of a language describes the concepts in the language and how they are related to each other. The following two notations are commonly used to define the abstract structure of a language: an abstract syntax and associated rules (as used in [3]), or as a MOF meta-model.
- The **concrete representation** specifies how the concepts in a language are actually represented. There are two different types of concrete representation: textual and graphical.
- The **semantics** of a language says something about the meaning of the concepts in the language.

This section will give an overview of the structure of eODL, while section 3 and 4 will present two different ways of representing the language graphically.

In the ITU-T Recommendation Z.130 [1], which specifies eODL, the definition of the structure is based on a meta-model, rather than a more traditional abstract syntax approach. The Recommendation says that "One advantage of the meta-model approach is to allow use of MOF related tools to support the automation of model transitions between the different software development phases. Another benefit is the ability to instantiate concrete models from the meta-model, which can be represented by existing languages, so an integration of different design approaches can be achieved."

Fig. 2 shows a small excerpt of the eODL meta-model. Since the entire eODL meta-model is quite large, we will only present the concepts that will be used in the examples later in this article.

The concept of *COType* (Computational Object type) comes from the Computational view and is used to specify the functional decomposition of a system. Instances of a *COType* are autonomous interacting entities, which encapsulate state and behaviour. COs interact with their environment via interfaces which are specified using the *InterfaceDef*. In order to introduce data types, operations, exceptions and interface types as modelling concepts in eODL, the eODL meta-model is also based on the meta-model of CORBA-IDL. The classes *InterfaceDef*, *Container* and *Contained* are all from the IDL meta-model [12]. A

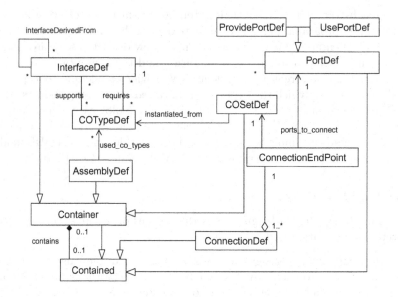

Fig. 2. Excerpt of the eODL Meta-model

COType may support or require an *InterfaceDef*. To support an interface type means that the COs of that *COType* provide interfaces of that interface type. To require an interface type means that COs of that *COType* use interfaces of that interface type. A COType is an instance of the class *COTypeDef* in the meta-model. The labels *supports* and *requires* identify the association between the *COTypeDef* and *InterfaceDef*. An *InterfaceDef* has an association to the class *PortDef*. A port is a named interaction port, where either a reference of a supported interface of a CO can be obtained or a reference of a used interface can be registered at runtime. The concepts *ProvidePortDef* and *UsePortDef* are used to model ports of a *COType* which are either used by the environment to obtain a reference to an interface (provide port) or to store a reference to an interface based on name (use port). The class *PortDef* inherits from the class *Contained*, meaning that a *COTypeDef* instance may contain provided and used port definitions. A provided and a used port definition are always associated to an interface definition.

The concept of assembly is used to model software systems by specifying the COTypes which are involved in the system and to model the initial configuration of the system. The initial configuration is the configuration which is established at the start of the execution time of the software system, and consists of initial COs and their initial connections. In the meta-model, the assembly is represented by the class *AssemblyDef* from the deployment view. The COTypes are associated with the introduction of an association between the metaclasses *AssemblyDef* and *COTypeDef*. To model initial COs, the meta-model contains the class *COSetDef*, which defines the creation of an arbitrary number of instances of the associated *COTypeDef*. A *COSetDef* is contained in an *AssemblyDef*. To model initial connections, the meta-model contains the class *ConnectionDef*. A connection is then established between ports of of the participating COs by exchanging interface references. These references are obtained from a CO where the COType has a provided port definition and is transferred to a CO whose type has a used port definition. In the meta-model, a *ConnectionDef* consists of a set of *ConnectionEndPoints*. A *ConnectionEndPoint* is associated with a *PortDef* of a *COTypeDef* and a *COSetDef*.

3   eODL Graphics in XMF

XMF-Mosaic from Xactium is a platform for building tailored tools that should provide high level automation, modelling and programming support for specific development processes, languages and application domains. The tool is implementing a layered executable meta-modelling framework called XMF that provides semantically rich meta-modelling facilities for the design of languages. This way, the Mosaic platform is realizing the Language Driven Development (LDD) process presented by Xactium in [13]. LDD is a model-driven development technology based on MDA [14] standards, and it involves adopting a unified and semantically rich approach to describe languages. A key feature of the approach is the possibility to describe all aspects of a language in a platform-independent way, including their concrete syntax and semantics. The idea is that these language definitions should be rich enough to generate tools that can provide all the necessary support for use of the languages, such as syntax-aware editors, GUI's, compilers and interpreters.

XMF provides a collection of classes that form the basis of all XMF-Mosaic defined tools. These classes form the kernel of XMF and are called XCORE. XCORE is a MOF-like meta-meta-modelling language, and it is reflexive, i.e. all XCORE classes are instances of XCORE classes. XMF provides an extensive language for describing language properties called XOCL (eXtensible Object Command Language). XOCL is built from XCORE and it provides a language for manipulating XCORE objects. In addition to XCORE, XMF provides a collection of languages and tools defined in XOCL. These include the following notations.

- OCL [15] is used to define the rules that relate the domain concepts (static constraints).
- XOCL is used to describe the behaviour of the language.
- XTools is used to specify the concrete graphical syntax of a language and to model user interfaces.
- XBNF is used to define the concrete textual syntax of a language and to build textual parsers.
- XMAP is used for model to model transformations.

The XTools are most important in this context and will be described in more detail in the following sections.

3.1   Specifying the Graphical Representation

The structure forms the fundament when specifying a language in XMF-Mosaic. In the context of XMF; the structure is called the domain model. The structure defines the (structural) concepts and their relation to each other. In this case the structure is the meta-model for eODL described in section 2. While the meta-model describes the concepts in a language, the concrete representation says something about how these concepts are represented. There are two main types of concrete representation: textual, where the instances of the meta-model are represented as text, and graphical, where the instances are represented as graphical diagram elements. The concrete graphical representation is the one we are discussing in this paper.

When specifying the concrete graphical representation of a language, we would like to say something about what the structure of a diagram in that language could look like. An important question in that context is: how to represent the graphical information? One way of doing this is by attaching the information about the concrete representation directly to the eODL meta-model. Another way is to describe a meta-model of the concrete representation and then match this with the eODL meta-model. Figure 3 shows Xactiums meta-model of how to handle the graphical representation. This model is in fact a mix of how to represent a diagram graphically and how to match it with the eODL meta-model. In addition, it covers an interchange aspect.

According to this meta-model, a diagram has a graph, which in turn has *Nodes* and *Edges*. A *Node* is displayed as a collection of one or more *Display* elements. In this meta-model, there are six different types of display elements defined:

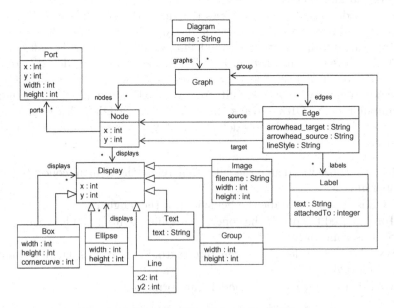

Fig. 3. A Diagram Meta-Model from XTools

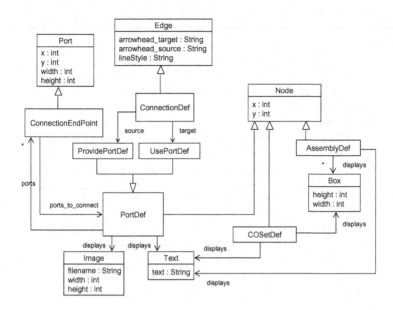

Fig. 4. The Diagram Meta-Model Specialiced for eODL

Box, Ellipse, Line, Text, Image, and *Group.* All *Display* elements have attributes which specify their position. Both *Ellipse* and *Box* can act as a container of other display elements. This means that a node could be represented as e.g. a *Box* with *Text* inside or as an *Ellipse* with an *Image* inside.

A *Node* has a number of *Attachment Ports* that are used to define where a *Node* could be connected to an *Edge*. A *Node* without any *Attachment Ports* cannot be connected to an *Edge*. An *Edge* has a source and a target *Node*. The model contains statements about the *line style* to an *Edge*, which defines how the *Edge* should be drawn, e.g. solid line or dashed line. If the *Edge* has any arrows, this is also specified here, by arrowhead_target and arrowhead_source. The *Labels* of an *Edge* are text fields that could be attached to the start, the middle, or the end of the *Edge*.

The general diagram meta-model in figure 3, is related to the eODL meta-model in figure 4. This connection is used later in the assembly model presented in figure 5. In figure 4, the used concepts from the eODL meta-model (see. figure 2) are brought together with the necessary metaclasses from the diagram meta-model. The relationships between the concepts from these two types of meta-models are represented using inheritance. For example, the concept *COSetDef* is a *Node*, and is graphically displayed as a *Box* and some *Text*. A *ConnectionDef* is an *Edge*, and as figure 3 points out, an *Edge* is associated with a source node and a target node. In this case, the *ProvidedPortDef* is the source and the *UsePortDef* is the target.

One of the biggest problem with Xactium's diagram meta-model is the abstraction level, which is too low when it comes to specifying the logical relations

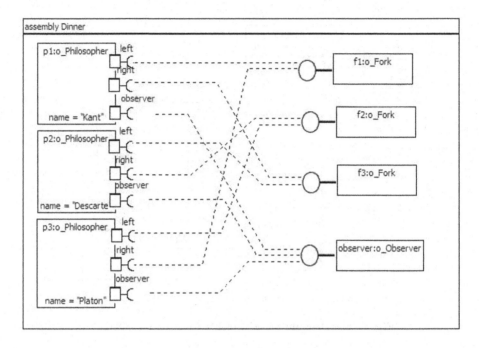

Fig. 5. An eODL Assembly Model from XMF

between the graphical components and describing the actual, graphical structure of the diagram. In this concrete representation, (physical) coordinates (x and y) are used extensively to specify the *Nodes* and *Display* Elements placed in the *Diagram*, but there is no possibility to describe the relationships between *Nodes* or *Display* Elements in an explicit way. Possible relationships to be expressed are *inside*, *above*, *leftOf*, *touching* etc. For example in eODL it would be desirable to express that a *COSetDef* is displayed as a *Box* with some *Text* inside. Figure 4 specifies that a *COSetDef* is displayed as a *Box* and some *Text* but says nothing about the explicit placement of these display elements according to each other.

The outcome of this specialiced diagram meta-model (figure 4) is an editor that can be used to create an assembly model (see figure 5). The model contains four node types: *assembly*, *CO set*, *provide port* and *use port*, and one edge type: *connection*. The *assembly Dinner* is represented as *Box* inside another *Box*. The innermost box has less height than the outermost. Inside the outermost box there is also some text telling the name of the assembly. The *assembly* contains a number of *CO Sets* with *ports*, and *connections* between the *provided ports* and the *used ports*. A *CO Set* is graphically represented by a *Box* with *Text* inside, while the *used ports* and the *provided ports* are represented by an *Image*. The *provided port* also has a *text label*. The *connections* are edges placed between the *ports*, and the line style of the edge are "dashed line". Neither the source nor the target of the edge have arrows.

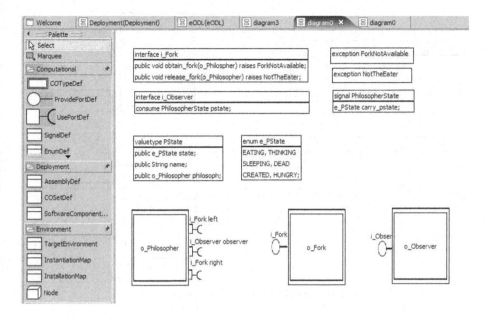

Fig. 6. An eODL Model Declaring Interface Types and CO Types

3.2   Some More Examples from the eODL Editor

When specifying the graphical syntax of eODL in XMF-Mosaic, we are at the same time building a graphical user-interface for a model editor for eODL diagrams. Figure 6 and 7 are showing some screenshots from the eODL diagram editor. The XTools are used to specify the graphical representation of the components in the language, but also provide support for specifying what the tool and menu bar in the editor should look like. It is additionally possible to describe the events that the user raises when creating nodes and edges in a diagram, and also when editing the display elements (see figure 6).

4   eODL Graphics as UML Profile

4.1   Profiling in UML

The *Unified Modeling Language* (UML, [4,5]) is a universal modelling language; it uses multiple modelling paradigms and several diagram types to model all aspects of a computer based system in all stages of its development. Thereby, UML allows to express the system under investigation in platform independent or platform dependent models. Based on this broad conception, the UML recommendation deliberately supplies only very loose semantics and flexible notations. The UML semantics, described in English text, is in some points open for interpretation, in others it explicitly offers different semantics, defined through *semantic variation points*, and UML's graphical syntax provides many notational options.

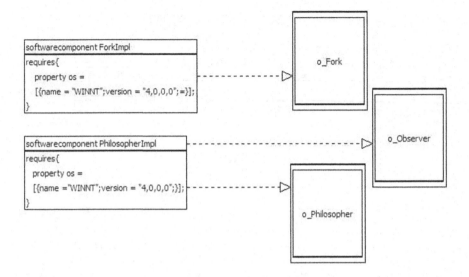

Fig. 7. An eODL Software Component Model

To define a modelling language with concrete specific semantics and notations, tailored for the use in a specific domain, UML offers the extension mechanism *profiles* [4]. UML profiles allow language extensions that formally specialise UML's language structure (meta-model) and informally clarify its semantics and notations. But UML profiles restrict extensions of UML to specialisations of already existing UML language concepts. Thus every model developed under a specific profile is still a UML model. This guarantees that such models can be constructed and used with existing UML tools.

A UML profile serves two general purposes: (1) it can provide a notation and tool support for this notation; (2) it can provide more precise semantics for UML by applying the specific semantics of the concrete notation as specialization to UML.

The language eODL has neither a concrete graphical notation nor tool support for it. But it has precise semantics and there are tools [16] that implement this semantics. ITU-T languages such as SDL, MSC, and eODL cover aspects or views that are also covered by UML. But the ITU-T languages provide more formal semantics and they are tailored for modelling systems in the specific domain of telecommunication.

In this section we want to present our experiences with developing a UML profile for eODL. In section 4.2 we describe the process of aligning the concepts of both languages. We will introduce some typical differences between the concepts of the two languages and explain how to capture those differences in a UML profile in section 4.3. Finally, we will visualize a part of the philosophers example as a UML model using this profile and discuss the results according to notations and language semantics in section 4.4.

4.2   Aligning the eODL Meta-model and the UML Meta-model

To develop a UML profile for an existing language, the concepts of that language have to be aligned with UML's concepts. For each language concept, the most specific UML concept that still generalises the original language concept has to be identified. The specialities of the language concepts must be modelled in stereotypes, expressed using formal constraints, tagged values, as well as additional notations and semantics.

The structure of UML concepts is modelled in UML's meta-model. The concepts of eODL are also modelled in a meta-model, as presented in section 2.2. The presence of the two meta-models makes it possible to define a precise profile for eODL. To find an appropriate UML concept for each eODL concept, we compared both meta-models with each other. For each eODL concept, i.e. for each class in the meta-model, we identify concepts in UML with similar semantics and compare the adjacent structure of the eODL concept class (associations, attributes, etc.) with those of the UML meta-classes. In the ideal case, we will find identical structures, where all associations, attribute, etc. have the same properties, except for different names. But this ideal is rare. In the next section we will provide some examples of structural differences in the meta-models, and we will find strategies to solve those problems.

4.3   Rendering the Differences Between eODL and UML in a Profile

Figure 8 depicts three examples from the meta-models of eODL and UML, showing the concepts (port, computational objects, and assemblies) on both sides. The first example regards the *port* concept; in this simple case eODL and UML are almost equivalent, except that the two concrete descendants of *PortDef* are rendered in the UML attribute *isService*. A corresponding stereotype *PortDef* must only constrain *redefinedPort* to be empty (there is no explicit port redefinition in eODL) and *isBehavior* to be false (this is what matches the eODL semantics best). The properties *required* and *provided* derive from *Port*'s *type* and *isService*. Therefore, *InterfaceDef* must be mapped to *Type*. The derivation from *required* and *provided* can be reversed, so that for each UML model, the analogous eODL model can be derived and eODL semantics can be applied to the UML model.

In the second example, showing the interfaces of computational objects, the *requires* and *supports* interfaces of computational object definitions seem to match with UML's *required* and *provided* interfaces, but they have different semantics. The set of *provided* interfaces in UML derives from all interfaces that are provided by the components ports, its realizing classifiers, and the explicitly modelled *realizedInterfaces*; where only the latter represents the obvious eODL counterpart. The same holds for *required* interfaces that should be modelled with *usedInterfaces* to match the eODL semantics.

The last example shows the composition of computational object sets in assemblies. This very specific eODL relationship has only a quite abstract equivalent in UML. Computational objects have to be modelled as properties, as structural features of a classifier (assembly); the *initial_instances* attribute can

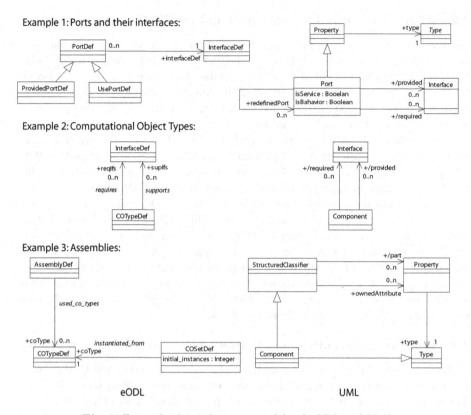

Fig. 8. Examples from the meta-models of eODL and UML

be modelled with the property's multiplicity. Only concrete concepts qualify as base classes for stereotypes, thus a concrete UML classifier has to be chosen. Both *class* and *component* are such classifiers, but only *component* is appropriate, because only it can contain connectors to connect different computational objects. The relation between *AssemplyDef* and *COTypeDef* has no concrete counterpart in UML, and is indeed not exactly necessary, because it could be derived from the computational objects contained in an *AssemplyDef*. To model the relation in UML, one has to use the *usage* relationship; this is a very abstract relation between two model elements that does not really match the specific eODL semantics.

4.4   Examination of the Results of the Philosophers Example

The previous section has shown that the eODL and UML concepts sometimes match very well and sometimes require more complex stereotypes, but basically eODL can be expressed in UML by restricting UML's concept space and semantics according to the rules for defining UML profiles. Furthermore, a UML specification can easily be mapped to an eODL specification using the eODL profile, whereby this mapping reflects the eODL semantics upon UML.

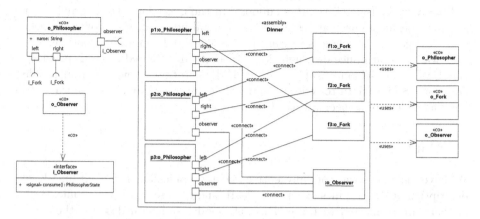

Fig. 9. An eODL model in UML using the eODL profile – Computational object types and assembly

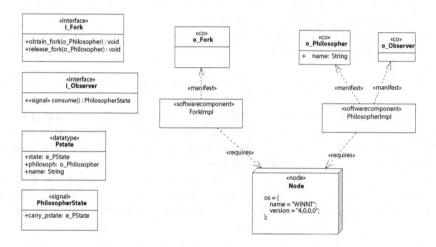

Fig. 10. More model elements in the eODL profile – Interfaces and software components

The other important point, besides semantics, is notation; can eODL be satisfyingly expressed in UML diagrams? Figure 9 shows an example that covers the concepts that we introduced by the meta-model; figure 10 shows diagram elements for other eODL concepts. Wherever eODL and UML concepts are very similar (e.g. eODL computational object definitions and UML components), the notation is very clean, and due to eODL bonds to the UML notation is almost identical to the notation introduced in section 3. The usage of more abstract UML concepts, on the other hand, requires a lot of stereotypes and results in diagrams that do not comply with typical UML practices. The *uses* dependency, for example, would probably never be used that way in a pure UML specification.

Finally we consider UML tool support. In the quest for a UML profile that leads to specifications that resemble the original notation, the profile engineer tends to utilize the whole spectrum of possible UML notational options and even wants to introduce own notations (theoretically allowed in UML profiles). But UML tools seldomly support every UML notation or even custom profile notations. So it is hard to write a good profile, in particular when one wants to be independent of a specific UML tool.

5   Conclusion

We have shown two ways of representing eODL graphically: an explicit high-level description of the graphics in terms of XMF and the use of a UML profile. Both of them are connected to the eODL meta-model and both describe the same language.

As the diagrams show, there is a strong similarity of the profile diagrams with UML. This is acceptable for some parts of eODL, that are similar to corresponding UML descriptions. For parts of eODL, that do not have a UML correspondence, this similarity is annoying.

For the XMF version, there is a high-learning curve to be taken before meaningful graphical descriptions can be generated. However, the end result is very appealing.

In summary, the result with XMF is more suitable than with UML profiles. Moreover, the concept of XMF is more powerful, because it allows arbitrary structures to be displayed. Profiles do only allow to constrain the existing UML concepts. The language used by XMF for displaying the graphical structure of eODL has a semantics and could be used as a description language for graphical specification languages (e.g. SDL and MSC).

Our experiments confirm that in both approaches a meta-model-based language definition allows a more efficient development of graphical editors. This is not surprising, considering the success of model driven development in general.

References

1. ITU-T: ITU-T Recommendation Z.130: Extended Object Definition Language (eODL). International Telecommunication Union (2003)
2. Böhme, H., Fischer, J., Neubauer, B.: Tutorial on eODL (11th International SDL Forum, Stuttgart 2003) (2003). http://casablanca.informatik.hu-berlin.de/wiki/index.php/EODL_projects
3. ITU-T: ITU-T Recommendation Z.100: Specification and Description Language (SDL). International Telecommunication Union (2002)
4. OMG: UML 2.0 Superstructure Specification. Object Management Group (2004). ptc/04-10-02
5. OMG: UML 2.0 Infrastructure Specification. Object Management Group (2003). ptc/03-09-15
6. OMG: Meta Object Facility (MOF) 2.0 Core Specification. Object Management Group (2003). ptc/03-10-04

7. Berndt, H., Darmois, E., Dupuy, F., Hoshi, M., Inoue, Y., Lapierre, M., Minerev, R., Minetti, R., Mossotto, C., Mulder, H., Natarajan, N., Sevcik, M., Yates, M.: The TINA Book. A co-operative solution for a competive world(SDL). Prentice Hall Europe (1999)
8. ITU-T X.903—X.904: Open Distributed Processing-Reference Model Part 3/4. International Telecommunication Union (1995)
9. OMG: CORBA Component Model, Version 3.0. Object Management Group (2002). formal/2002-06-65
10. Auerbach, A.: Integration eines komponentenorientierten Client-Programmier-modells in das CORBA-Komponentenmodell. Master's thesis, Humboldt-Universität zu Berlin (2004)
11. The netCCM Platform. URL http://www.netccm.com/
12. OMG: Interface Definition Language, Part of CORBA. Object Management Group (2002). formal/2002-06-07
13. Clark, T., Evans, A., Sammut, P., Willans, J.: Applied Metamodeling – A Foundation for Language Driven Development. Xactium (2004). http://www.xactium.com/
14. OMG: Model Driven Architecture Guide, Version 1.0.1. Object Management Group (2003). omg/03-06-01
15. OMG: Object Constraint Language Specification (OCL). Object Management Group (1997). ad/1997-08-08
16. Böhme, H., Schütze, G., Voigt, K.: Component development: MDA based transformation from eODL to CIDL. In: A. Prinz, R. Reed, J. Reed (eds.), SDL 2005: Model Driven: 12th International SDL Forum, Grimstad, Norway, June 20-23, 2005. Proceedings, volume 3530 / 2005 of Lecture Notes in Computer Science. Springer-Verlag GmbH (2005). ISBN 3-540-26612-7. ISSN 0302-9743, 68

Distributed Real-Time Behavioral Requirements Modeling Using Extended UML/SPT

Abdelouahed Gherbi and Ferhat Khendek

Electrical and Computer Engineering Department
Concordia University
1455 de Maisonneuve Blvd. W.
Montreal, Quebec H3G 1M8 Canada
{gherbi, khendek}@ece.concordia.ca

Abstract. Distributed real-time systems call for expressive modeling languages to capture and express their functional and nonfunctional requirements at early stages of the development process. The UML profile for Schedulability, Performance and Time (UML/SPT) is an object-oriented real-time modeling language. UML/SPT has been designed using the built-in extension mechanisms of UML, which makes it flexible and customizable. In this paper, we propose an extension for UML/SPT to capture multicast communications. We define a metamodel that encapsulates the main concepts involved in multicast communications, we show its relationship to UML/SPT domain model, and we introduce new stereotypes corresponding to these concepts. We illustrate the extension with the modeling of the Reliable Multicast Transport Protocol (RMTP2). Finally, we compare our approach to extend UML/SPT for multicast communications with an extension for MSC having the same purpose.

1   Introduction

The Unified Modeling Language (UML) [14] is widely accepted as the *defacto* standard specification and modeling language of software. It is a graphical, object-oriented modeling language that uses a variety of diagrams to describe different aspects of the software: its structure, dynamic behavior and deployment. The abstract syntax of the different UML modeling elements is defined using a metamodel [14]. In addition, UML can be adapted/specialized to a variety of domains. This can be achieved by means of its built-in extension mechanisms.

Particularly, UML is aimed to be effectively used for the design and analysis of real-time software. Indeed, several UML profiles for real-time systems [5] have been proposed as a result of active research in the academia in addition to the standardization activities at the OMG. For instance, the OMG standardized profile for Schedulability, Performance and Time [12], hereafter referred to as UML/SPT, is a UML-based modeling language that allows for capturing and analyzing the real-time requirements and designs. UML/SPT is, however, based on UML 1.4 and presents many drawbacks pointed out in different research papers and experiments. UML/SPT is, nowadays, undergoing a major revamp

R. Gotzhein and R. Reed (Eds.): SAM 2006, LNCS 4320, pp. 34–48, 2006.

that will lead to MARTE [13]. The objective is to inline UML/SPT with UML 2.0 and to handle many of the weaknesses of UML/SPT pointed out in various research works.

In order to model the behavioral requirements of distributed real-time systems, we need expressive, flexible and customizable specification languages. Message Sequence Charts (MSC) is a well-established specification language for high-level behavioral requirements modeling. It is extensively used in the telecommunication software engineering. MSC has evolved through its successive versions to enable the expression of time constraints, object orientation, data, and scenario composition [9]. However, the extensibility of MSC is hindered by a lengthy standardization process. This led to ad-hoc extensions (e.g., [10], [17], [18]) that need to go through the standardization process before being accepted and effective. On the other hand, UML/SPT is designed leveraging the UML built-in extensibility mechanisms to capture the concepts necessary for the modeling of resource, concurrency and time. UML/SPT inherits this extensibility allowing for simple and natural extensions. This is illustrated in this paper with an UML/SPT extension enabling for the modeling of multicast communications, which are required to model multicast protocols such as RMTP2 [15].

The main goal of this paper is to demonstrate the easiness of extending UML/SPT in comparison to languages such as MSC. Its main contribution is an extension of UML/SPT for modeling multicast communications. In order to achieve this, we introduce a metamodel capturing the main concepts involved in multicast communications along with their corresponding stereotypes. We model the main requirements of the RMTP2 protocol using this extended version of UML/SPT. Finally, we compare this extension and modeling exercises with the ones performed and conducted in [8] using MSC.

This paper is structured as follows. Section 2 presents the main features of UML/SPT. We introduce the extension for UML/SPT for multicast communications modeling in Section 3. The application of the extended UML/SPT is illustrated in Section 4 with the modeling of RMTP2 protocol requirements. In Section 5, we compare the extension and modeling exercises using UML/SPT with the ones presented in the literature using MSC. In Section 6, we discuss the related work. We conclude in Section 7.

2   UML Profile for Real-Time Systems

UML/SPT [12] is a UML framework to model resources and quality of service; time concept and time-related mechanisms; and concurrency. UML/SPT provides also models for schedulability and performance analysis. The end-user perceives UML/SPT as a set of stereotypes and tagged values used to annotate the UML design models with quantitative information. This enables for predicting key properties at early stages of the software development process, using quantitative analysis (schedulability and performance analysis).

The structure of the UML/SPT profile, illustrated in Figure 1, is composed of a number of sub-profiles. The core of the profile represents *the General Resource*

Model framework, and it is further partitioned into three sub-profiles: *RTre-sourceModeling* for the basic concepts of resource and quality of service; *RTcon-currencyModeling* for concurrency modeling; and *RTtimeModeling* for the time concept and time-related mechanisms. Furthermore, UML/SPT is composed of extensible analysis sub-profiles, including: *PAprofile* for the performance analysis modeling and *SAprofile* for the real-time schedulability analysis modeling.

At the top of UML/SPT lays an abstract definition of the resource and quality of service concepts. These are refined and extended progressively while going down the profile's structure to find the concepts of time and concurrency. These represent a modeling framework that is extended further to define the concepts required for schedulability and performance analysis. Several research works in the literature (e.g., [3], [6], [16]) take advantage of UML/SPT extensibility either to add modeling capabilities or enable other model analysis. In this paper, we show how to extend UML/SPT to enable the modeling of multicast communications and use it to model the requirements of RMTP2 protocol.

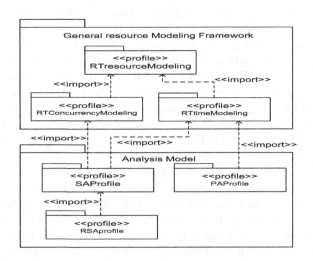

Fig. 1. The Structure of UML/SPT Profile

For each of the aforementioned sub-profiles, UML/SPT provides a domain model encapsulating the main concepts and a set of associated stereotypes that a developer uses to annotate UML models. Hereafter, we illustrate only the features needed in this paper. For an exhaustive presentation of UML/SPT domain models and the associated stereotypes, the reader is referred to [12].

We have used mainly the time-related mechanisms for modeling the RMTP2 protocol behavioral requirements. The domain model defined in UML/SPT to encapsulate the time-related mechanisms is illustrated in Figure 2. The corresponding stereotypes allow for expressing time values (e.g., ≪RTtime≫), times constraints (e.g., ≪RTdelay≫, ≪RTinterval≫) and time-related mechanisms such as a timer ≪RTtimer≫. UML/SPT provides also stereotypes to model timer-related operations: creating a new timer ≪RTnewTimer≫, setting a timer ≪RTset≫, stoping a timer ≪RTpause≫ and unsetting a timer ≪RTreset≫. The timeout generated by a timer is stereotyped ≪RTtimeout≫. Finally, timer periodicity is modeled using the tag *RTperiodic* and its duration is modeled with the tag *RTDuration*. A subset of these stereotypes is used in the RMTP2 protocol requirements model presented in Section 4.

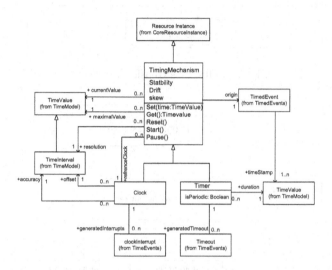

Fig. 2. UML/SPT Time-related Mechanisms Domain Model

3 Multicast Communication Extension for UML/SPT

The extension presented here allows to model *multicast communications*, which are important for communication protocols such as the protocol RMTP2. In order to do so, we present a metamodel capturing the main concepts in multicast communications. The package encapsulating this metamodel and its relationship with the structure of UML/SPT profile are illustrated in Figure 4.

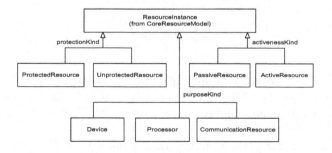

Fig. 3. UML/SPT Resource Type Domain Model

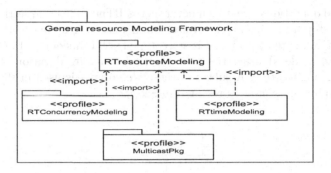

Fig. 4. Multicast Extension Package

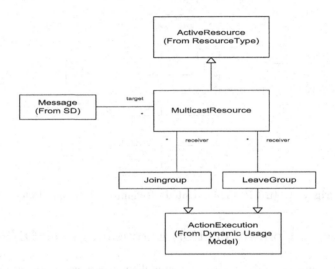

Fig. 5. Multicast Extension Metamodel

Table 1. Multicast Communication Extension Stereotypes

Stereotype	UML Model Element
≪Multicast≫	Object
≪Joingroup≫	Message, Stimilus
≪Leavegroup≫	Message, Stimilus

A *multicasting resource* is a specialization of the *ActiveResource* concept. The latter is defined in UML/SPT *resource type* domain model, illustrated in Figure 3, as an autonomous and concurrent entity able to generate stimuli independently. The multicasting resource is composed of a *dynamic group* of members. Each message targeting a multicasting resource is implicitly forwarded to all the group members by the multicasting resource. The configuration of this group is dynamic where the members could join and leave at will using *Joingroup* and *LeaveGroup* actions, derived from *ActionExecution*. The latter is defined in the *dynamic usage model* of UML/SPT. Figure 5 illustrates this metamodel extension and how it is linked to UML/SPT domain model.

The metaclasses *Joingroup* and *Leavegroup* represent respectively the actions of joining and leaving a multicasting resource. A specification of *Joingroup* meta-classe semantics should ensure that an entity joining a multicasting resource does not belong to it before the action is executed and that it does after the action is executed. Reciprocally, for *Leavegroup*, it should specify that an entity does no more belong to a multicasting resource after the execution of the action of leaving it. Such a specification could use *executionHost*, which is the role of the instance in its association with the *executionAction* as defined in the *Causality Model Package* domain model of UML/SPT, to identify the leaving member.

For each message targeting a multicasting resource corresponds a message having the same signature and that is sent to all the members of this multicasting resource. To specify this, the UML modeling elements related to message exchange such as *message*, *sendEvent*, *receiveEvent*, and *lifeline*, defined in the UML sequence diagram metamodel [14], might be used.

We introduce three new stereotypes as illustrated in Table 1. They correspond to the main concepts introduced in our extension, and that are used to annotate UML models to express multicast communication requirements such as joining a multicast group, leaving a multicast group, and/or sending a message to a multicast group. The example illustrated in Figure 6 shows a UML sequence diagram annotated using these stereotypes. According to the semantics of our extension, the message *M1* will be received by both *A* and *B* since they both joined the multicast group, but *M2* will be received by B only because A has left the multicast group.

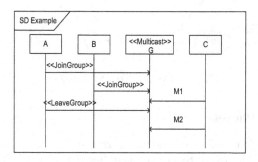

Fig. 6. UML/SPT Multicast Extension Example

4   Application: RMTP2 Behavioral Requirement Modeling

The main features of RMTP2 [11], [15] are guaranteed reliability, high through-put, and low end-to-end delay regardless of the underlying network. RMTP2's reliability is achieved through acknowledgments, but the network congestion that would be caused by a growing number of direct ACKs is avoided using a tree-based organization of the network.

The *sender node*, the top of the *global multicast tree* that spans all the receivers, multicasts the data on the data channel. The receivers are grouped into local regions with a special *control node*. The control node could be: (1) an *aggregate node* which maintains the receivers membership, and aggregates the acknowledgements from the receivers to the sender and forward missing packets; (2) a *designated receiver* node which keeps a copy of the data and retransmits it to the subtree below. Eventually, the acknowledgments are aggregated at the top level control node, which retransmits them to the sender node.

We have used the extended version of UML/SPT to model the main requirements of the protocol RMTP2. We have used the UML sequence diagrams for the basic interactions. The latter are composed using UML interaction overview diagrams, and the real-time requirements are captured using the extended UML/SPT profile. In the following, we present the UML/SPT models for heartbeat packets, parent failure detection and join algorithm behavioral requirements of RMTP2.

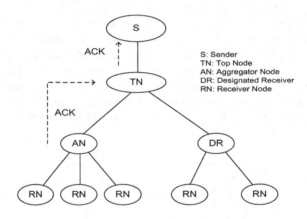

Fig. 7. RMTP2 Tree Structure

4.1   Heartbeat Packets

The nodes cooperate to maintain the multicast tree integrity. Parent nodes send periodic heartbeat messages to notify their liveliness to the child nodes. This enables the child nodes to detect the parent failure and join another parent. This requirement calls for periodicity and multicast communication modeling. We use a periodic timer modeled using the stereotype ≪RTTimer≫ from the time sub-profile of UML/SPT to model periodicity and our ≪Multicast≫ stereotype to model multicast communication. Figure 8 illustrates how this requirement could be described using UML Sequences Diagrams and UML/SPT stereotypes.

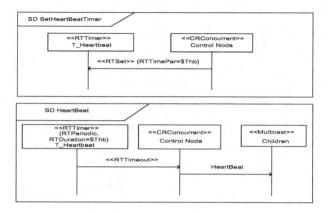

Fig. 8. Heartbeat Packets Requirement Model

4.2 Parent Failure Detection

If a child node does not receive his parent heartbeat for a time interval specified by $F * Thb$, where F is a failure threshold constant, a parent failure is detected. Figure 9 illustrates the different scenarios modeling this requirement and Figure 10 is a UML overview interaction diagram composing these scenarios.

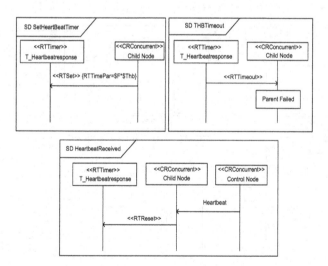

Fig. 9. Parent Failure Requirement Scenarios

4.3 Join Algorithm

A receiver node must join a multicast tree in order to be able to send acknowledgments or ask for retransmissions. The receiver node sends a *Joinstream* packet to its parent node and waits a period of time of *T_joinresponse* for the response.

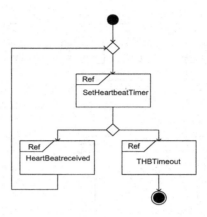

Fig. 10. Parent failure Requirement Model

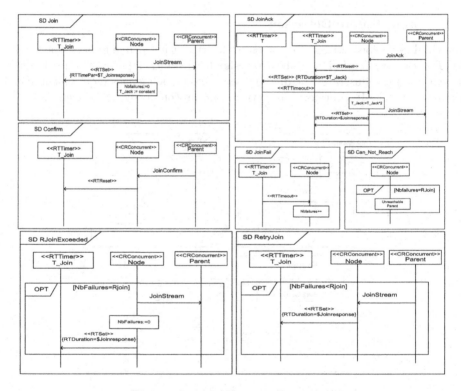

Fig. 11. Scenarios for Tree Connection

This is specified with the UML/SPT annotated sequence diagram *SD Join* in Figure 11. The parent node sends as response either a *JoinConfirm* packet or a *JoinAck* in the case where it cannot handle the request immediately. The behavior of the receiver node in both cases is specified respectively in the *SD Confirm*

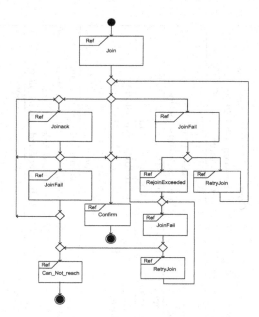

Fig. 12. Tree Connection Requirement Model

and *SD JoinAck* in Figure 11. If no response is received upon receiving a *T_join*
timeout, the receiver node retransmits the *JoinStream* request (*SD JoinFail*)
in Figure 11. This is repeated for a maximum of *RJoin* times before reporting
parent unreachable error (*SD Can_Not_Reach*) in Figure 11. In the case where
a receiver node receives an *JoinAck* from its parent node, it keeps transmitting
JoinStream requests with waiting times growing exponentially. This is modeled
with the sequence diagram (*SD JoinAck*) as illustrated in Figure 11. The whole
join connection algorithm is specified by composing the different scenarios using
a UML interaction overview diagram as illustrated in Figure 12.

5   UML/SPT-Based vs. MSC-Based RMTP2 Requirement Modeling

We compare the extension and modeling exercises using UML/SPT with the
ones presented in [8] using MSC. The main criteria used for this comparison are:
the language built-in constructs, the time-related mechanisms, the multicast
communication extension, the extension approach, and the notation used for
the extension. This comparison is shown in Table 2 and can be summarized as
follows:

- **Language built-in constructs:** MSC and UML are comparable in terms of
  expressiveness to model behavioral requirements [7]. Both languages provide
  constructs allowing for the expression of control flow, basic scenarios and
  their composition. In [8], bMSCs have been used to model the basic scenarios

Table 2. MSC vs. UML/SPT Behavioral Modeling Summary

Criterion	MSC-based Model	UML/SPT-based Model	Comments
Language built-in construct	bMSC hMSC MSC operators	UML Sequence Diagrams UML Interaction Overview Diag. UML Interaction operators	Comparable Expressiveness between MSC-2000 UML interactions [7]
Time-related mechanisms	Timer + HMSC loop composition Time constraints + MSC loop operator	Periodic Timer «RTtimer» + tag value *RTperiodic*	With UML/SPT it is easier to express time constraints, periodicity
Concurrency	MSC instances are implicitly concurrent	Explicit concurrency modeling «CRConcurrent»	UML/SPT allows explicit concurrency modeling
Multicast communications extension	Needed Not standardized	Needed Easy and natural	UML/SPT extensibility using UML built-in mechanisms facilitates the extension
Approach	Tentative formal semantics [8]	Metamodel	MSC extension in [8] is formal but not standardized. Our extension is not formal but take advantage of the standard extensibility
Introduced notation	Simple note attached to an MSC instance modeling a multicast group	New Stereotypes	UML Standard way to introduce new modeling elements

and HMSC have been used to compose them. We have used simple UML sequence diagrams for basic scenarios and interaction overview diagrams to compose them expressing more complex behavior as in the join algorithm requirement.

- **Time-related mechanisms:** MSC-2000 allows for expressing time constraints as well as time-related mechanisms such as timers. UML/SPT is probably more expressive in this regard. It is easier, for instance, to express periodicity, which is useful for periodic behavioral requirement such as the heartbeat packet requirement of RMTP2. With UML/SPT, periodicity can be modeled using a periodic timer (using the ≪RTtimer≫ with the tag value RTperiodic). With MSC, this can be modeled, as this was emphasized in [8], using either a time interval inside a loop or a loop composition of two basics MSC using an HMSC. On the other hand, the instance delay concept introduced in [18] can also be used to express process periodicity in general.
- **Concurrency:** RMTP2 behavior involves the interaction of concurrent communicating entities. These are modeled in [8] by MSC instances which are implicitly concurrent. UML/SPT, on the other hand, allows a more explicit modeling of concurrency. We have used the ≪CRConcurrent≫ stereotype to identify the concurrent entities.
- **Multicast communication extension:** Both MSC and UML/SPT needed to be extended to model multicast communication.
- **Approach:** In [8], a formal semantics has been proposed for the multicast communication extension. We have defined our extension through a meta-model and an informal definition of the introduced concepts' semantics.
- **The extension notation:** In [8], an MSC instance representing a multicast group is indicated by a simple note attached to the instance. We have proposed new stereotypes to model multicast communications. Stereotyping is UML's standard way to introduce new and specific modeling elements.

6   Related Work

MSCs have been extensively used to capture the high-level behavioral requirements in telecommunication software engineering. In addition to the official extensions of MSC through its successive versions MSC'92, MSC'96 and MSC'2000, many other extensions have been proposed in the literature including [10], [17], [18]. In particular, Hélouët presented in [8] an MSC-based model for the requirements of the RMTP2 protocol. In order to model multicast communication, Hélouët proposed an extension of his semantics for MSC. For this extension as well as the aforementioned ones to be effective, they should be integrated to the standard.

Our proposal for an extension of UML/SPT is inspired by Hélouët's extension for MSC. It is, however, easier and more natural because of the built-in extensibility mechanisms provided by UML. Moreover, the UML/SPT model presented in this paper takes advantage of the time concept and time-related mechanisms offered by UML/SPT profile. For instance, expressing periodicity, which is necessary to model the heartbeat requirement, is simply modeled using a periodic timer ≪*RTTimer*≫ {*RTperiodic, RTDuration=value*} such as in the basic scenario *SD Heartbeat* in Figure 8, while this called for either the introduction of a non standard notation and a loop or an HMSC loop composition in [8].

Several other proposals of extensions to UML/SPT using UML extensibility mechanisms have been presented in the literature. Cortellessa et al. presented in [3] a similar approach to extend UML/SPT to represent the concepts used in the reliability analysis domain. A metamodel for these concepts was presented and their relationship to UML/SPT domain model was illustrated. A set of new stereotypes was introduced as well. Rodrigues et al. defined in [16] a profile for reliability analysis. It is also an approach to bridge the gap between UML/SPT models and MSC enabling early reliability prediction. Addouche et al. presented in [1] a UML profile called DAMRTS aiming at adding stochastic and probabilistic information to real-time systems models to enable their dependability analysis. This profile is an extension for UML/SPT, but neither its domain model was extended nor new stereotypes were presented.

7   Summary and Perspective

UML is becoming the standard notation for the description of software models. It is also adapted to various domains through its profiling mechanisms. In particular, UML/SPT is used to express real-time models and quantitative analysis models, such as models for performance and schedulability. We motivated and presented an extension for UML/SPT profile enabling multicast communications modeling. Specifically, we have presented a metamodel encapsulating the main concepts involved in multicast communications and provided the corresponding UML stereotypes. We illustrated the application of this extension with the modeling of the main behavioral requirements of RMTP2 protocol. We have used the UML sequence diagrams to express the basics scenarios and the UML interaction overview diagrams to compose those scenarios. The extended version of UML/SPT has been used to model the time-related mechanisms, concurrency and multicast communication requirements of this protocol. Finally, we have contrasted this exercise with the extension of MSC for the modeling of RMTP2 [8].

As proof of concept, the proposed extension is being implemented in a general setup that consists of a tool chain including an implementation of the General Resource Framework extended with our proposed multicasting sub-package as depicted in Figure 4 and the schedulability analysis sub-profile (SAProfile). The tool is an Eclipse plug-in leveraging the Eclipse Modeling Framework (EMF) plug-in [2]. In addition, the tool chain includes an implementation of a schedulability analysis technique as another Eclipse plug-in. This will allow for the analysis of the UML models annotated with the UML/SPT stereotypes. The derivation of the schedulability analysis task models from UML/SPT models is an implementation of the model transformation presented in [4].

There is an interesting issue, related to the metamodel-based approach to extend UML and its profiles, that needs further investigation. Indeed, the concepts required for a certain domain could be expressed in different manners leading to different metamodels. For instance, two different metamodels have been proposed in [3] and [16] for the reliability prediction domain and used to extend UML/SPT domain model. It would be interesting to assess the consistency between the extended profiles.

Acknowledgments. This work has been partially supported by the Natural Sciences and Engineering Research Council of Canada (NSERC).

References

1. Nawal Addouche, Christian Antoine, and Jacky Montmain. UML Models for Dependability Analysis of Real-time Systems. In *Proceedings of the IEEE International Conference on Systems, Man & Cybernetics*, pages 5209–5214, The Hague, Netherlands, 10-13 October 2004. IEEE.
2. Frank Budinsky, David Steinberg, Ed Merks, Raymond Ellersick, and Timothy J. Grose. *Eclipse modeling framework : a developer's guide*. The eclipse series. Addison-Wesley, 2004.
3. Vittorio Cortellessa and Antonio Pompei. Towards a UML Profile for QoS: a Contribution in the Reliability Domain. In *WOSP '04: Proceedings of the 4th international workshop on Software and performance*, pages 197–206, New York, NY, USA, 2004. ACM Press.
4. Abdelouahed Gherbi and Ferhat Khendek. From UML/SPT Models to Schedulability Analysis: a Metamodel-Based Transformation. In 9th *IEEE International Symposium on Object-Oriented Real-Time Distributed Computing (ISORC 2006), 24-26 April 2006, Gyeongju, Korea*, pages 343–350. IEEE Computer Society, 2006.
5. Abdelouahed Gherbi and Ferhat Khendek. UML Profiles for Real-Time Systems and their Applications. *Journal of Object Technology*, 5(4):149–169, May-June 2006.
6. Vincenzo Grassi, Raffaela Mirandola, and Antonino Sabetta. UML Based Modeling and Performance Analysis of Mobile systems. In Simonetta Balsamo, Carla-Fabiana Chiasserini, and Lorenzo Donatiello, editors, *Proceedings of the 7th International Symposium on Modeling Analysis and Simulation of Wireless and Mobile Systems, MSWiM 2004*, pages 95–104. ACM, 2004.
7. Øystein Haugen. Comparing UML 2.0 Interactions and MSC-2000. In *System Analysis and Modeling, 4th International SDL and MSCWorkshop, (SAM' 2004)*, volume 3319 of *Lecture Notes in Computer Science*, pages 65–79, Ottawa, Canada, June 2005. Springer.
8. L. Hélouët. Distributed System Requirements Modeling with Message Sequence Charts. *International Journal of Information and Software Technology*, 45:701–714, 2003.
9. IUT-T. Message Sequene Charts (MSC-2000). *ITU-T Recommendation Z.120*, November 1999.
10. Ingolf Krüger, Wolfgang Prenninger, and Robert Sandner. Broadcast MSCs. *Formal Aspects of Computing*, 16(3):194–209, 2004.
11. T. Montgomery, B. Whetten, M. Basavaiah, S. Paul, N. Rastogi, J. Conlan, and T. Yeh. The RMTP2 protocol IETF draft. IETF (Internet Engineering Task Force), April 1998.

12. OMG. UML Profile for Schedulability, Performance, and Time Specification. *Version 1.1, formal/05-01-02*, January 2005.
13. OMG. UML Profile for Modeling and Analysis of Real-Time and Embedded systems (MARTE). *Request For Proposals OMG Document: realtime/05-02-06*, Fubruary 2005.
14. OMG. Unified Modeling Language: Superstructure. *version 2.0 formal/05-07-04*, August 2005.
15. Sanjoy Paul, Krishan K. Sabnani, John C.-H. Lin, and Supratik Bhattacharyya. Reliable Multicast Transport Protocol (RMTP). *IEEE Journal On Selected Areas In Communications*, 15(3):407–421, April 1997.
16. Genana Nunes Rodrigues, David S. Rosenblum, and Sebastian Uchitel. Reliability Prediction in Model-Driven Development. In *Proc. ACM/IEEE 8th Int'l Conf. on Model Driven Engineering Languages and Systems*, Springer Lecture Notes in Computer Science 3713, pages 339–354, 2005.
17. Gwang Sik Yoon and Yong Rae Kwon. Extending MSC for Reactive Systems. In *IEEE CS International Symposium on Human-Centric Computing Languages and Environments (HCC'2001)*. IEEE Computer Society, 2001.
18. Tong Zheng and Ferhat Khendek. An Extension for MSC-2000 and Its Application. In Edel Sherratt, editor, *Telecommunications and beyond: The Broader Applicability of SDL and MSC, Third International Workshop, (SAM 2002)*, volume 2599 of *Lecture Notes in Computer Science*, pages 221–232. Springer, 2003.

Formal Operations for SDL Language Profiles

Rüdiger Grammes

Computer Science Department, University of Kaiserslautern
Postfach 3049, D-67653 Kaiserslautern, Germany
grammes@informatik.uni-kl.de

Abstract. Expressive system modelling languages lead to language definitions that are long and hard to understand. Tool support for these languages is hard to implement, and often only parts of the language are supported. In this paper we introduce the concept of language profiles as well-defined subsets of a language with formal syntax and semantics as the basis for tool support. We outline two approaches to generate language profiles for SDL from the complete formal semantics definition, and provide a formalisation for a reduction-based approach, on which a tool for this approach is based.

1 Introduction

In order to support a wide range of applications, system modelling languages are often complex and expressive. The complexity of the languages leads to language definitions that are long and hard to understand, and can limit their applicability in domains for which specialised, tailor-made languages are preferred. Another drawback is that tool support for complex languages usually covers only parts of the language. For example, there is no tool that supports the whole of SDL-96 [1,2], and only a few of the language constructs introduced in SDL-2000 [3,4,5] are supported.

Language profiles divide a language into a core language and a set of language modules that can be used as language building blocks. The language core represents a minimal subset of the language that a tool for the language should implement. This core is a profile that can be extended by language modules, yielding further language profiles that represent well-defined subsets of the language which a tool provider can implement. Thus, using language profiles it is possible to define sublanguages of a language that are of lesser complexity and are tailor-made for certain application areas.

Formal semantics gives a precise definition of the language and eliminate the ambiguities that come with an informal language definition. Operational mathematical formalisms like Abstract State Machines [6,7] can be executed and used to generate a compiler and runtime system [8], giving a reference for tool developers. Defining language profiles, we focus on the formal semantics of the language. Formal semantics allow us to formulate precise criteria for valid language extension and reduction. SDL-2000 [3] is a language with a complete formal semantics [9,10,11], defined using ASMs, which makes it well-suited for the definition of language profiles.

R. Gotzhein and R. Reed (Eds.): SAM 2006, LNCS 4320, pp. 49–63, 2006.

In this paper, we introduce language profiles of SDL (section 2). We define a process for the generation of language profiles for SDL from a formal semantics defined with Abstract State Machines. This process is based on the reduction of the semantics by formally defined operations (section 3), and formalised and implemented in an SDL-profile tool (section 4).

2   Language Profiles and Modules

2.1   Problem and Definition

SDL has become a sophisticated and complex language with many language features. SDL-2000, the most recent version, has added several new language constructs, for example composite states, exceptions, agents (a harmonisation of the concepts of systems, blocks and processes) and textual notation of algorithms. This results in a large and extensive language definition. In the formal semantics of SDL-2000, the operational nature of ASMs and the extensive use of modularisation lead to a readable formal semantics definition. However, due to the complexity of the language, the formal semantics is large and requires substantial effort to be understood completely: the dynamic semantics of SDL-2000 consist of more than 3000 lines of ASM specification.

The problem of the complexity of SDL-2000 has been identified, and the definition of simpler sublanguages of SDL has been proposed. One such language is defined by the SDL Task Force as the simplest useful subset of SDL [12]. This language is implemented by the SAFIRE tool, and here is called SAFIRE. SAFIRE focuses on the state machine aspect of SDL, and enhances it with functionality needed for testing. However, although a formal semantics exists for SDL, none is provided for SAFIRE.

A sublanguage like SAFIRE is a language profile. Tools for a language profile can be developed faster, leading to less expensive tools and enabling code optimisations. Possible language profiles could also be derived from the supported features of the code generators Cbasic and Cadvanced in Telelogic Tau.

Apart from being subsets of the complete language, language profiles can be subsets of other language profiles, forming a hierarchy profiles. For SDL, we have defined four language profiles. The smallest profile is *Core*, which contains a minimal set of features. *Static$_1$*, *Static$_2$* and *Dynamic* extend *Core*, each profile adding additional features to the preceding one, *Dynamic* being roughly the equivalent of SDL-96. The subset relationships between different language profiles are shown in Figure 1.

A *language module* encapsulates a language feature, defining its syntax, semantics and dependencies to other language modules. Some language modules of SDL are timers, exceptions, save, and inheritance. Figure 2 shows the (graphical) syntax elements of the timer feature, ASM-Listing 1 parts of the formal semantics of timers. ASM macro SETTIMER describes the setting of a timer by inserting a new timer instance into the schedule of the process. If a time t is

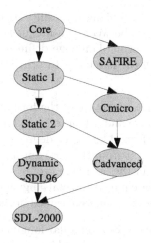

Fig. 1. Superset Relationship between Language Profiles

given, the arrival is set to this time, otherwise the arrival is computed from the current time and the standard duration defined for the timer. Signals in the schedule are sorted by time of arrival. They are invisible to the process until the current time is equal or greater than their time of arrival.

```
1  SETTIMER(tm: TIMER, vSeq: VALUE*, t: [TIME]) ≡
2      let tmi = mk−TimerInst(Self.self, tm, vSeq ) in
3          if t = undefined then
4              Self.inport.schedule := insert(tmi, now + tm.duration, delete(tmi, Self.
                   inport.schedule))
5              tmi.arrival := now + tm.duration
6          else
7              Self.inport.schedule := insert(tmi, t, delete(tmi, Self.inport.schedule))
8              tmi.arrival := t
9          endif
10     endlet
```

ASM-Listing 1. Setting SDL Timers

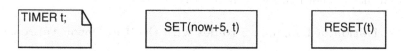

Fig. 2. Syntactical Elements of the Timer Module

2.2 Approach for the Generation of Language Profiles

SDL-2000 is a language with formal semantics, and this property should be retained for its sublanguages. However, it is not feasible to define a new formal semantics from scratch for every sublanguage, since it requires substantial effort and can lead to inconsistencies between the language profiles. A sensible approach is to take the existing formal language definition, and to systematically modify it to match a subset of the language. In principle, there are two ways to achieve this goal:

- *bottom-up:* Given a modular structure of the formal language definition, i.e. consisting of a core language and a hierarchy of language modules that can be added to the core, the formal language definition for the language profile is obtained by constructing it from the core and the modules corresponding to the features contained in the language profile.
- *top-down:* Starting from the complete formal language definition, we remove all parts that correspond to features not contained in the subset of the language.

The bottom-up approach requires a modular language definition with a small core language, language features encapsulated in language modules, and a way to compose the language modules with the core and other modules, both syntactically and semantically. Feature interaction plays a crucial role with the bottom-up approach, as language features like exceptions may interact with other language features. This affects the order in which the language modules are composed. Another problem of the bottom-up approach is that it is very difficult to encapsulate the formal semantics of a language module in a way that it can be easily composed with a given language profile, while at the same time maintaining readability of the formal semantics. For these reasons, we are choosing the top-down approach.

2.3 Consistency of Language Profiles

The goal is for a specification defined with a language profile to behave in the same way with all supersets of the language profile. In order to accomplish this goal, we need to assure *consistency* between the language profiles. Deriving the profiles from a common language definition enables us to make statements about consistency, because, unlike profiles defined from scratch, the derived profiles share many common parts. With the bottom-up approach, we need to ensure that adding modules does not interfere with existing specifications. With the top-down approach, only parts of the language definition that do not apply to features contained in the subset may be removed (that is, parts of the ASM formalism that are not reached in the subset).

2.4 Derivation of Language Profiles with the Top-Down Approach

Reduction of the formal language definition consists of reduction of the formal syntax and reduction of the formal semantics. The formal syntax is reduced by deleting all syntax elements corresponding to features to be deleted from both the concrete and abstract syntax. In order to remove a feature from the formal semantics of SDL-2000, we start by identifying domains and functions from the signature of the formal semantics definition. The signature consists of names of domains, functions and relations of the ASM. We identify the parts of the signature that correspond to the feature to be removed. Several domains in the formal semantics can be identified that correspond to a particular feature, for example the domains TIMER and TIMERINST are used to specify the timer feature of SDL. Furthermore, for each non-terminal in the abstract syntax, there is a domain in the formal semantics definition. As the abstract grammar is reduced, the respective domains can be removed, too.

1 TIMER $=_{def}$ *Identifier*
2 TIMERINST $=_{def}$ PID ×TIMER ×VALUE∗
3 SET $=_{def}$ TIMELABEL ×TIMER ×VALUELABEL ×CONTINUELABEL
4 RESET $=_{def}$ TIMER ×VALUELABEL ×CONTINUELABEL

ASM-Listing 2. Domains Corresponding to the TIMER Feature

Reduction of the signature of the formal semantics definition affects the ASM-rules of the definition, which have to be reduced accordingly. All occurrences of removed functions and domains must be removed from the definition. This leads to the removal of entire rule blocks, for example when the guard of an if-rule has to be removed. The rules should be reduced as much as possible, in order to get a concise formal semantics definition without any remaining parts of the removed features. On the other hand, care must be taken that the removal only affects language constructs that should be removed and no other language constructs are affected. In cases where this is not possible, there is very likely a feature interaction, which is either inherent to the language or was introduced in the formal semantics. For example, procedures and composite states share common parts in the formal semantics of SDL-2000, because their underlying concepts are very similar.

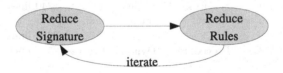

Fig. 3. Process of Feature Removal

A way to approach the removal of rules is to assign fixed default values to the functions and domains to be removed, and then to remove unreachable parts of the formal semantics accordingly. Possible default values for domains would be the empty set, for partial functions the special ASM element **undefined**, for boolean functions (predicates) it would be either **true** or **false**. For example, the default value for the predicate *Spontaneous* would be **false**, so that the triggering of a spontaneous transition during transition selection would never occur, disabling spontaneous transitions entirely. Listing 3 shows the rule fragment that defines how spontaneous transitions are triggered. Since the fixed default value **false** is assigned to *Spontaneous*, the entire **elseif**-block of the rule fragment can be removed. Consistency is guaranteed for specifications that do not use spontaneous transitions, since it can be proven that mode *selectSpontaneous* has no effect in this case. That is, no updates are fired in this mode, except for updates that set the agent mode functions to the previous mode.

```
1  monitored Spontaneous: AGENT →BOOLEAN (default False)
2
3      if  Self.stateNodeChecked = undefined then
4          NEXTSTATENODETOBECHECKED
5      elseif Self.Spontaneous then
6          Self.agentMode4 := selectSpontaneous
7      else
8          ...
9      endif
```

ASM-Listing 3. Triggering Spontaneous Transitions

Assigning the default value `false` to *Spontaneous* disables spontaneous transitions, however, unreachable parts of the formal semantics of spontaneous transitions still remain in the formal semantics definition. In order to remove them, a further reduction of the formal semantics definition is necessary. This reduction includes, for example, guarded rule fragments that check for the agent mode *selectSpontaneous*.

Table 1. Definition Size for Profiles

Profile	Features	Lines of Spec.
Core	System, Block, Process, Channel Simple Statemachines	1500 lines
Static$_1$	*Core* +Timer, +Actions, +Data, ...	1900 lines
Static$_2$	*Static$_1$* +Services, +Inheritance, +Data +Priority Input, +Continuous Signal, ...	2240 lines
SAFIRE		2280 lines
Dynamic ∼ SDL 96	*Static$_2$* +Procedures, +Dynamic Process Creation	2570 lines
SDL-2000		3130 lines

Table 1 shows the size of the reduced dynamic part of the formal semantics of SDL for several language profiles of SDL-2000. *Core*, *Static$_1$*, *Static$_2$* and *Dynamic* build a hierarchy of language profiles, starting from *Core* with minimal features and going up to the dynamic subset, which roughly equals SDL'96. The formal semantics of SAFIRE is slightly larger than the second static subset, though *Static$_2$* contains features not covered by SAFIRE. However, SAFIRE contains procedures, which are not part of *Static$_2$*.

3   Formalisation

In this section, we introduce a formalisation of the process for the derivation of language profiles with the top-down approach. The formalisation gives an exact definition of the removal process, leading to deterministic results. It provides the foundation for tool support for the removal process. Finally, a formal definition is necessary in order to make precise statements about the consistency of language profiles. Since the formal syntax definition can be easily defined in a modular fashion, making reduction of the syntax straightforward, we focus on the reduction of the formal semantics definition.

The formal semantics definition consists of two parts, the static semantics and the dynamic semantics. The static semantics consists of well-formedness conditions and transformation rules. Where language modules are removed, corresponding well-formedness conditions and transformation rules have to be removed accordingly. However, in this paper we focus on the dynamic semantics of SDL.

For the formal definition of the removal process, we are looking for a mathematical formalism that is readable and easy to understand. Therefore, we have decided to use a functional approach, defining functions that recursively map the original formal semantics to the reduced formal semantics. These functions are based on a concrete grammar for Abstract State Machines.

3.1 Formalisation Signature

To formalise the extraction, we define a function *remove*, which maps a term from the grammar G of ASMs and a set of variables V - an initially empty set of locally undefined variables from the ASM formal semantics - to a reduced term from the grammar G. Additionally, we introduce three *mutually exclusive* binary predicates, namely *undefined*, *true* and *false*, that control the reduction. The profile definition is given as a globally defined set of elements r from the signature of the formal semantics definition, annotated by default values $\mathtt{true}$ and $\mathtt{false}$ for predicates. This set represents the elements to be removed from the formal semantics definition, and is therefore called the *reduction profile*. For all elements in the reduction profile, *undefined* (*true* or *false* for predicates) holds.

$$remove_r : G \times V \to G$$
$$undefined_r : G \times V \to \mathsf{Boolean}$$
$$true_r : G \times V \to \mathsf{Boolean}$$
$$false_r : G \times V \to \mathsf{Boolean}$$

The *remove* function is defined on all elements of the grammar G. It is defined recursively - a given term is mapped to a new term by applying the mapping defined by *remove* to the subterms. In case the predicates *undefined*, *true* and *false* do not hold, nothing more is done. This assures that *remove* corresponds to the identical mapping if the signature of the formal semantics definition is not reduced (that is, the reduction profile is empty). In other cases, subterms can be replaced or omitted depending on which of the predicates hold.

Predicates *true* and *false* are explicitly defined on boolean and first-order logic expressions. On all other elements of G, the predicates do not hold. Predicate $true(e, v)$ ($false(e, v)$) holds only if expression e always evaluates to $\mathtt{true}$ ($\mathtt{false}$) in any state of the ASM with reduced signature. These predicates are determined using formal criteria and heuristics.

Predicate *undefined* is defined on all expressions and domains. It holds on any expression or domain that can not be reduced to a defined expression/domain. A defined expression or domain contains only elements that are not in the reduction profile r. For example, if *undefined* holds for expression e_1 and expression e_2, *undefined* also holds for expression $e_1 \vee e_2$.

3.2 Formal Reduction of ASM Rules

Rules specify transitions between states of the ASM. The basic rule is the *update rule*, which updates a location of the state to a new value. All together, there are seven kinds of rules for ASMs, for all of which we have formalised the reduction. Below, we show the formalisation of the reduction for two representative rules.

The mapping of the **if**-rule (see below) depends on which predicate holds for the guard *exp* of the rule. If the guard always evaluates to `true` (`false`), the **if**-rule can be omitted, and removal continues with subrule R_1 (R_2). If the guard is undefined, the rule is syntactically incorrect, and should not be reachable[1]. If none of the predicates hold, the removal is applied recursively to the guard and the subrules of the **if**-rule, leaving the rule itself intact.

$remove($**if** exp **then** R_1 **else** R_2 **endif**, $\mathcal{V}) =$

$remove(R_1, \mathcal{V})$	iff	$true(exp, \mathcal{V})$
$remove(R_2, \mathcal{V})$	iff	$false(exp, \mathcal{V})$
skip	iff	$undefined(exp, \mathcal{V})$
if $remove(exp, \mathcal{V})$ **then** $remove(R_1, \mathcal{V})$		else
else $remove(R_2, \mathcal{V})$ **endif**		

The **extend**-rule dynamically imports a fresh ASM element from the reserve (an infinite store of unused ASM elements), binding it to a variable x in the context of the subrule R and including it in the ASM domain D. In case the domain name D is undefined, i.e. has been removed from the ASM signature, the **extend**-rule can be omitted, since elements of domain D belong to a removed feature. However, the subrule R might still contain parts not related to this feature - although it would be better style to move these parts outside the **extend**-rule. Therefore, the subrule is not omitted by default, but replaced with its mapping by the remove function, including the now unbound variable x in the set of locally undefined variables. This leads to all occurrences of x being removed from the rule R.

$remove($**extend** D **with** x R **endextend**, $\mathcal{V}) =$

$remove(R, \mathcal{V} \cup \{x\})$	iff	$undefined(D, \mathcal{V})$
extend D **with** x $remove(R, \mathcal{V})$ **endextend**		else

---

[1] This is a proof obligation that we have to verify manually. However, so far this has only occurred in very few cases, which were the result of errors in the reduction profile.

3.3   Formal Reduction of ASM Expressions

Expressions are terms over the signature of the formal semantics definition. Additionally, ASMs include common mathematical structures like boolean algebra, or natural numbers. Our formal reduction covers all operations defined in [13]. Below is an excerpt of the formal reduction of ASM expressions, covering boolean and relational operators.

Boolean operators take boolean expressions as arguments, therefore the predicates *true*, *false* and *undefined* apply. With binary boolean operators, we have to consider sixteen different combinations of predicates holding for subexpressions - four for each subexpression. In order to improve readability, we combine the definitions of *true*, *false*, *undefined* and *remove* for boolean operators in a four-valued truth table. Valid boolean expressions always evaluate to either **true** or **false**. Therefore, it is undesirable that the predicate *undefined* holds for such an expression. However, this can not be avoided in every case.

Table 2. Truth Table for Negation

$\neg e_1$	T	F	U	-
	F	T	U	$\neg e_1$

Table 3. Truth Table for Disjunction

e_1 \ e_2 ∨	T	F	U	-
T	T	T	T	T
F	T	F	F	-
U	T	F	U	-
-	T	-	-	-

T Predicate *true* holds
F Predicate *false* holds
U Predicate *undefined* holds
- $\neg T \wedge \neg F \wedge \neg U$

We define truth tables for all boolean operators from the concrete syntax of ASMs: negation ($\neg$, see Table 2), disjunction ($\vee$, see Table 3), conjunction ($\wedge$), implication ($\rightarrow$) and equivalence ($\leftrightarrow$). In order to ensure consistent results, we derive the definition of conjunction, implication and equivalence from the definitions of negation and disjunction.

A special relational operator is the element-of operator $e_1 \in e_2$, where e_1 denotes an element and e_2 denotes a set. It is important as it often appears in the guard of **if**-statements. The expression e_2, denoting a set, is interpreted as the empty set if *undefined* holds. Therefore, *false* (*true*) holds for the element-of (not element-of) expression if e_2 is undefined. Likewise, an undefined expression should not be an element of any set. Note that according to this definition, *undefined* can not hold for an element-of expression.

In the same way as with the examples given above, the function *remove* is formally defined for all elements of the concrete grammar of ASMs, and the predicates *true*, *false* and *undefined* are formally defined for the elements of the grammar for which they apply. This gives us a complete formalisation of the reduction process.

4   SDL-Profile Tool

Based on the formalisation provided in section 3, we have implemented an SDL-profile tool in order to validate the reduction process, providing visible results. The tool reads the formal semantics definition, performs the *remove* operation based on a *reduction profile*, and outputs a reduced version of the formal semantics. The reduction profile is a list of domain names, function names and macro names that are removed from the ASM signature (or from the set of rules, in the case of macro names), possibly defining default values. Figure 4 shows the sequence of steps performed during the removal, and the tools used for each step.

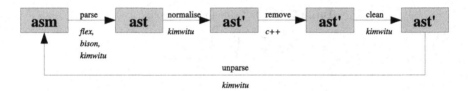

Fig. 4. Toolchain of the SDL-Profiling Tool

4.1   Toolchain

Parser. The *parser* takes an ASM specification as input and creates an abstract syntax tree representation of the specification as output. It is generated out of definitions of the lexis, grammar and abstract syntax of Abstract State Machines, as used in the formal semantics of SDL-2000. The definition of the abstract syntax is translated by kimwitu++ [14] to a data structure for the abstract syntax tree, using C++ classes. Scanner and parser are generated by flex and bison, respectively. Apart from minor differences, the parser is identical to the parser used in [8].

Normalisation. The *normalisation* step transforms the abstract syntax tree to a pre-removal normal form. The transformation is specified by rewrite rules on the abstract syntax tree. The rewrite rules are translated to C++ functions by the kimwitu tool. The main function of the normalisation step is to split up complicated abstract syntax rules, in order to make the definition of the remove function easier. For example, during the normalisation step, **extend**-statements containing a list of variables to be bound to new elements in a domain are rewritten. The result is a set of nested **extend**-statements containing only one variable each.

```
Extend(dom, ConsnameList(nhead,nrest), rul)
-> < normal: ExtendSingle(dom, nhead, Extend(dom, nrest, rul)) >;
```

Remove. The *remove* step is the implementation of the removal formalised in section 3. For each type of node (called *phyla* in kimwitu) in the abstract syntax definition, a remove function is introduced. The remove function performs removal for each term of the respective phylum, for example the terms `Assign`, `Choose`, `Extend`, ... for the *rule* phylum. It returns a term of the respective phylum as result – for example the remove function for rules always returns a term of type rule.

The remove functions for phyla follow a pattern. Formal arguments of the function are a phylum and a set of casestrings (the locally undefined ASM names). The return type is the same as the phylum used as formal argument, ensuring the resulting term has the correct type in the context in which it occurs. The outermost statement is a switch over all terms of the phylum, using the kimwitu control structure *with*. For each term, the actions for removal are defined separately.

For a term of a phylum, removal starts by checking conditions consisting of the predicates *true*, *false* and *undefined*, as defined in the formalisation of the removal process. If a condition evaluates to **true**, a modified term is returned, calling remove recursively on the subterms of the term if necessary. For example, for the rule term `IfThenElse`, if the predicate *true* holds for expression *exp*, removal continues with the **then**-part, if the predicate *false* holds for expression *exp*, removal continues with the **else**-part. If *undefined* holds for the expression *exp* the rule term `Skip` is returned.

```
IfThenElse(exp, r1, r2):  {
   if (eval_true(exp,V)) { return remove(r1,V); };
   if (eval_false(exp,V)) { return remove(r2,V); };
   if (eval_undef(exp,V)) { return Skip(); };
   return IfThenElse(remove(exp,V), remove(r1,V), remove(r2,V));
}
```

Cleanup. Removal starts at the root of the abstract syntax tree and works towards the leaves, without any backtracking. Therefore, removal on a subtree does not take the context of the subtree into account. However, the removal can affect the context and make it obsolete. If the entire rule body of an **extend**-statement is reduced to skip, the **extend**-statement itself could be removed. The *cleanup* step transforms superfluous rules resulting from the removal step to a post-removal normal form. The normal form is achieved by defining term rewrite rules in kimwitu. Unlike removal, the rewrite rules apply anywhere where their left hand side matches, and are applied as long as a match is found.

Cleanup performs the following modifications to the formal semantics:

– The rule skip is removed from parallel rule blocks.
– Rules with subrules are replaced with skip if all subrules of the rule are skip-rules.

- **if**-rules with identical subrules in the **then**- and **else**-part are replaced by the subrule in the **then**-part.
- All local definitions of a rule macro with a skip-rule as rule-body are removed. These definitions are not visible outside of the rule macro, and are not referenced by the rule-body.

The cleanup step only removes trivial parts of the ASM specification. The resulting specification is semantically equivalent to the specification before the cleanup step.

Iteration. Given a completely defined reduction profile, only one run of the SDL-profile tool is needed to generate a reduced formal semantics definition. In case the reduction profile is incomplete, the SDL-profile tool can identify further names in the signature that can be removed, and iterate the removal process. For example, a function with a target domain that has been removed during the previous removal step is included in the reduction profile of a subsequent iteration.

Unparsing. Unparsing traverses the abstract syntax tree and outputs a string representation of every node. The result is a textual representation of the formal semantics tree in the original input format. Therefore, the output of the SDL-profile tool can be used as the input for a subsequent run of the tool. It is also possible to output the result as a latex document, for better readability. A partial compilation of ASM rules to C++ exists as a third output format. This compilation is still in an early development phase.

4.2   Results

Given a formal semantics definition in ASM and a reduction profile, the SDL-profile tool generates a reduced formal semantics definition in the original format. In order to validate the removal process, we compared the original semantics definition with the reduced version. For this, we have used graphical diff-based tools (for example, tkdiff) to highlight the differences between the versions. Using the SDL-profile tool, we have created reduction profiles for several language features, such as timers, exceptions, save, composite states and inheritance. We have also created reduction profiles for language profiles like SAFIRE, resulting in a formal semantics definition that, with small modifications, matches that language profile.

Listings 4 and 5 show the results of applying the SDL-profile tool on the formal semantics definition for the macro SELECTTRANSITIONSTARTPAHSE, using a reduction profile for exceptions. The reduction profile contains, besides other function and macro names, the function name *currentExceptionInst*, which is interpreted as *undefined* in the context below. Therefore, the predicate *false* holds for the guard of the if-rule, and the first part of the **if**-statement is removed.

```
1  SELECTTRANSITIONSTARTPHASE ≡
2    if ( Self. currentExceptionInst ≠ undefined) then
3      Self. agentMode3 := selectException
4      Self. agentMode4 := startPhase
5    elseif ( Self. currentStartNodes ≠ ∅) then
6      ...
7    else
8      ...
9    endif
```

ASM-Listing 4. Macro SELECTTRANSITIONSTARTPHASE before Removal

```
1  SELECTTRANSITIONSTARTPHASE ≡
2    if ( Self. currentStartNodes ≠ ∅) then
3      ...
4    else
5      ...
6    endif
```

ASM-Listing 5. Macro SELECTTRANSITIONSTARTPHASE after Removal

5 Related Work

A modular language definition as described in this paper can be found in the language definition of UML [15]. The abstract syntax of UML is defined using a meta-model approach, using classes to define language elements and packages to group language elements into medium-grained units. The core of the language is defined by the Kernel package, specifying basic elements of the language such as packages, classes, associations and types. Each meta-model class/language element has a description of its semantics in an informal way.

UML has a profile mechanism that allows metaclasses from existing metamodels to be extended and adapted, using stereotypes. Semantics and constraints may be added as long as they don't conflict with existing semantics and constraints. For example, the profile mechanism is used to define a UML profile for SDL, enabling the use of UML 2.0 as a front-end for SDL-2000.

In [16], the concept of program slicing is extended to Abstract State Machines. For an expressive class of ASMs, an algorithm for the computation of a minimal slice of an ASM, given a slicing criterion, is presented. While the complexity of the algorithm is acceptable in the average case, the worst case complexity is exponential.

ConTraST [17] is an SDL to C++ transpiler that generates a readable C++ representation of an SDL specification by preserving as much of the original structure as possible. The generated C++ code is compiled together with a runtime environment that is a C++ implementation of the formal semantics defined in Z100.F3. ConTraST is based on the textual syntax of SDL-96, and supports language profiles syntactically by allowing the deactivation of language features. In particular, the language profiles *Core*, *Static₁*, *Static₂* and *Dynamic* - as described in section 2 - are supported. In order to support language profiles semantically, we can use the results of the formally defined derivation of language profiles from the complete formal semantics definition. Using the SDL-profile tool, the translation from the reduced formal semantics definition into a C++ runtime environment can be performed semi-automatic. The resulting runtime environment is smaller, leading to a more efficient execution.

6   Conclusions and Outlook

In this paper, we have introduced the concept of language profiles as well-defined subsets of a language, leading to smaller, more understandable language definitions. Tool support can be based on these language profiles, leading to faster tool development and less expensive tools. Based on the smaller language definitions, code optimisations can be performed when generating code from a specification.

We have argued for the importance of formal semantics for language definitions, and the importance of deriving the formal semantics of language profiles from a common formal semantics definition. This allows us to compare the formal semantics of different language profiles, and to make assertions about the consistency of language profiles.

To achieve deterministic results, we have formalised the process of deriving formal semantics for language profiles from a complete formal semantics definition, based on Abstract State Machines and applied to the formal semantics of SDL-2000. This process is based on reducing the signature of the ASM, subsequently leading to the reduction of parts of ASM-rules that become unreachable. We have implemented this formally defined process in an SDL-profile tool, making it possible to validate the results of the reduction. This tool was used to create several language profiles for SDL-2000, by removing language features from the formal semantics definition, such as exceptions, timers, save and composite states.

Based on the formally defined process for the derivation of SDL language profiles, we can define precise criteria for the consistency of language profiles. However, currently the consistency has to be verified manually. Our future work will focus on modifying the derivation process, so that as many automatic guarantees as possible can given for the consistency of the derived profiles.

References

1. ITU Recommendation Z.100 (03/93): Specification and Description Language (SDL). Geneva (1993)
2. ITU Recommendation Z.100 Addendum 1 (10/96): Specification and Description Language (SDL). Geneva (1996)
3. ITU Recommendation Z.100 (08/02): Specification and Description Language (SDL). Geneva (2002)
4. ITU Recommendation Z.100 (2002) Corrigendum 1 (08/04): Specification and Description Language (SDL). Geneva (2004)
5. ITU Recommendation Z.100 (2002) Amendment 1 (10/03): Specification and Description Language (SDL). Geneva (2003)

6. Gurevich, Y.: Evolving Algebras 1993: Lipari Guide. In Börger, E., ed.: Specification and Validation Methods. Oxford University Press (1995) 9–36
7. Gurevich, Y.: May 1997 draft of the ASM guide. Technical Report CSE-TR-336-97, EECS Department, University of Michigan (1997)
8. Prinz, A., von Löwis, M.: Generating a Compiler for SDL from the Formal Language Definition. In Reed, R., Reed, J., eds.: SDL 2003: System Design. Volume 2708 of LNCS., Springer (2003) pp. 150–165
9. ITU Study Group 10: Draft Z.100 Annex F1 (11/00) (2000)
10. ITU Study Group 10: Draft Z.100 Annex F2 (11/00) (2000)
11. ITU Study Group 10: Draft Z.100 Annex F3 (11/00) (2000)
12. SDL Task Force: SDL+ - The Simplest, Useful 'Enhanced SDL-Subset' for the Implementation and Testing of State Machines (2004) www.sdltaskforce.org/sdl-tf-draftresult_4.pdf, www.sdltaskforce.org/sdl-plus_syntax.html, www.sdltaskforce.org/sdl-plus_codec.html.
13. Glässer, U., Gotzhein, R., Prinz, A.: An Introduction To Abstract State Machines. Technical Report 326/03, Department of Computer Science, University of Kaiserslautern (2003)
14. von Löwis, M., Piefel, M.: The Term Processor Kimwitu++. In Callaos, N., Harnandez-Encinas, L., Yetim, F., eds.: SCI 2002: The 6th World Multiconference on Systemics, Cybernetics and Informatics, Orlando, USA (2002)
15. OMG Unified Modelling Language Specification: Version 2.0 (2003) www.uml.org.
16. Nowack, A.: Slicing Abstract State Machines. In Zimmermann, W., Thalheim, B., eds.: Abstract State Machines 2004 - Advances in Theory and Practice. Volume 3052 of LNCS., Wittenberg, Germany, Springer (2004) pp.186–201
17. Weber, C.: Entwurf und Implementierung eines konfigurierbaren SDL Transpilers für eine C++ Laufzeitumgebung. Master's thesis, University of Kaiserslautern, Germany (2005)

Automating Scenario Merging

Loïc Hélouët[1], Thibaut Hénin[2], and Christophe Chevrier[3]

[1] IRISA/INRIA, Campus de Beaulieu, 35042 Rennes Cedex, France
loic.helouet@irisa.fr
[2] ENS Cachan, Campus de Ker Lann, 35170 Bruz
thibaut.henin@irisa.fr
[3] France Télécom R&D, 2. av Pierre Marzin,22300 Lannion, France
christophe.chevrier@francetelecom.com

Abstract. The design of distributed systems requirements often ends with a collection of redundant use cases or scenarios, each of which illustrating a peculiar functionality or a typical execution of the system. The actual behavior of the system under design can be considered as a superposition of all use cases. However, current scenario languages do not propose such superposition mechanism. An operator for Message Sequence Charts defined as a sum of MSCs was proposed recently. However, the designer must provide explicitly the common parts in operands (called the interface) to compute a sum. This paper proposes an automatic construction of this interface based on a heuristic search.

1 Introduction

Scenarios are a popular formalism describing runs of distributed systems. They often appear in protocol descriptions or as illustrations of a system's use. They are also proposed to design use cases in the UML standard. Several scenario languages have been proposed: Message Sequence charts [4], Live Sequence Charts [2], UML's sequence diagrams [9]. MSCs, LSCs and sequence diagrams represent scenarios as compositions of basic diagrams which are more or less finite chronograms. A natural formal representation of these basic diagrams is labeled partial orders. In addition to the basic diagrams, all notations propose several composition operators such as sequence, iteration, alternative, etc. These extensions are available in MSCs since 1996 [11], and came later for sequence diagrams in UML 2.0 [9]. However, even a high-level description is not sufficient to capture all the behaviors of a system. Of course scenarios cannot be considered as a programming language, and their role is not to be exhaustive. Scenarios should rather be considered as an abstraction of a system's behavior, attached to a particular functionality, or to a particular point of view (the user's view of the system, for example). As a consequence, the requirement phase in design often ends with a collection of different scenarios describing the system from different points of view, hence with some similarities (see [3] for an example of scenario collection for the same system). The behavior of the system under study is not a parallel composition of these descriptions. It is not either an alternative or a sequence, but rather a superposition of scenarios.

R. Gotzhein and R. Reed (Eds.): SAM 2006, LNCS 4320, pp. 64–81, 2006.

Superposition is an usual preoccupation for telecommunication services composition. Superposition operators have already been proposed for parallel programs by [1], or for other formalisms such as automata (see for example [6,12]). Let us illustrate the expected outcome of a superposition operator for basic Message Sequence Charts (or bMSCs). A bMSC is roughly speaking a chronogram, depicting communications an actions of a set of processes. Figure 1 shows several examples of bMSCS. BMSC M_1 describes an exchange of three messages $m1$, $m2$ and $m3$, in this order. M_2 depicts the exchange of two messages $m1$ and $m3$, but specifies that an internal action a must take place on instance A between the sending of $m1$ and $m2$. The desired result is the bMSC M_3, that can be considered as a "sum" of M_1 and M_2. Note that as M_1 and M_2 do not specify any ordering between the sending of $m2$ and action a, these two events are kept unordered in the sum, and appear in a coregion.

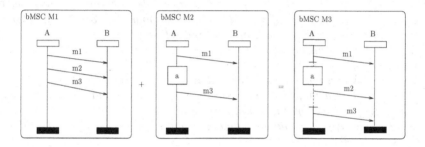

Fig. 1. Superposition of two scenarios

If all scenarios obtained after the requirement phase are seen as partial views of an actual behavior, then a composition of two abstractions should be a more concrete scenario that refines both views. A superposition operator for MSCs called *amalgamated sum* was proposed in [7]. To sum two bMSCs, the common part (also called *interface*) of the operands have to be defined. The result of the sum is an union of both scenarios where the common part is not duplicated. The main drawback so far is that the identical parts in operands have to be explicitly given before composition. Automating the product is not always possible, as there is more than one possible interface and amalgamated sum hence requires some directives from an user. In this work, we investigate how to compute efficiently the best possible interfaces between two bMSCs to reduce the work of end users. Note that [7] also defines a superposition operator for HMSCs, but this is out of the scope of this work. The paper is organized as follows: Section 2 recalls some usual notations on scenarios and defines the notion of amalgamated sum of bMSCs. Section 3 defines the notion of common part of two bMSCs and highlights some of their properties. Section 4 shows how the search for an interface can be brought back to an heuristic search algorithm. Section 5 shows an example of automatic composition of bMSCs, and section 6 concludes this work. Due to lack of space, proofs of propositions are not included in this paper. They can however be found in a preliminary version of this work available on the first author's web page.

2   Scenarios

Message Sequence Charts is a scenario formalism standardized by ITU [4]. It is composed of two description levels. At the lowest level, basic Message Sequence Charts (bMSCs for short) define interactions among objects called *instances*. BMSCs can be considered as a formal definition of chronograms. In a bMSCs, interactions among instances are performed using asynchronous communications. The second level of this formalism is called High-level Message Sequence Charts [11], and allows for the definition of more elaborated descriptions containing iterations, and alternatives. In this section, we will only consider bMSCs and their amalgamated sum. Formally, bMSCs can be considered as labeled partial orders [5] and can be defined as follows:

Definition 1. *A bMSC is a tuple* $B = (E, \leq, A, I, \alpha, \phi, m)$, *where:*

- $E = E_S \cup E_R \cup E_A$ *is a set of events that can be partitioned into a set of message sendings, a set of message receptions, and a set of atomic actions.*
- $\leq$ *is a preorder on* E, *i.e a transitive and reflexive relation*
- A *is a set of action names,*
- I *is a set of instances,*
- $\alpha : E \longrightarrow A$ *is a mapping that associates a label to each event.*
- $\phi : E \longrightarrow I$ *is a mapping that associates an instance name to each event.* $\phi(e)$ *will sometimes be called the locality of* e.
- $m : E_S \longrightarrow E_R$ *is a mapping that associates a message reception to each message sending.*

Note that $\leq$ *is not necessarily a partial order, i.e. from our definition, a bMSC may not describe a valid execution of a system. When* $\leq$ *is a partial order, we will say that* B *is* well-formed. *Let us also define the empty bMSC* $B_\epsilon = (E_\epsilon, \leq_\epsilon, A_\epsilon, I_\epsilon, \alpha_\epsilon, \phi_\epsilon, m_\epsilon)$ *such that* $E_\epsilon = \emptyset$.

Figure 2 shows an example of bMSC. Three instances *Sender*, *Medium*, and *Receiver* exchange messages *Data*, *ack*, and *info*. An atomic action *action* is performed by instance *Sender*. Note that the ordering on an instance lifeline is not

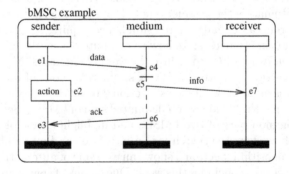

Fig. 2. An example of bMSC

necessarily a total order. This is symbolized by a dashed part called a *coregion* on the lifeline. In our example, the sending of messages *info* and *ack* are unordered.

For a given bMSC B, we will denote by $\downarrow (e) = \{e' \in E \mid e' \leq e\}$ the *causal past* of event e in B. Similarly, we will define the *future* of an event by $\uparrow (e) = \{e' \in E \mid e \leq e'\}$. A well-formed bMSC describes a set of *executions*, each of which is a linearization of its partial ordering (i.e an execution of a bMSC $B = (E, \leq, A, I, \alpha, \phi, m)$ is a word $w = e_1 \ldots e_{|E|}$ such that any event of E appears exactly once in w, and furthermore, for all e_i, e_{i+k} in w, $e_{i+k} \not\leq e_i$). The set of linearizations of a bMSC will be denoted by $Lin(B)$. For a given linearization $w \in Lin(B)$, $w_{[i]}$ will denote the ith event of word w.

The usual operators proposed for Message Sequence Charts are sequential composition, parallel composition, alternative and iteration. As already mentioned, these operators do not allow superposition as described in Figure 1. In a recent paper, [7] has proposed an operator called *amalgamated sum*, that allows for this kind of composition. In this sum, the common part between two bMSCs B_1 and B_2 is defined by another bMSC called the *interface*, that is related to B_1 and B_2 by *bMSC morphisms*. Roughly speaking, a bMSC morphism $f : B_I \longrightarrow B$ from an interface B_I to a bMSC B exists if and only if B_I is "contained" in B, and describes how B_I is injected in B.

Definition 2. *Let $B_1 = (E_1, \leq_1, A_1, I_1, \alpha_1, \phi_1, m_1)$, $B_2 = (E_2, \leq_2, A_2, I_2, \alpha_2, \phi_2, m_2)$ be two bMSCs. A morphism from B_1 to B_2 is a triple $f = (f_1, f_2, f_3)$, where:*

- *$f_1 : E_1 \longrightarrow E_2$ is an injective function from E_1 to E_2.*
- *$f_2 : A_1 \longrightarrow A_2$ is an injective mapping from A_1 to A_2.*
- *$f_3 : I_1 \longrightarrow I_2$ is an injective mapping from I_1 to I_2.*

Furthermore, the morphisms should satisfy the following properties:

i) *$\forall e, e' \in E_1, e \leq_1 e' \Rightarrow f_1(e) \leq_2 f_1(e')$: the ordering among events is preserved by the morphism.*

ii) *$\forall e, e' \in E_1, m(e) = e' \Rightarrow m(f_1(e)) = f_1(e')$: messages are preserved by the morphisms*

iii) *$\forall e_1 \in E_1, e_2 \in E_2$ such that $e_2 = f(e_1)$, $\exists e'_2 \in E_2, m(e_2) = e'_2 \Longrightarrow \exists e'_1 \in E_1$ such that $m(e_1) = e'_1 \wedge f(e'_1) = e'_2$ and $\exists e'_2 \in E_2, m(e'_2) = e_2 \Longrightarrow \exists e'_1 \in E_1$ such that $m(e'_1) = e_1 \wedge f(e'_1) = e'_2$. This condition means that messages are mapped integrally by bMSC morphisms, and that we cannot associate a single event with a message sending or reception.*

iv) *$f_3 \circ \phi_1 = \phi_2 \circ f_1$: this property means that the locality of events is coherent: two events located on the same instance in B_1 will be located on the same instance in B_2.*

v) *$f_2 \circ \alpha = \alpha' \circ f_1$: this property means that the labeling of events remains coherent through morphisms. The images of two events with identical label are events with identical labels.*

Note that in this definition, nothing forces labeling or locality to be similar in B_1 and B_2. Figure 3 shows two examples of bMSC morphisms. Consider

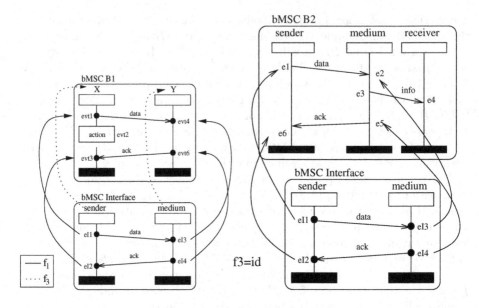

Fig. 3. Two example morphisms

the leftmost morphism. Event morphism is represented as a plain arrow and instance morphism as a dashed arrow. For the sake of clarity, labels morphism is not represented, but is obvious on this example. bMSC *Interface* can clearly be injected in bMSC $B1$. Each event of *Interface* has an image in $B1$, messages and order are preserved. Instances *Sender* and *Medium* are renamed by the instance mapping into X and Y.

Definition 3 (Amalgamated Sum of Two Sets). *Let I, J and K be three finite sets. Let $f : I \to J$ and $g : I \to K$ be two injective maps. The amalgamated sum $J_f +_g K$ is defined as $J_f +_g K = (J \backslash f(I)) \uplus (K \backslash g(I)) \uplus I$. The amalgamated sum yields two injections $\tilde{f} : J \to J_f +_g K$ and $\tilde{g} : K \to J_f +_g K$ defined as follows:*

$$\begin{cases} \forall i \in f(I), & \tilde{f}(i) = f^{-1}(i) \\ \forall i \in J \setminus f(I), \tilde{f}(i) = i \end{cases} \qquad \begin{cases} \forall i \in g(I), & \tilde{g}(i) = g^{-1}(i) \\ \forall i \in K \setminus g(I), \tilde{g}(i) = i \end{cases}$$

Amalgamated sum of sets is a disjoint union of these sets where events that are identified through the interface are not duplicated. It will be used to amalgamate sets of instances, events or actions of two bMSCs.

Definition 4. *Let B_1, B_2, B_I be three bMSCS and let $f : B_I \longrightarrow B_1$ and $g : B_I \longrightarrow B_2$ be two bMSC morphisms. The amalgamated sum of B_1 and B_2 with respect to interface B_I and morphisms f and g is denoted $B_1 {}_f +_g B_2$, and is defined as $B_1 {}_f +_g B_2 = (E, \leq, A, I, \alpha, \phi, m)$, where:*

- $E = E_1 \, {}_{f_1}\!+_{g_1} E_2$
- $\leq$ is the preorder relation obtained by transitive closure of $\tilde{f}_1(\leq_1) \cup \tilde{g}_1(\leq_2)$;
- $A = A_1 \, {}_{f_2}\!+_{g_2} A_2$
- $I = I_1 \, {}_{f_3}\!+_{g_3} I_2$
- $\forall e \in E,\, \alpha(e) = \begin{cases} \alpha_1(e) \text{ if } e \in E_1 \backslash f_1(E_I) \\ \alpha_2(e) \text{ if } e \in E_2 \backslash f_2(E_I) \\ \alpha_0(e) \text{ otherwise} \end{cases}, \quad \phi(e) = \begin{cases} \phi_1(e) \text{ if } e \in E_1 \backslash f_1(E_I) \\ \phi_2(e) \text{ if } e \in E_2 \backslash f_2(E_I) \\ \phi_0(e) \text{ otherwise} \end{cases}$
- $m = \tilde{f}_1(m_1) \cup \tilde{g}_1(m_2)$

Using the two morphisms of Figure 3, the amalgamated sum between bMSCs $B1$ and $B2$ with bMSC $Interface$ produces the bMSC of Figure 2. Note that $\leq$ is not always acyclic, even when B_1 and B_2 are well-formed bMSCs. We will say that an amalgamated sum is *well-formed* whenever $\leq$ is a partial order relation (transitive, reflexive, antisymmetric). Figure 4 shows an example of amalgamated sum for which the orderings between actions a and b defined by $M1$ and $M2$ are inconsistent. The result produces a bMSC that is not well-formed.

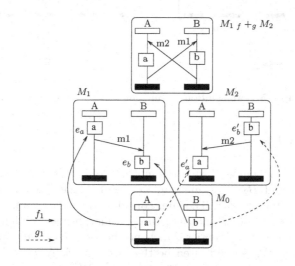

Fig. 4. An amalgamated sum that is not well-formed

Proposition 1. *Let* B_1, B_2, B_I, *be three bMSCs and* $f : B_I \longrightarrow B_1, g : B_I \longrightarrow B_2$ *be two bMSC morphisms. Let us denote by* $\mathcal{P}_{f,g} : E_1 \longrightarrow E_2$ *the partial bijective function that pairs events of* E_1 *and* E_2, *i.e.* $\mathcal{P}_{f,g}(e_1) = e_2$ *iff* $\exists e_i \in B_I, f(e_i) = e_1$ *and* $g(e_i) = e_2$. *The following propositions are equivalent:*

1. $B_1 \, {}_f\!+_g B_2$ *is well-formed*

2. $\forall e_1 \in f(B_I), \uparrow (e_1) \cap \mathcal{P}_{f,g}^{-1}\!\left(\downarrow \left(\mathcal{P}_{f,g}(e_1) \right) \right) = \{e_1\}$

3. $\forall e_2 \in g(B_I), \uparrow (e2) \cap \mathcal{P}_{f,g}\!\left(\downarrow \left(\mathcal{P}_{f,g}^{-1}(e_2) \right) \right) = \{e_2\}$

From this proposition, we know that checking for well-formedness of an amalgamated sum resumes to finding connected components in $\leq_2 \cup \leq_2 \cup \mathcal{P} \cup \mathcal{P}^{-1}$. This can be done in polynomial time using Tarjan's algorithm [13]. Note however that the complexity of finding a valid interface from a pair of bMSCs is due to the number of possible interfaces more than to the complexity of checking whether $B_1 {}_f+_g B_2$ is well-formed.

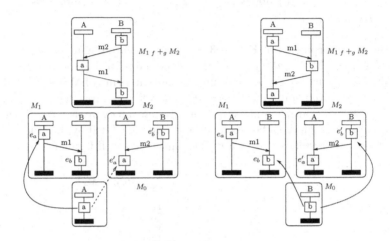

Fig. 5. Two solutions to merge bMSCs of Figure 4

3   Common Part

Intuitively, in an amalgamated sum, the interface bMSC B_I represents the common part of B_1 and B_2. The amalgamated sum merges B_1 and B_2 without duplicating the common part. The sum considers that two events that are the image of a single event of the interface through morphisms are identical. These events do not need to have identical labels nor be located on the same instance. Note however that this should often be the case, especially when labeling and location of events is the only information available. When an amalgamated sum is not well formed, it means that operands do not agree of the respective orders of common events. Then either some events that were identified in the interface should not be considered as identical, or the two descriptions are not compatible and should not be composed. To resolve this inconsistency, an user can either withdraw some events that cause the ordering relation in the sum to be cyclic from the morphims definitions, or redesign one of the composed scenarios to obtain a well-formed sum.

If we consider again the example of Figure 4, considering $a's$ and b's as common events in both views produces an ill-formed bMSC. However, if we chose to consider only $a's$ or only $b's$ as common events, then there is a way to compose $M1$ and $M2$ to obtain a well-formed behavior, as depicted in Figure 5. Note that well formedness could be used to define a notion of coherence: if we try to match all occurrences of events with similar label and similar rank on an instance, and obtain an ill-formed bMSC, then we can consider that the composed bMSCs are inconsistent.

For a well-formed amalgamated sum $B_1 {}_f +_g B_2$, we will often call the triple (B_I, f, g) the *common part* of B_1 and B_2. The empty common part C_ϵ is a common part such that $B_I = B_\epsilon$.

Automating the amalgamated sum resumes to finding common parts for a pair of bMSCs B_1, B_2. Note however that the design of an interface for a couple of bMSCs can be a difficult task. In our definition, nothing forces the interfaced events to have the same label, nor to be located on the same instance. The only restriction in the general case is that the bMSC morphisms should be injective. That is, an interface can have up to the size of the smallest operand of the sum. Kleitman and Rotschild gave a bound for the number of partial orders of size n which is in $O\left(2^{\frac{n^2}{4} \cdot \frac{3n}{2} \cdot \ln(n)}\right)$ [8]. Note however that the number of interfaces of size n describing the behavior of l instances (without considering labeling, that may yeld an infinite number of different bMSCs) is much lower, as it is in l^n (everytime you add an event, it can be located on l instances, and ordering does not matter as it can be deduced from the ordering in $B1, B2$). Anyway, this number remains too big to consider searching exhaustively the whole set of interfaces and morphisms: if m is the size of the minimal operand (and M the size of the largest operand) for an amalgamated sum, the number of possible interfaces is $\sum_{i \in 1..m} l^i$, and the worst number of possible common parts is hence in $\sum_{i \in 1..m} l^i \cdot \frac{m!}{(m-i)!} \cdot \frac{M!}{(M-i)!}$. A sensible restriction of the amalgamated sum is to consider that when two events in B_1 and B_2 are the image of a single event in the interface, then they are located on the same instance and have identical labels, i.e. $\forall e_1 \in E_1, e_2 \in E_2$, when $\exists e \in E_I, f_1(e) = e_1$ and $g_1(e) = e_2$ we have $\phi(e_1) = \phi(e_2)$ and $\alpha(e_1) = \alpha(e_2)$. With this restriction in mind, the interface can be built using the same labels and the same instances as the summed operands (i.e. $A_I \subseteq A_1 \cap A_2$ and $I_I \subseteq I_1 \cap I_2$). Hence, if we call $K = |\alpha^{-1}(A_1 \cap A_2) \cap \phi^{-1}(I_1 \cap I_2)|$, the number of possible interfaces becomes $\sum_{i \in 1..K} l^i \cdot \frac{m!}{(m-i)!} \cdot \frac{M!}{(M-i)!}$. So, from now, we will consider that in any bMSC morphism $f = (f_1, f_2, f_3)$, $f_2 = id$ and $f_3 = id$. But even with this restriction, the number of common parts remains huge.

Now, we have to remind that the main justification of amalgamated sum is to exploit redundancy in different views. Hence a common part with a large interface can be considered as better than the empty common part C_ϵ, but also as any smaller interface. The notion of *extension* of a common part formalizes this intuition, and provides a structure to the set of common parts.

Definition 5. *Let $C = (B_I, f, g)$ be a common part for a pair of bMSCs B_1, B_2. We will say that $C' = (B'_I, f', g')$ is an extension of C and write $C \sqsubseteq C'$ if and only if:*

- *(B'_I, f', g') is a common part of B_1, B_2*   *$- E_I \subseteq E'_I$*
- *$\forall e \in E_I, f'(e) = f(e)$ and $g'(e) = g(e)$*

We will say that (B'_I, f', g') is a sequential extension of (B_I, f, g) when no event of $E'_I \setminus E_I$ (respectively $f'(E'_I \setminus E_I)$ and $g'(E'_I \setminus E_I))$ is located in the causal past of E_I (respectively $f(E_I)$ and $g(E_I))$.

For a common part C, let us denote by $Ext(C)$ the set of extensions of C and by $SExt(C)$ the set of sequential extensions of C. These extension sets contain a set of maximal elements $\widehat{C}$ and $\overline{C}$ such that $Ext(\widehat{C}) = \widehat{C}$ and $SExt(\overline{C}) = \overline{C}$.

Proposition 2. *For any pair of bMSCs B_1, B_2, $\widehat{C_\epsilon} \subseteq \overline{C_\epsilon}$.*

This proposition gives the intuition for an efficient and incremental search for interfaces. The set of common parts is in fact the search space that has to be explored to produce the best interfaces. $(Ext(C_\epsilon), \sqsubseteq)$ and $(SExt(C_\epsilon), \sqsubseteq)$ form two lower semi-lattices. However, the size of $SExt(C_\epsilon)$ is lower than the size of $Ext(C_\epsilon)$. Furthermore, the maximal elements in the lattice of extensions are also maximal elements in the lattice of sequential extensions, i.e. no optimal solution is lost. This means that the best maximal common part can be built incrementally (and more efficiently) by exploration of a linearization of one of the operands. Let us clarify this intuition with the example bMSCs of figure 6. The semi-lattices of common parts extensions and sequential extensions for this pair of bMSCs are represented in Figure 7. The table in Figure 7 describes how events are matched in each common part: common part $C1$ identifies two events e_1 and e'_1, $C2$ identifies e_2 and e'_2, $C3$ e_3 and e'_3, etc. We know that $e_1 \leq e_2 \leq e_4 \leq e_3$, and furthermore, no common part may contain at the same time e_2 and e_4. Note also that events associated to messages m, n, o and t, u, v never appear in a common part (one cannot find events with similar labels). The leftmost graph in Figure 7 shows the Hasse diagram of the extension semi-lattice: vertices represent common parts, and an arrow between two vertices C_i, C_j indicates that $C_i \sqsubseteq C_j$.

Maximal elements in this semi-lattice are depicted by squares. The rightmost graph represents the semi-lattice of sequential extensions. Note that due to the ordering among events, some edges do not appear anymore in the diagram.

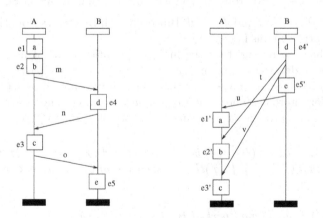

Fig. 6. A pair of bMSCs

Hence, some common parts (such as $C3$, $C6$, and $C7$) become maximal w.r.t the sequential extension relation. However, they are not maximal w.r.t extension, and most of them will be ignored during the heuristic search.

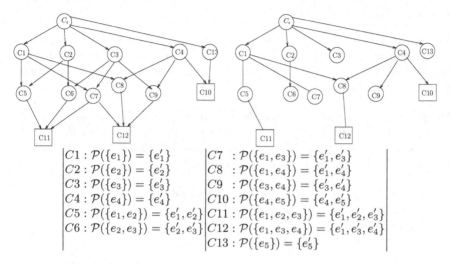

$$C1 : \mathcal{P}(\{e_1\}) = \{e'_1\}$$
$$C2 : \mathcal{P}(\{e_2\}) = \{e'_2\}$$
$$C3 : \mathcal{P}(\{e_3\}) = \{e'_3\}$$
$$C4 : \mathcal{P}(\{e_4\}) = \{e'_4\}$$
$$C5 : \mathcal{P}(\{e_1, e_2\}) = \{e'_1, e'_2\}$$
$$C6 : \mathcal{P}(\{e_2, e_3\}) = \{e'_2, e'_3\}$$
$$C7 : \mathcal{P}(\{e_1, e_3\}) = \{e'_1, e'_3\}$$
$$C8 : \mathcal{P}(\{e_1, e_4\}) = \{e'_1, e'_4\}$$
$$C9 : \mathcal{P}(\{e_3, e_4\}) = \{e'_3, e'_4\}$$
$$C10 : \mathcal{P}(\{e_4, e_5\}) = \{e'_4, e'_5\}$$
$$C11 : \mathcal{P}(\{e_1, e_2, e_3\}) = \{e'_1, e'_2, e'_3\}$$
$$C12 : \mathcal{P}(\{e_1, e_3, e_4\}) = \{e'_1, e'_3, e'_4\}$$
$$C13 : \mathcal{P}(\{e_5\}) = \{e'_5\}$$

Fig. 7. Semi lattices of extensions and sequential extensions

4 Automation of MSC Sums

According to [10], performance of heuristic search depends on two criterions: a good representation and organization of the search space, and a good evaluation function for a place in this search space. For each place of the search space, we have to be able to compute a set of successors, and chose to explore the more promising among them (w.r.t. the evaluation function). The semi-lattice of sequential extensions is smaller than the lattice of extensions. Furthermore, the maximal elements w.r.t extension are the same in both lattices, and the extension relation guarantees that we are progressing toward a better solution. Hence the lattice of sequential extensions can be considered as a good organization of the search space. A good way to explore the lattice of sequential extensions of a pair of bMSCs B_1, B_2 is to study events of the smallest operand according to the causal ordering (i.e. chose a peculiar linearization). For each event e, we have to find a similar event e' in the other operand (same label and same instance), and make sure that after identifying e and e', the amalgamated sum of B_1 and B_2 is still well-formed.

In the sequel, we will denote by $B \circ \{e\}$ the bMSC obtained by sequential concatenation of B and an event e, and slightly abusing the morphisms notation, we will denote by $f' = f \cup \{(e, e')\}$ the morphism f' defined on $dom(f) \cup \{e\}$ such that : $f'(x) = \begin{cases} f(x) \text{ if } x \neq e \\ e' \text{ otherwise} \end{cases}$

Proposition 3. *Let $C = (B, f, g)$ be a common part of B_1, B_2, let e be an atomic action of $E_1 \setminus \downarrow f(E_B)$ and e' be an atomic action of $E_2 \setminus \downarrow g(E_B)$ such that $\phi(e) = \phi(e')$ and $\alpha(e) = \alpha(e')$. Let e_i be a freshly created event such that $\phi(e_i) = \phi(e)$ and $\alpha(e_i) = \alpha(e)$. Then, $C' = (B \circ \{ei\}, f \cup \{(e_i, e)\}, g \cup \{(e_i, e')\})$ is a sequential extension of C.*

This property shows that atomic actions can be easily paired as long as they do not appear in the past of an already matched event. Hence, searching for a paired event for an atomic action resumes to finding this event in the future of already matched events.

Proposition 4. *Let $C = (B, f, g)$ be a common part of B_1, B_2, and let e be an event of $E_1 \setminus \downarrow f(E_B)$ and e' be an event of $E_2 \setminus \downarrow g(E_B)$ such that $\phi_1(e) = \phi_2(e')$ and $\alpha_1(e) = \alpha_2(e')$. If e is a message sending, then there is an extension $C' = (B', f', g')$ of C containing e and $m(e)$ iff:*

- *$\exists e' \in E_2 \setminus \downarrow g(E_B)$ such that $\phi(e) = \phi(e')$ and $\alpha(e) = \alpha(e')$.*
- *$\exists e'' \in E_2 \setminus \downarrow g(E_B)$ such that $\phi(m(e)) = \phi(e'')$ and $\alpha(m(e)) = \alpha(e'')$.*
- *$m(e') = e''$*
- *$\mathcal{P}_{f',g'}^{-1}(\downarrow (e'')) \cap \mathcal{P}_{f',g'} \uparrow (e) = e$*

This proposition means that if we try to build a common part by exploring a linearization of one of the operands and matching its events one after another, then we cannot conclude immediately that a message sending will appear in a common part, and we have to study its reception before concluding. Figure 8 shows a situation where events e_1 and e_1' cannot be identified through an interface when e_2 and e_2' have already been matched.

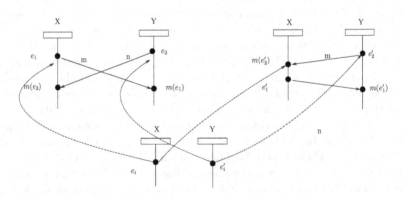

Fig. 8. Matching messages

These properties show how to explore the semi-lattice of sequential extensions, following a linearization. However, we may still explore the complete search space, and we need a way to discriminate common parts which extensions cannot be among the best ones to avoid exploring the whole lattice. This can be done through the definition of a quality criterion to guide the exploration and abandon hopeless interfaces. Of course, to fit the properties of extensions and their lattices, quality should be a function of the size of a common parts.

Definition 6. *The* quality *of a common part is* $Q(B_I, f, g) = \frac{|B_I|}{min(|B_1|,|B_2|)}.$

With the definition of a quality criterion, the search for the best common parts can be defined as the construction of the set $C_{Best} = \arg\max\{Q(B_I) \mid \exists (B_I, f, g)$ common part of $B_1, B_2\}$. The notion of quality is useful to help finding the best common parts, but also to quantify the coherence of two bMSCs. A pair of bMSCs which best common parts have a high quality can be considered as very coherent.

Proposition 5. *Let* B_1, B_2 *be two bMSCs, and let* C_{Best} *be the best common parts found w.r.t quality Then* $C_{Best} \subseteq \overline{C_\epsilon}$.

Note however that this property only holds when the quality of an interface is a function of its size. The main idea is to avoid searching the whole space of possible common parts by pruning systematically parts of the lattice for which the best reachable sequential extensions will have a lower quality than the best quality already computed. And of course, we must take this decision without exploring the abandoned part. We adopt a classical approach in operational research: common parts are built sequentially and incrementally. The exploration is guided by the quality that must be maximized on all maximal common parts, and by an heuristic, that gives an upper approximation of the maximal quality reachable from a common part. For a detailed survey on heuristics, interested readers may consult [10].

The estimated quality $\mathcal{E}Q(C) = qs(C) + h(C)$ of an common part C is an over approximation of the quality of any extension of C. It is defined as the sum of two functions: a fixed value $qs(C)$, the quality of C (i.e. the number of events matched for sure so far in C and in any extension of C), and an heuristic $h(C)$ that is an over approximation of the number of events that can still be matched in an extension of C. At each step, we chose to extend the part that has the best estimated quality.

The heuristic should satisfy two main principles :

– when a common part C is maximal, then $h(I) = 0$.
– For any extension C' of a common part C, $qs(C') + h(C') \leq qs(C) + h(C)$

The first requirement means that when no extension is possible for a common part C, then the estimated quality which is also the best quality reachable should be the actual quality of C. The second requirement means that the heuristic should always provide an over-approximation of the quality that may be achieved from a common part. This way, we can be sure that a path leading to a solution is never forgotten due to underestimation of the reachable maximal quality. Hence, the problem of automating the amalgamated sum is brought back to an exploration of a subset of common parts such that if a common part C' is explored after a common part C, then $\mathcal{E}Q(C') \geq \mathcal{E}Q(C)$.

During the exploration we will study events one after another in a linearization of the smallest operand. To keep track of the events explored so far, we just need to recall an integer n. However, we cannot be sure that a message sending will be eventually matched in the maximal extension reachable from the state of our research. Hence, we will keep some events as matched for sure in an interface B_I, with associated morphisms f and g, and we will also memorize temporary events in another potential interface B_I', with associated morphisms f' and g'. During the exploration, we will compute an estimated quality associated to an exploration state rather that to a common part (in a state, some potential solutions have already been ruled out). For a pair of bMSCS B_1, B_2, and in a given state $s = (n, B_I, B_I', f, g, f', g')$, we will have $\mathcal{E}Q(s) = qs(s) + h(s)$, where:

$$qs(n, B_I, B_I', f, g, f', g') = \frac{|B_I|}{min(|B_1|, |B_2|)},$$

and

$$h(n, B_I, B_I', f, g, f', g') = \frac{\left| \left\{ \begin{array}{c} e \in E_1 \setminus \downarrow (f(B_I) \cup f(B_I')) \mid \\ \exists e' \in E_2 \setminus \downarrow (g(B_I) \cup g'(B_I')), \\ \alpha(e) = \alpha(e') \wedge \phi(e) = \phi(e') \end{array} \right\} \right|}{min(|B_1|, |B_2|)}$$

Here, function qs describes the ratio between the number of event matched in a state and the size of bMSCs. Function h gives the ratio between events that may still be matched in an exploration state and the size of bMSCs. Obviously, the estimated quality of common part can only decrease with sequential extension. Hence, if we have a maximal sequential extension $C \in \overline{C_\epsilon}$, and an extension C' such that $Q(C) \geq \mathcal{E}Q(C')$, then for any sequential extension C'' of C', $Q(C) \geq \mathcal{E}Q(C'')$. This means that we do not have to explore successors of some states, as we already know (using the evaluation function) that the quality of their sequential extensions will be lower than a local maxima that was previously discovered. This also holds for exploration states.

From previous results, the exploration algorithm is rather straightforward: start from the empty common part, and find its best extensions. The heuristic is used to avoid exploring common parts for which we already know a better extension of C_ϵ. Extensions are computed as follows: events are studied one after another. For each event, we can decide to match it or not, hence creating two exploration paths. For atomic actions, events can be matched without the risk to create a cyclic preorder in the sum $B_1 {}_f +_g B_2$. Whether a sending can be matched depends on the future extensions, hence these matching are just potential. A reception must be matched if the corresponding sending is matched and if it does not create a cycle in the preorder relation of the amalgamated sum.

The complete exploration algorithms are described by algorithms 1 and 2 next pages. Note that the algorithm does not exactly explore the set of extensions, as when a message sending is under study, we have to guess whether it should be matched or not (this guess is depicted by B_I'). Note also that the heuristic allows to rule out automatically some parts of the search space. For the example

---

Algorithm 1 BestCommonParts(B_1, B_2)

1: Chose a linearization $w \in Lin(B_1)$
2: $T = \{(0, \emptyset, \emptyset, f_\epsilon, g_\epsilon, f_\epsilon, g_\epsilon)\}$
3: $Best = \{\}$
4: $fbest = 0$
5: **while** $T \neq \emptyset$ **do**
6:     select $t \in T$ such that $\forall t' \in T, qs(t') + h(t') \leq qs(t) + h(t)$
7:     $T = T \setminus \{t\}$
8:     $Succ = Successors(t, w)$
9:     **for all** $s \in Succ$ **do**
10:        **if** s is a leaf **then**
11:            **if** $qs(s) \geq fbest$ **then**
12:                $fbest = qs(s)$
13:                $Best = \{s' \in Best \cup \{s\} \mid qs(s') \geq fbest\}$
14:            **end if**
15:        **else**
16:            $T = T \cup \{s\}$
17:        **end if**
18:     **end for**
19:     $T = \{t \in T | qs(t) + h(t) \geq fbest\}$
20: **end while**
21: $C_{Best} = \emptyset$
22: **for all** $(n, E_I, E_I', f, g, f', g') \in Best$ **do**
23:     $B = (E_I, \{(e, e') \mid f(e) \leq_1 f(e') \wedge g(e) \leq_2 g(e')\}, \phi(E_I), \alpha(E_I), \alpha_1 \circ f, \phi_1 \circ f, m_1 \circ f)$
24:     $C_{Best} = C_{Best} \cup \{(B, f, g)\}$
25: **end for**
26: return (C_{Best})

---

of Figure 6, the linearization among events is $e1.e2.!m.?m.e4.!n.?n.e3.!o.?o.e5$, and the set of extensions explored would be $C_\epsilon, C1, C2, C4, C5, C6, C7, C8, C11,$ $C12, C13$. The best common parts computed by the algorithm are $C11$ and $C12$.

5   Example

Let us show on a concrete example how amalgamated sum can be used to compose services. Figure 9 presents an example of a cartography service built over an SOA architecture. In this kind of architecture, a service is described as an orchestration of basic services that are designed independently. The expected behavior is thus a combination of the individual basic services behaviors.

BMSC $UserServiceInteraction$ (USI) describes the behavior expected by an user. BMSC $ServiceDirectoryInteraction$ (SDI) describes the service from the directory provider's point of view: when an user asks for a map, the service calls the directory provider to obtain the destination address. BMSC $ServiceLocali-$ $zationInteraction$ (SLI) describes the relation between the service and the localization provider: when an user asks for a map and the destination address

Algorithm 2. Successor$((n, I, I', f, g, f', g'), w))$, where

- n number of events studied so far in the linearization of B_1
- E_I events of the interface computed so far
- E'_I events that may appear in the maximal interface reachable from current state (essentially sending events).
- $f : E_I \longrightarrow E_1$ morphism from I to E_1
- $g : E_I \longrightarrow E_2$ morphism from I to E_2
- $f' : E'_I \longrightarrow E_1$ potential morphism from I' to E_1
- $g' : E'_I \longrightarrow E_2$ potential morphism from I' to E_2

1: $Succ = \emptyset$; choose $e_1 = w_{[n+1]}$
2: **if** e_1 is an atomic action **then**
3:     $Succ := Succ \cup \{(n + 1, E_I, E'_I, f, g, f', g')\}$ /* e1 may not be matched */
4:     $Match = \{e_2 \in E_2 \backslash \downarrow (g(E_I) \cup g'(E'_I))$ such that $\phi(e') = \phi(e_2)$ and $\alpha(e_2) = \alpha(e')$ and $\uparrow (e_1) \cap \mathcal{P}_{f,g}^{-1} \downarrow (\mathcal{P}_{f,g}(e_1)) = e_1\}$
5:     **for all** $e_2 \in Match$ **do**
6:         Create a new event e_i
7:         $Succ := Succ \cup \{n + 1, E_I \cup \{e_i\}, E'_I, f \cup \{(e_i, e_1)\}, g \cup \{(e_i, e_2)\}, f', g')\}$
8:     **end for**
9: **end if**
10: **if** e_1 is a message sending **then**
11:     $Succ := Succ \cup \{(n + 1, E_I, E'_I, f, g, f', g')\}$ /* e1 may not be matched */
12:     $Match = \{e_2 \in E_2 \backslash \downarrow (g(E_I) \cup g'(E'_I))$ such that $\phi(e') = \phi(e_2)$ and $\alpha(e_2) = \alpha(e')$ and $\uparrow (e_1) \cap \mathcal{P}_{f,g}^{-1} \downarrow (\mathcal{P}_{f,g}(e_1)) = e_1\}$
13:     **for all** $e_2 \in Match$ **do**
14:         Create a new event e_i
15:         $Succ := Succ \cup \{(n + 1, E_I, E'_I \cup \{e_i\}, f, g, f' \cup \{(e_i, e_1)\}, g' \cup \{(e_i, e_2)\})\}$
16:     **end for**
17: **end if**
18: **if** e_1 is a reception **then**
19:     **if** $m^{-1}(e_1) \notin dom(f')$ **then**
20:         /* The corresponding sending was not matched: e_1 must not be matched */
21:         $Succ := Succ \cup \{(n + 1, E_I, E'_I, f, g, f', g')\}$
22:     **else**
23:         $e_i = f'^{-1}(m^{-1}(e_1))$
24:         /* e_i represents the sending of message received in e_1 in the interface */
25:         $e_2 = m(g'(e_i))$
26:         **if** pairing e_1, e_2 does not create cycles in the sum **then**
27:             create a new event e'_i
28:             $Succ := Succ \cup \left\{ \begin{pmatrix} n + 1, E_I \cup \{e_1, e_2\} \\ f \cup \{(ei, f'(e_i))\} \cup \{(e'_i, e_1)\}, \\ g \cup \{(ei, g'(e_i))\} \cup \{(e'_i, e_2)\}, \\ f' \setminus \{(ei, f'(e_i))\}, \\ g' \cup \{(ei, g'(e_i))\} \end{pmatrix} \right\}$
29:         **else**
30:             $Succ := Succ \cup \left\{ (n + 1, E_I, E'_I, f, g, f' \setminus \{(ei, f'(e_i))\}, g' \cup \{(ei, g'(e_i))\}) \right\}$
31:         **end if**
32:     **end if**
33: **end if**

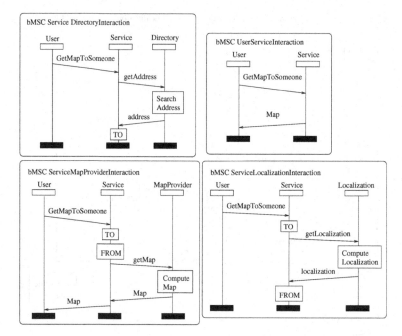

Fig. 9. A complete example

has been found, the service asks the localization provider for the user's location. Finally, the last bMSC *ServiceMapProviderInteraction* (SMPI) describes the service as seen by the Map Provider: when the destination address and the user location are found, the service asks for a map.

All these bMSCs can be automatically composed to obtain a single behavior, that refines the UserServiceInteraction. The bMSC provided in Figure 10 can be computed as the amalgamated sum $((USI_{f1+g1} SDI)_{f2+g2} SLI)_{f3+g3} SMPI$. Note that in this example, the best common parts are unique, and hence do not require interaction with an user. This may not always be the case, and the integration order for bMSCs may also influence the final result.

6 Conclusion

We have proposed an algorithm to compute efficiently the common parts of two bMSCs. This should facilitate the use of amalgamated sum to merge scenarios. Several other merging operator were proposed in previous works. The operator proposed in [6] merges two automata. The final result is an automaton that accepts the languages of both specifications. The operator proposed in [12] is very similar, and starts from a set of timed automata. These automata are merged as long as they agree on played sequences of events and on time constraints. The operators defined in [6,12] can be seen as products of scenarios. The major difference between a product and a sum is that as soon as both specifications

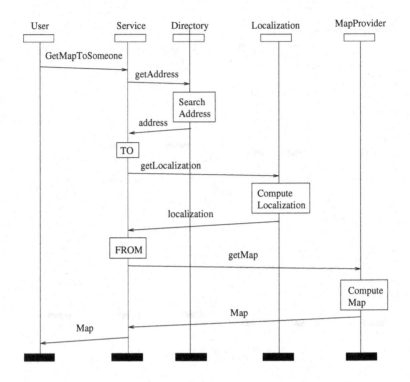

Fig. 10. Automatic composition of bMSCs of Figure 9

disagree on which event should be fired, the product provides no way to consider that other events of the specification are common. An amalgamated sum considers common events located at arbitrary places in a bMSC. The only requirement for merging is that the respective order on common events must be the same in both operands. Hence, two scenarios mays start with different sequences of events, and eventually agree on the rest of the description. Furthermore, events with identical label may not be considered as common if the result of a sum is ill-formed. For the example of Figure 4, a product would provide a specification that can play either M1 or M2. Amalgamated sum provides another interpretation that allows to consider events labeled by a or events labeled by b as common. Indeed, the amalgamated sum and the product are of different nature: the former considers merging of two different view of the same behavior, while the latter merges different behaviors of a specification.

The common part construction method proposed in this paper is an heuristic search. At the end of the algorithm, the result may not be unique. The final choice of which interface to chose to compose the bMSCs can be left to the end-user, or we may assume that the sum of two bMSCs produces a set of new bMSCS and consider all results as valid. Another possible solution is to add new quality criteria to discriminates solutions. However, we believe that in most cases the number of possible choices should remain small. We have shown that in the worst case, the number of possible solutions that have to be searched is really huge ($\sum\limits_{i\in 1..K} l^i \cdot \frac{m!}{(m-i)!} \cdot \frac{M!}{(M-i)!}$). The heuristic proposed does not guarantee that the complete search space is not explored. We may hence still have an exponential number of states to explore, and an exponential time complexity. Note however that the exploration of the semi-lattice only needs to recall the best solutions, and never memorizes at the same time a solution and one of its ancestors. The space complexity of heuristic search should then be a function of the width of the lattice (which vary with each example). Note also that as soon as a large enough number of events are successfully paired, all solutions that embed fewer events located at the end of composed scenarios have lower quality. Hence, they will probably not be considered during exploration. Furthermore, operational research algorithms have shown good average complexities. Tests on small examples gave a quasi instantaneous answer. Of course, additional case studies are needed, but after the first tests we think that the automatic composition problem should be feasible in practice. A possible extension of this work is to consider similar automation for HMSCs.

References

1. K. M. Chandy and J. Misra. *Parallel Program Design, A Foundation*. Addison-Wesley, 1988.
2. W Damm and D. Harel. Live sequence charts: Breathing life into message sequence charts. *Journal of System Design*, 2001.
3. L. Hélouët. Distributed system requirements modeling with message sequence charts. *International Journal of Information and Software Technology*, 2002.
4. ITU-TS. *ITU-TS Recommendation Z.120: Message Sequence Chart (MSC)*. ITU-TS, Geneva, September 1999.
5. J.P. Katoen and L. Lambert. Pomsets for message sequence charts. In *Proceedings of SAM98:1st conference on SDL and MSC*, pages 281–290, Berlin, Juin 1998.
6. F. Khendek and G.V. Bochmann. Merging behavior specifications. *Journal of Formal Methods in System Design*, 6(3):259–294, 1995.
7. J. Klein, B. Caillaud, and L. Hélouët. Merging scenarios. In *9th International Workshop on Formal Methods for Industrial Critical Systems (FMICS)*, number 133 in ENTCS, pages 209–226, sep. 2004.
8. D.J Kleitman and B.L Rotschild. Asymptotic enumeration of partial orders. *Transactions of the American Mathematical Society*, (205):205–220, 1975.
9. OMG. Uml superstructure specification, v2.0. OMG Document number formal/05-07-04, 2005.
10. J. Pearl. *Heuristics: Intelligent Search Strategies for Computer Problem Solving*. Addison-Wesley, 1995.
11. E. Rudolph, P. Graubmann, and J. Grabowski. Tutorial on Message Sequence Charts. *Computer Networks and ISDN Systems*, 28(12):1629–1641, 1996.
12. A. Salah, R. Dssouli, and G. Lapalme. Compiling real-time scenarios into a timed automaton. In *proc. of FORTE 2001*, pages 135–150, 2001.
13. R. Tarjan. Depth-first search and linear graph algorithms. *SIAM Journal of Computing*, 1(2), 1972.

Timed High-Level Message Sequence Charts for Real-Time System Design*

Tai Hyo Kim and Sung Deok Cha

Division of Computer Science,
Korea Advanced Institute of Science and Technology,
Daejeon, Republic of Korea
{taihyo, cha}@dependable.kaist.ac.kr

Abstract. Existing notations for expressing time constraints in high-level message sequence charts (HMSC) may cause ambiguity when used with HMSC compositions such as alternative and iteration. To overcome such limitation, we propose *timed high-level message sequence charts* (THMSC) which include an unambiguous subset of time constraints and timed edges as a new complementary notation. THMSC is effective in accurately specifying popular requirement patterns such as watchdog timers and periodic tasks. We present the formal semantics and demonstrate the effectiveness of THMSC using a real-world example that formalizes timing requirements for Korea Multi-Purpose Satellite (KOMPSAT) software.

1   Introduction

Message sequence charts (MSC) describe scenarios in terms of message exchanges and local actions. In order to support specification of large and complex real-time systems, MSC standard [10] includes HMSC and time constraints. However, current notation for time constraints has limitations in that formal semantics are not fully defined. In particular, when used with HMSC compositions such as alternative or iteration, ambiguities arise. As time constraints for HMSC are essential when specifying requirements for real-time systems such as periodic tasks, watchdogs, and time triggered actions. Thus, ambiguity must be resolved in order to avoid misunderstanding and enable automated analysis such as time consistency [5,23].

In this paper, we propose *timed high-level message sequence charts* (or THMSC in short) which includes unambiguous subset of time constraints and *timed edges* as a new complementary notation for specifying timing requirements. The formal semantics of THMSC is defined using labeled partially ordered set. To avoid ambiguities which will be presented in section 2, the subset accepts constraints only between *strongly and consistently ordered pairs* which we formalized.

---

* This work was partially supported by the KOSEF through the AITrc, by the Defence Software Research Center, and by the MIC under the ITRC support program supervised by the IITA.

R. Gotzhein and R. Reed (Eds.): SAM 2006, LNCS 4320, pp. 82–98, 2006.

Timed edges are directed time constraints between two consecutive MSCs. They can be safely harmonized with the proposed subset as well as HMSC compositions such as alternatives and loops. Moreover, timed edges permit us to specify essential features of embedded systems such as watchdogs and periodic tasks intuitively.

We applied THMSC to specify scenarios for timing requirements of KOMPSAT software. In this case study, our notation concisely and intuitively captured various types of requirements. Current notations are only partially capable of expressing such requirements and often result in complex scenarios.

This paper is organized as follows: Section 2 briefly reviews basics of MSC and issues on time constraints for HMSC. Section 3 proposes THMSC, our main contribution, and Section 4 demonstrates the usefulness and effectiveness of it using KOMPSAT case study. The formal semantics of THMSC is given in Section 5 and further issues are discussed in Section 6. Section 7 presents related works, and Section 8 concludes the paper.

2   Message Sequence Charts

In this section, we briefly explain the syntax and semantics of MSC and HMSC with focus on time-related constructors (e.g. timers and time constraints) and present some examples demonstrating ambiguity of time constraints for HMSC. While the standard [10] provides both of visual and textural notations for each description type, this paper uses the visual notation.

2.1   Message Sequence Charts

Figure 1(a) shows a simple MSC specification. Vertical lines ($P1$ and $P2$) and horizontal arrows ($m1$ and $m2$) denote instances (or processes) of a system and message exchanges among them, respectively. Rectangles stand for local actions (lat). In each instance, events (message sending, receiving, and local actions) occur sequentially from top to bottom. For example, $P2$ receives $m1$, performs local action lat, and then sends $m2$. We will use '$!m$' to denote the event sending message m, and '$?m$' for receiving.

The MSC standard includes timers and time constraints as notations to specify timing requirements. In Figure 1(a), the symbol $\overline{\mathrm{X}}$ denotes that a timer T is set to 2 time units, and the corresponding timeout event is consumed at the symbol $\overline{\mathrm{X}}$ after 2 time units.

The MSC standard introduced additional notations, *time constraints*, to specify a relative time between two events and an absolute time of an event. A time constraint is labeled with an interval representing quantitative timing requirements. A label for an absolute time is prefixed by the symbol '@'. Figure 1(a) shows that event $!m1$ must occur at one time unit after startup ($@[1,1]$), and it takes up to six time units from $!m1$ to $?m2$ of the process $P1$ ($[0,6]$). We use the term 'untimed MSC' if an MSC contains neither timers nor time constraints; otherwise, 'timed MSC' will be used.

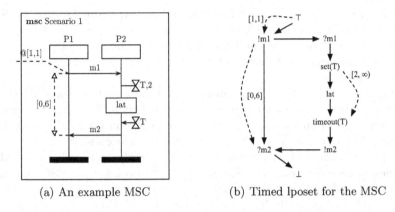

(a) An example MSC   (b) Timed lposet for the MSC

Fig. 1. A message sequence chart and its timed lposet

Many papers defined formal semantics of untimed and timed MSC using process algebra [19], automata [15], partial order [11,2,24], and petri-net [9]. This paper uses *timed lposet* [24], a timing extension of labeled partially ordered set (lposet) [20].

There are two classes of partial order among MSC events. That is, events of an instance must occur in the downward order and every message sending event must precede the corresponding receipt. The sequences of events accepted by an untimed MSC must satisfy these partial orders, and they are representable using a lposet [11]. Timed lposet extends lposet to have an additional timing function $\mathcal{T}$ for time constraints. The timed lposet for an MSC is formally defined as follows. In the definition, two special events $\top$ and $\bot$ denote the start and the end of a system, respectively.

Definition 1 (Timed lposet). *Let L be a set of labels. Timed lposet for a MSC is a tuple $M = (V, <, \lambda, \mathcal{T})$, where*

- *V is a set of events including two special events $\top$ and $\bot$,*
- *$<: V \times V$ is a reflexive, anti-symmetric, and transitive order on V,*
- *$\lambda : V \to L$ is a labeling function, and*
- *$\mathcal{T} : V \times V \to \mathbb{I}$ is a timing function that maps two events to their relative time interval, where $\mathbb{I} : 2^{\mathbb{R}}$ denotes all possible intervals.*

Figure 1(b) depicts the partial order $<$ and the timing function $\mathcal{T}$ for Figure 1(a) as solid lines and dashed lines, respectively. Note that the absolute time constraint @$[1, 1]$ is represented as the relative time constraint $[1, 1]$ between $\top$ and $!m1$. All ordered pairs in Figure 1(b) are assumed to have time constraints $[0, \infty)$ if constraints are not depicted explicitly. An untimed MSC is a timed MSC that all ordered pairs of events have time constraints $[0, \infty)$.

2.2   High-Level Message Sequence Charts

An HMSC is a tuple $H = (Q = N \cup P, E, \mathcal{R}, \mathcal{C})$ which consists of nodes (N), parallel frames (P) and edges $(E : Q \times Q)$. Nodes refer to other MSCs (M), and edges imply execution flows among nodes. Relation $\mathcal{R} : Q \to 2^M$ maps nodes to lposets for their reference MSCs and parallel frames to HMSCs. Two types of special nodes, $\triangledown$ and $\triangle$ ($\{\triangledown, \triangle\} \in N$), represent the start and the end of HMSC. They are defined as special timed lposets: $\triangledown = (V = \{\top\}, <= \emptyset, \lambda(\top) = start, \mathcal{T} = \emptyset)$, and $\triangle = (V = \{\bot\}, <= \emptyset, \lambda(\bot) = end, \mathcal{T} = \emptyset)$.

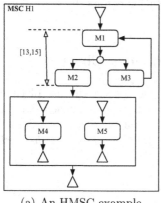 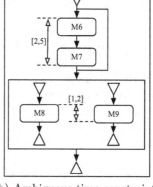

(a) An HMSC example   (b) Ambiguous time constraints

Fig. 2. High-level message sequence charts and ambiguous time constraints

Figure 2(a) shows an HMSC. A split edge indicates alternatives (M_2 and M_3), whereas a cycle expresses a repetition (M_1 and M_3). A parallel frame denotes concurrent execution of contained HMSCs (M_4 and M_5). Execution of an HMSC begins with the start node ($\triangledown$), and performs MSC indicated by nodes along edges. The execution is finished when an end node ($\triangle$) is encountered. Note that execution may not be terminated if a chart includes a repetition. Formally, a possible execution (or a *run*) of an HMSC $H = (Q, E, \mathcal{R}, \mathcal{C})$ is $q_1 q_2 \cdots q_n$ or $q_1 q_2 \cdots$ such that $\forall i \in \mathbb{N} : q_i \in Q \bigwedge (q_i, q_{i+1}) \in E \bigwedge q_1 = \triangledown \bigwedge q_n = \triangle$. MSC *language* is a set of all possible runs.

Time constraints are also specifiable in HMSC with the same notation for MSC. The MSC standard gives example HMSCs containing time constraints such as Figure 2(a). In this example, it takes $[13, 15]$ time units from the start of *M1* to the end of *M2*. We use a notation $Q^+ = \{q, \overline{q} \mid q \in Q\}$ to distinguish the start and the end of nodes Q. Thus, time constraints $\mathcal{C} : Q^+ \times Q^+ \to \mathbb{I}$ maps node pairs to intervals. For example, the constraint in Figure 2(a) is represented as $\mathcal{C}(\overline{M1}, \underline{M2}) = [13, 15]$.

Unfortunately, the formal semantics of time constraints for HMSCs is not fully defined in that time constraints mixed with HMSC compositions may result in *ambiguity*. For example, *M8* and *M9* in Figure 2(b) can interleave in an arbitrary order. As a result, the time constraint $[1, 2]$ in the parallel frame becomes ambiguous, since two different interpretations are possible: a constraint from the start of *M8* to the end of *M9* or from the end of *M9* to the start of *M8*. This ambiguity stems from that a time constraint, which is an undirected notation, is used with two independent MSCs having undefined precedence.

Besides, the time constraint $[2, 5]$ in Figure 2(b) can be interpreted as various meanings, although an explicit dependency exists between $M6$ and $M7$. Let M_i denotes the i-th iteration of scenario M. Possible interpretations include a constraint from the start of $M6_3$ to the end of $M7_3$ and one from the end of $M7_2$ to the start of $M6_3$. Actually, for any i and j, every time constraint $[2, 5]$ between the start of $M6_i$ and the end of $M7_j$ is represented as the same form. This ambiguity stems from that the current notation cannot distinguish iteration numbers.

3   Timed High-Level Message Sequence Charts

To resolve the ambiguity of time constraints, we restrict the use of time constraints in HMSC to unambiguous cases (section 3.1) and propose a complementary notation *timed edges*, directed time constraints between two consecutive MSCs (section 3.2). We termed this variant of HMSC as *Timed High-Level Message Sequence Charts*, or *THMSC* in short.

3.1   A Safe Subset of Time Constraints

Before we restrict the use of time constraints, we present some preliminaries. As we mentioned, an HMSC contains many runs. We define that two nodes are *ordered* if there exists a run containing both nodes. Even if two nodes are ordered, a unique prior node may not be determined: neither two nodes $D2$ nor $D3$ in Figure 3(c) precedes the other, because both types of runs $D1D2D3\cdots$ and $D4D3D2\cdots$ are possible.

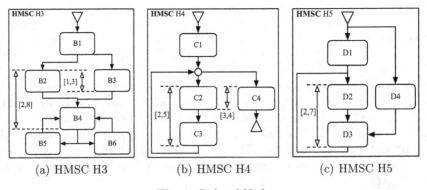

(a) HMSC H3   (b) HMSC H4   (c) HMSC H5

Fig. 3. Ordered Nodes

Thus, we refine the notion of ordered nodes: two nodes are *consistently ordered* if they are ordered and one node must precede the other; otherwise the nodes are *inconsistently ordered*. In an HMSC $H = (Q, E, \mathcal{R}, \mathcal{C})$, let $\Pi_{type1}, \Pi_{type2} \subseteq \mathcal{L}(H)$ be two sets of possible runs that $\Pi_{type1} = \nabla \cdots p \cdots q \cdots (\triangle)$ and $\Pi_{type2} = \nabla \cdots q \cdots p \cdots (\triangle)$. The notion of consistently ordered nodes is formally defined as follows.

Definition 2 (Consistently Ordered). *Two nodes $p, q \in Q$ are **ordered** if $(\Pi_{type1} \cup \Pi_{type2}) \neq \emptyset$. An ordered pair p and q is **consistently ordered** if $(\Pi_{type1} = \emptyset \wedge \Pi_{type2} \neq \emptyset) \bigvee (\Pi_{type1} \neq \emptyset \wedge \Pi_{type2} = \emptyset)$.*

On the other hand, ordered pairs can be categorized into two classes according to whether a run contains only one of the two nodes. That is, two ordered nodes are *strongly ordered* if both or none of them occur in all possible runs; otherwise *weakly* ordered.

Definition 3 (Strongly Ordered). *Two ordered nodes p and q are **strongly ordered** if $(\Pi_{type1} \cup \Pi_{type2} \cup \Pi_{type3}) = \mathcal{L}(H)$, where $\Pi_{type3} = \{ \pi \in \mathcal{L}(H) \mid \pi = \nabla q_1 q_2 \cdots (\triangle) \bigwedge \forall i \in \mathbb{N} : q_i \neq p \wedge q_i \neq q \}$.*

Note that the notions of consistently ordered and strongly ordered are independent, and all combinations are possible. Figure 3 shows weakly and inconsistently (*B5* and *B6*), weakly and consistently (*B1* and *B2*), strongly and inconsistently (*D2* and *D3*), and strongly and consistently (*B1* and *B4*) ordered pairs.

THMSC accepts time constraints only between consistently and strongly ordered pairs, which are termed as *well-formed time constraints*. The reason is that time constraints between unordered, weakly ordered, and inconsistently ordered nodes are responsible for ambiguity. For example, the time constraint $[1, 3]$ between *B2* and *B3* in Figure 3(a) is a representative case prohibited by THMSC, because *B2* and *B3* are unordered and mutually exclusive. Time constraint $[2, 7]$ in Figure 3(c) is ambiguous as mentioned in section 2, since *D2* and *D3* are inconsistently ordered.

Time constraint $[3, 4]$ between *C2* and *C4* in Figure 3(b) is also disallowed by THMSC because they are weakly ordered. We argue that prohibition of this case is more recommendable for the following reasons: this type of constraints may lead to a misunderstanding that the subsequent node must be executed to fulfill a constraint. For example, *C4* may not be executed if the loop of *C2* and *C3* iterates infinitely.

We particularly regard *C2* and *C3* as a strongly and consistently ordered pair. Obviously, they are strongly ordered, but the order is unclear because of the loop. All appearing pairs of *C2* and *C3* are, however, consistently ordered, supposing an infinite linearization of the loop. That is, $C2_i$ and $C3_i$ are consistently ordered for all positive integer i. THMSC interprets the time constraint $[2, 3]$ as a set of constraints between *C2* and *C3* whose iteration number is identical.

3.2   Timed Edges in THMSC

The restriction of time constraints in THMSC is imperative to prevent the ambiguities. However, some timing requirements for the embedded systems are hard to specify only with the restricted notations. Thus, we propose a complementary new notation, *timed edges*, which can be used with the conventional compositions of HMSC safely and to describe many timing requirements for real-time systems intuitively.

The syntax of timed edges uses dashed arrows labeled with intervals, distinguished from normal edges of HMSC depicted as solid arrows. We introduce two

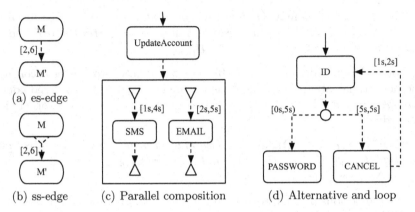

Fig. 4. Timed edges and THMSC Compositions

types of timed edges having different scopes: a typical dashed arrow denotes a timing requirement between the end of the source node and the start of the target (Figure 4(a)), whereas a split-tailed dashed arrow (Figure 4(b)) represents a requirement between the start of the source and the start of the target. We termed the former *es-edge* and the latter *ss-edge*. An unlabeled timed edge is an instantaneous timed edge with interval [0, 0] oppositely to an unlabeled normal edges having interval [0, ∞) implicitly.

Differently from time constraints, timed edges can be safely used with the HMSC compositions, namely, parallel composition, alternative composition, and iteration.

Parallel composition of HMSC is effective in describing requirements for independent tasks. For example, suppose an ATM system that sends a confirming message by email [2, 5] seconds later (*EMAIL* in Figure 4(c)) and by SMS [1, 4] seconds later (*SMS*) if an account is updated (*UpdateAccount*). If sending email and SMS are independent, a parallel composition containing two scenarios *EMAIL* and *SMS* can be used as depicted in Figure 4(c); two timing requirements for SMS and EMAIL, [1s, 4s] and [2s, 5s] are specified using two timed edges connected to the start nodes. Because an unlabeled timed edge is instantaneous, the completion of *UpdateAccount* immediately initiates the parallel frame triggering two independent scenarios *SMS* and *EMAIL* with different timing requirements.

A requirement, *"ATM gets an ID card (ID in Figure 4(d)) and then waits 5 seconds until the user enters a password (PASSWORD). If the user does not enter any password within 5 seconds, ATM cancels the process (CANCEL)"*, can be described with two alternative scenarios *PASSWORD* and *CANCEL* as shown in Figure 4(d). In the example, the time constraints [0s, 5s] and [5s, 5s] are used as conditions to decide which scenario will be selected. Note that nondeterminism may occurs if intervals of two timed edges overlap and this can be analyzed statically.

In Figure 4(d), the timed edge [1s, 2s] represents a requirement *"ID card can be reentered [1s, 2s] seconds after the cancellation."* without any ambiguity. The time constraint [5s, 5s], moreover, is assigned in the loop safely without modification.

4   Formalization of KOMPSAT Software Requirements Specification

We use KOMPSAT software requirements specification [12] to demonstrate the usability of THMSC. KOMPSAT was developed by Korean Aerospace Research Institute with TRW Inc. We categorize 80 time related requirements of KOMPSAT into several groups according to their patterns. This section presents THMSCs for three representative types of requirements in different groups.

Before we proceed the demonstration in detail, we assume the followings to describe patterns rigorously. An instantaneous action is represented as an event using symbols $e, e', e_1, e_2, \cdots, e_n$. Tasks consumes some time to complete a goal or sub-goal and $\tau, \tau', \tau_1, \tau_2, \cdots, \tau_n$ are used for them. Symbols τ_i^s and τ_i^e are the start and the end time of τ_i, respectively. A time function $tm : E \mapsto \mathbb{T}$ maps an event to its occurrence time.

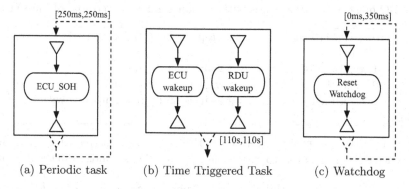

  (a) Periodic task   (b) Time Triggered Task   (c) Watchdog

Fig. 5. KOMPSAT THMSC Scenarios

Periodic Tasks. Because KOMPSAT software is executed in a periodic manner, there exist many requirements related to periodic tasks. We define periodic tasks more rigorously as follows: time slots appear regularly with a given duration d, and periodic tasks are executed within the time slots. Let τ' be a periodic task and τ be a time slot with a duration d. Requirements for a periodic task have the following pattern:

$$\forall i : \ \tau_i^s \leq \tau'^s_i \leq \tau'^e_i \leq \tau_i^e \ \land \ \tau_{i+1}^s = \tau_i^e = \tau_i^s + d$$

This constraint implies that a task can be executed at any moment within the time slots. The following is a representative KOMPSAT requirement related to periodic tasks.

> The software shall:
>   a. read SOH info. from the ECU component via the 1553B bus.
>   b. read SOH info. from the ECU once every 250ms.

To describe a periodic task, we specify both time slots and the task as scenarios: the time slots can be regarded as a task that repeats periodically and has subtasks. The parallel frame, depicted in Figure 5(a), describes the time slot and the timed edge enforce the time slot to repeat every $[250ms, 250ms]$. This example is hard to specify with the current notation because it cannot express a timing requirement between two consecutive iterations as mentioned in section 2.

Time Triggered Tasks. The KOMPSAT software includes time triggered tasks that start after a certain delay from different tasks. Let τ_1 and τ_2 be tasks and $\delta \in \mathbb{I}$ be a time interval. Task τ_2 is a time triggered task of τ_1 if they are constrained by the following timing requirements.

$$\tau_2^s = \tau_1^s + \delta \ \vee \ \tau_2^s = \tau_1^e + \delta$$

In the following requirements, the OBC component reads two wakeup-clue messages from both components RDU and ECU, and then executes other tasks. The OBC must wait 110 seconds without concerning the receipts of messages.

A. During the 110 second wait of step A, the OBC shall perform steps 1 and 2 below.
    1. read the RDU processor wakeup clues message.
    2. read the ECU processor wakeup clues message.
B. If both messages of step A were successfully read, proceed with step below.· · ·

In Figure 5(b), we specified step A as a HMSC component (parallel frame) and used timed edge $[110s, 110s]$ to express that it waits 110 seconds from the its start.

Watchdog Timers. Watchdog timer is a popular component of real-time systems to check the normal functionality. KOMPSAT also has the following requirement related to the watchdog timer.

During all phases of initialization, the software shall reset the watchdog timer at least once every 350 msec.

The requirement means that time intervals between any two consecutive reset signals do not exceed 350ms as the following constraint.

$$\forall i.tm(reset_{i+1}) \leq tm(reset_i) + 350ms$$

Figure 5(c) shows the corresponding THMSC, which is similar to the pattern of periodic tasks. However, this scenario can reset the watchdog timer irregularly unless it exceeds $350ms$ from the previous update.

5   Formal Semantics of THMSC

This section presents the formal semantics of THMSC. The semantics of a node in THMSC were defined as a lposet in section 2. Because a run of a HMSC is a sequence of nodes, it can be defined as sequential compositions of lposets for the involving nodes. Analogously, we define timed sequential composition for timed edges in order to define a run of a THMSC. In this setting, language of a THMSC is a set of these runs.

5.1   Sequential Composition

An edge of HMSC means that its source and target nodes are sequentially composed. That is, execution of the source node must precede that of the target. A sequential composition can be interpreted in two different ways according to the enforced partial order [6]. A *synchronous sequential composition* enforces that all instances of the source MSC have to be completely finished before the system enters the next MSC. An *asynchronous sequential composition* allows that an instance of the target MSC can start its execution only if all events of the corresponding instance in the previous MSC are completed. In this case, the other instances of the previous chart may not be finished. In Figure 6, $?a$ should precede $!b$ when we interpret the edge between $M1$ and $M2$ as the synchronous manner, while $!b$ can precede $?a$ in the asynchronous interpretation. In this paper, all edges are assumed to be synchronous sequential compositions.

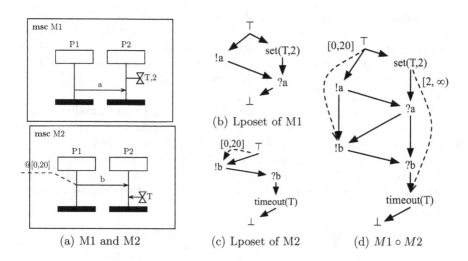

(a) M1 and M2   (b) Lposet of M1   (c) Lposet of M2   (d) $M1 \circ M2$

Fig. 6. Sequential Composition with Timers

Let $p = (V_p, <_p, \lambda_p, \mathcal{T}_p)$ and $q = (V_q, <_q, \lambda_q, \mathcal{T}_q)$ be two lposets such that $V_p \cap V_q = \{\top, \bot\}$ and $p \circ q = (V, <, \lambda, \mathcal{T})$ be the sequential composition of p and q. Trivially, V and λ are $V_p \cup V_q$ and $\lambda_p \cup \lambda_q$ respectively. Note that $V_p \cup V_q$ preserves the uniqueness of $\top$ and $\bot$, because they are common events.

Sequential composition introduces new ordered pairs $<_{poq}$ between the end of p and the start of q, namely, $<_{poq} = \{(a, b) \mid (a, \bot) \in <_p \wedge (\top, b) \in <_q\}$. Therefore, the order becomes $< = <_p \cup <_q \cup <_{poq}$.

Time constraints of p and q are preserved by the sequential composition. However, timers may introduce additional time constraints during the composition. The sequential composition of $M1$ and $M2$ in Figure 6 introduces a time constraints $[2, \infty)$ owing to timer T. Thus, $\mathcal{T}$ of $p \circ q$ is defined as follows.

- $\mathcal{T} = \mathcal{T}_p \cup \mathcal{T}_q \cup \mathcal{T}_{timer}$, where $\mathcal{T}_{timer} = \mathcal{T}_{set/timeout} \cup \mathcal{T}_{set/reset} \cup \mathcal{T}_{reset/timeout}$
  such that
  - $\mathcal{T}_{set/timeout} = \{(\,(e, e'), [n, \infty)\,) \mid (e, e') \in V_p \times V_q \wedge \lambda(e) = set(i, T_i, n) \wedge \lambda(e') = timeout(i, T_i)\}$
  - $\mathcal{T}_{set/reset} = \{(\,(e, e'), [0, n)\,) \mid (e, e') \in V_p \times V_q \wedge \lambda(e) = set(i, T_i, n) \wedge \lambda(e') = reset(i, T_i, n)\}$
  - $\mathcal{T}_{reset/timeout} = \{(\,(e, e'), [n, \infty)\,) \mid (e, e') \in V_p \times V_q \wedge \lambda(e) = reset(i, T_i, n) \wedge \lambda(e') = timeout(i, T_i)\}$

In the previous definition, $set(i, T_i, n)$ stands for a set-timer event that assigns the time value n to the timer variable T_i of the instance i. We can interpret $reset(i, T_i, n)$ and $timeout(i, T_i)$ in the same way. Figure 6(d) shows the resulting partial orders and timing function of $M1 \circ M2$.

5.2 Timed Sequential Composition

We formalize a timed edge as a timed sequential composition. Timed edges of THMSC can refer only two points of a node, i.e. the start and the end of a node. Rigorously, the start and end of a node are a set of the first and last events. Note that an MSC has several start and end events because events in the MSC are not totally ordered but partially ordered. For example, the starting events of $M1$ in Figure 6(a) are $!a$ and $set(P2, T, 2)$.

The start and the end events of a MSC $M = (V, <, \lambda, \mathcal{T})$ are formally minimal and maximal events with respect to the ordering relation $<$. We represent the first events as $pre(M)$ and the last events as $post(M)$, respectively.

A timed edge is also a sequential composition except that it compels pairs of two events to occur within a given duration. Such durations of timed edges are also denotable as elements of timing function $\mathcal{T}$ of the composed lposets.

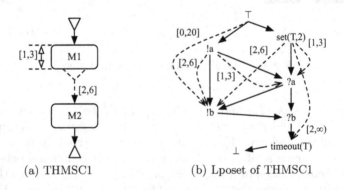

(a) THMSC1   (b) Lposet of THMSC1

Fig. 7. THMSC with Time Constraints

Figure 7(b) shows the partial order and the time constraints with respect to THMSC1 in Figure 7(a). The time constraint $[2, 6]$ is depicted as dashed arrows between the starting events of $M1$ ($!a$ and $set(P2, T, 2)$) and the starting event of $M2$ ($!b$) in the sequentially composed lposet.

Timed sequential composition $\circ_{i \in \mathbb{I}}$ is an extension of the sequential composition $\circ$ of HMSC considering a time interval i. Timed edges are formally defined as the follows. In the definition, $\mathcal{N}$ is the set of event pairs for each type of timed edges. Each element of the set is mapped to the time interval i given in the timed edge.

Definition 4 (Timed Sequential Composition). *Let* $p = (V_p, <_p, \lambda_p, \mathcal{T}_p)$ *and* $q = (V_q, <_q, \lambda_q, \mathcal{T}_q)$ *be two timed lposets, and* $p \circ q = (V, <, \lambda, \mathcal{T})$ *be the sequentially composed lposet.* ***Timed sequential compositions*** $p \circ_{i \in \mathbb{I}}^{ss} q$ *and* $p \circ_{i \in \mathbb{I}}^{es} q$ *are lposets* $(V, <, \lambda, \mathcal{T}')$ *such that*

- $\mathcal{T}' = \mathcal{T} \cup \{(r, i) | r \in \mathcal{N}\}$, *where*
  - $\mathcal{N} = \{(a, b) | a \in pre(p) \wedge b \in pre(q)\}$ *for ss-edge* $(p \circ_{i \in \mathbb{I}}^{ss} q)$.
  - $\mathcal{N} = \{(a, b) | a \in post(p) \wedge b \in pre(q)\}$ *for es-edge* $(p \circ_{i \in \mathbb{I}}^{es} q)$.

5.3   Formal Semantics of THMSC

We extend HMSC to THMSC as follows. A THMSC TH is a tuple $TH = (Q, E, \mathcal{R}, \mathcal{T}, \mathcal{T}_E)$, where $\mathcal{T}_E : E \rightarrow \{normal, es, ss\} \times \mathbb{I}$ maps an edge into its type (normal, es-, or ss-timed edge) and the others are identical to those of HMSC. Let Π of a THMSC TH be the set of finite runs and Π^* be the set of infinite runs. The *language* of a THMSC TH, $\mathcal{L}(TH)$, is the union of Π and Π^*.

In THMSC, no time constraints can be specified among events belong to different components of parallel frames. Thus, if sub-charts are two lposets $TH_1 = (Q_1, E_1, \mathcal{R}_1, \mathcal{T}_1, \mathcal{T}_E^1)$ and $TH_2 = (Q_2, E_2, \mathcal{R}_2, \mathcal{T}_2, \mathcal{T}_E^2)$, a parallel composition of TH_1 and TH_2 becomes a lposet $TH_1 \| TH_2 = (Q = Q_1 \cup Q_2, E = E_1 \cup E_2, \mathcal{R} = \mathcal{R}_1 \cup \mathcal{R}_2, \mathcal{T} = \mathcal{T}_1 \cup \mathcal{T}_2, \mathcal{T}_E = \mathcal{T}_E^1 \cup \mathcal{T}_E^2)$. Therefore, every node can be regarded as a lposet, and a behavior corresponding to a run $r = q_0 q_1 q_2 \cdots (q_n)$ of a THMSC $TH = (Q, E, \mathcal{R}, \mathcal{T}, \mathcal{T}_E)$ becomes $q_0 \circ_? q_1 \circ_? q_2 \circ_? \cdots (\circ_? q_n)$, where

$$q_i \circ_? q_j = \begin{cases} q_i \circ q_j & \text{if } \mathcal{T}_E((q_i, q_j)) = (normal, [0, \infty)) \\ q_i \circ_k^{es} q_j & \text{if } \mathcal{T}_E((q_i, q_j)) = (es, k) \\ q_i \circ_k^{ss} q_j & \text{if } \mathcal{T}_E((q_i, q_j)) = (ss, k) \end{cases}$$

5.4   Time Consistency of Finite Paths

To improve reliability of real-time systems, rigorous analysis is essential. It is also a main usability of formal specification such as THMSC. Several studies have focused on application of MSC to real-time system specification and analysis of various aspects such as time consistency [23], performance evaluation [16], and task scheduling based on schedulability analysis [21].

Time consistency of THMSC is a question whether a system is implementable performing scenarios without any violation of time constraints of THMSC. Analysis techniques of time consistency for MSC have been already proposed [5,17,23]. Time consistency of finite timed lposets is analyzable with the negative cost cycle algorithms analogous to the previous techniques [5,2]. Since the semantics of THMSC is a set of lposets if it is finite, this technique remains applicable. The finite timed lposet is time consistent if the timing graph has no negative cost cycle as proven in [5,2].

6   Discussion

6.1   Experimental Results

Table 1 shows the formalization result of KOMPSAT software. Among 61 time-related requirements, 45 requirements could be specified with THMSC. However, the remaining 16 requirements needed additional notations for *timed exception* and *time variables*.

Table 1. Formalization results of KOMPSAT software

Type	Example	N#	Notes
Definition	a minor cycle is 0.250 seconds	6	Constants
Duration	perform items A and B within 64msec	3	Time constraints
Time Triggered	start X at the beginning of every minor frame	3	THMSC
Watchdog	reset Watchdog timer at least once every 350ms	8	THMSC
Periodic Task	distribute the current OBT once each second	25	THMSC
Exceptions	If 24h elapse without a code being received ...	4	Timed exception
Clock variable	Time tags for stored commands	12	Time variable

A timed exception is a preemptive time constraint. Currently, the violation of time constraint is detected by time consistency. Suppose a case that an alternative scenario describes exception handling to be executed if a scenario fails completion within a duration. Such behavior requires the notion of preemption. Time consistency alone is insufficient in that every run of consistent scenarios must include all events of the involving scenarios.

On the other hand, KOMPSAT software has some requirements related to real world time. Examples include scheduled tasks that need a way to transmit time values with messages. While the MSC standard includes time marks to save occurring time of an event, they are insufficient in that a time value being transmitted may be for a future event.

6.2   Implementability of THMSC

Each implemented process must decide its behavior deterministically according to the context of related scenarios. H. Ben-Abdallah and S. Leue presented the notion of *non-local choice* [5]. The idea is that deadlock can be occurred if a process cannot determine its next behavior deterministically only with locally available information. R. Alur, K. Etessami and M. Yannakakis formalized the realizability problem which address a question whether a scenario can be implemented in a distributed environment where local information is invisible to others [1]. Since time constraints are not local information, a process may not determine its behavior related to a time constraint.

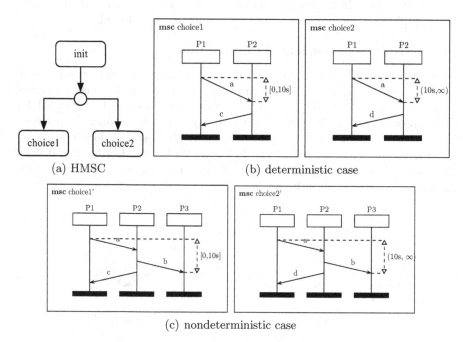

(a) HMSC   (b) deterministic case

(c) nondeterministic case

Fig. 8. Alternative Scenario

Figure 8(b) shows alternative scenarios. Difference between scenarios *choice1* and *choice2* is that process *P2* responses differently according to the amount of time between events sending and receiving message *a*. Although *P2* receives the same message *a*, it can determine the response, *c* or *d*, deterministically if the sending time is transferred with the message. The reason is that *P2* knows how long it takes to transmit message *a*. Note that this case can be regarded as a local choice if one distinguishes a message according to its sending time.

On the other hand, process *P2* in Figure 8(c) cannot determine how it responses, since only process *P3* can decide whether time to exchange message *a* and *b* meets the time constraint [0, 10s] or not. That is, the time to exchange two messages is determined when *P3* receives message *b*. Process *P2*, however, cannot get any information from *P3*.

Each process is implemented independently so that they do not share any local informations without message exchanges. Thus, satisfaction of a time constraint should be shared through message exchanges among the related processes. Without this, a process which does not know whether the constraint is satisfied cannot behave deterministically.

In [24], T. Zheng, F. Khendek, and L. Helouët also addressed a similar problem with time constraints between two independent events. The standard allows time constraints to be used only between causally related events as *"relative timing uses pairs of events - preceding and subsequent events, where the preceding event enables (directly or indirectly, i.e. via some intermediate events) the subsequent event."* However, as demonstrated in Figure 8, some scenarios may not be implementable even when the constraints are causally related.

6.3   Asynchronous Sequential Composition

Our semantics of THMSC is based on the synchronous sequential composition, which is a special case of the asynchronous composition. Because the asynchronous composition is more expressive, our semantics can be extended for it. Two possible approaches are possible. First, one can define only the resulting partial order asynchronously. Figure 9(a) shows the resulting lposet for asynchronous composition of Figure 7(a). In Figure 9(a), partial order < is defined as asynchronous composition, but timing function $\mathcal{T}$ has no difference with the synchronous composition in Figure 7(b).

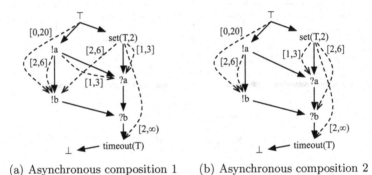

(a) Asynchronous composition 1   (b) Asynchronous composition 2

Fig. 9. Asynchronous timed sequential compositions of Figure 7(a)

Alternatively, one can define not only partial order < asynchronously, but also timing function $\mathcal{T}$ differently as Figure 9(b) where time constraints and timed edges are bound to each process locally. For example, timed edge $[2, 6]$ restricts the occurrence of events $set(T, 2)$ and $?b$ instead of events $set(T, 2)$ and $!b$, because $?b$ is the first event of process $P2$ in $M2$.

7   Related Works

Time constraints for MSC were explored in different works. R. Alur, G. Holzmann, and D. Peled proposed the semantics of MSC using partially ordered set and also presented timed semantics and time consistency problem [2]. H. Ben-Abdallah and S. Leue addressed analysis issues on time constraints in MSC [5]. These approaches mainly focused on basic message sequence charts.

P. Maigat and L. Helouët proposed partial order and (max,+) automaton based semantics and analysis for timed MSC considering HMSC and compositions [18]. P. Lucas proposed an approach using timed automata for timed MSC. T. Zheng, F. Khendek, and L. Helouët used timed lposet for the formal semantics [24]. This work also addressed various composition of MSCs including inline expressions and high-level message sequence charts.

However, these works did not consider time constraint at the inter-scenario level, although they presented cases that different scenarios are related by a timer. Timing function for a timer is determined when an execution encounter timer operations. Thus, constraint events can be bound dynamically. Thus, timer does not introduce ambiguity such as time constraint in a loop.

On the other hand, M. Belachew and R. K. Shyamasundar proposed MSC+ [4], an extension of MSC for reactive systems. In the work, they generalized HMSC with the notion of preemption. However, they did not conver timing aspects related to the proposed features.

8   Conclusion

In this paper, we defined THMSC which includes a safe subset of HMSC and timed edges as a new notation. The formalization of requirements for KOMPSAT software demonstrated that THMSC is simple but effective in description of many timing requirements for real-time systems. Especially, our notation was useful to specify periodic tasks and time triggered tasks, which are popular patten of timing requirements for real-time systems but hard to specify with the current standard notations.

As future works, expressiveness of THMSC can be extended to include timed exception. Timed exception are useful to describe scenarios for error handling routines. We plan to rigorously define the implementability problem of time constraints and to develop an algorithm to synthesize a design for implementable THMSC. Because time constraints are not implementable entities, they must transformed into timer operations that satisfy the original constraints. We expect that this technique give a help to construct design for realtime systems more conveniently and effectively.

Acknowledgment. The authors thank Ho Jung Bang for helpful comments on the revision. We also thank anonymous reviewers for their valuable comments and suggestions.

References

1. R. Alur, K. Etessami, and M. Yannakakis. Realizability and verification of msc graphs. In *Proceedings of the 28th International Colloquium on Automata, Languages, and Programming*, 2001.
2. R. Alur, G. Holzmann, and D. Peled. An Analyzer for Message Sequence Charts. In *Proceedings of the 2nd International Workshops on Tools and Algorithms for the Construction and Analysis of Systems, LNCS 1055*, 1996.

3. C. Andre, M. A. Peraldi-Frati, and J. P. Rigault. Scenario and property checking of real-time systems using a synchronous approach. In *Proceedings of the 4th International Symposium on Object-Oriented Real-Time Distributed Computing*, 2001.
4. M. Belachew and R. K. Shyamasundar. MSC+: From Requirement to Prototyped Systems. In *Proceding of the 13th EuroMicro Conference on Real-Time Systems*, 2001.
5. H. Ben-Abdallah and S. Leue. Expressing and analyzing timing constraints in message sequence chart specifications. Technical Report 97-04, Dept. of Electrical and Computer Engineering, University of Waterloo, 1997.
6. H. Ben-Abdallah and S. Leue. Syntactic detection of process divergence and non-local choice in message sequence charts. In *Proceedings of the 3rd International Workshop on Tools and Algorithms for the Construction and Analysis of Systems*, 1997.
7. Y. Bontemps, P. Heymans, and P. Schobbens. From live sequence charts to state machines and back: A guided tour. *IEEE Transactions on Software Engineering*, 31(12), 2005.
8. D. Harel and R. Marelly. *Come, Let's Play: Scenario-Based Programming Using LSCs and the Play-Engine*. Springer, 2003.
9. S. Heymer. A Semantics for MSC based on Petri–Net Components. Technical Report A-00-12, Schriftenreihe der Institute für Informatik/Mathematik, Medical University at Lübeck, Germany, 2000.
10. ITU-T. *Z120: Message Sequence Charts 2000*. ITU-T, 2001.
11. J. P. Katoen and L. Lambert. Pomsets for message sequence charts. In *Proceedings of the 1st Workshop of the SDL Forum Society on SDL and MSC*, 1998.
12. Korean Aerospace Research Institute (KARI). *GX-SDA-001B : KOMPSAT (Korea Multi-Purpose Satellite) Software Requirements Specification*, Jan 1999.
13. I. Krüger. Capturing Overlapping, Triggered, and Preemptive collaborations using MSCs. In *Proceedings of the 6th International Conference on Fundamental Approaches to Software Engineering, FASE 2003, LNCS 2621*. Springer, 2003.
14. I. Krüger, R. Grosu, P. Scholz, and M. Broy. From MSCs to Statecharts. *Distributed and Parallel Embedded Systems*, 1999.
15. P. B. Ladkin and S. Leue. Interpeting message flow graph. *Formal Aspects of Computing*, 7(5), 1995.
16. L. Lambert. PMSC for Performance Evaluation. In *Proceedings of the 1st Workshop on Performance and Time in SDL/MSC*, 1998.
17. X. Li and J. Lilius. Timing analysis of message sequence chart. Technical Report Technical Report 255, Turku Centre for Computer Science TUCS, 1999.
18. P. L. Maigat and L. Helouët. A (max,+) approach for time in message sequence charts. In *Proceedings of the 5th Workshop on Discrete Event Systems*, 2000.
19. S. Mauw and M. A. Reniers. Operational Semantics for MSC'96. *Computer Networks and ISDN Systems*, 35(17), 1999.
20. V. Pratt. Modeling Concurrency with Partial Orders. *International Journal of Parallel Programming*, 15(1), 1986.
21. F. Slomka, J. Zant, and L. Lambert. MSC-based Schedulability Analysis. In *Proceedings of Workshop on Performance and Time in SDL and MSC*, 1998.
22. S. Uchitel, J. Kramer, and J. Magee. Synthesis of bahavioral models from scenarios. *IEEE Transactions on Software Engineering*, 29(2), 2003.
23. T. Zheng and F. Khendek. Time Consistency of MSC 2000 Specifications. *Computer Networks*, 42(3), 2003.
24. T. Zheng, F. Khendek, and L. Helouët. A Semantics for Timed MSC. In *Proceedings of the International Workshop on Validation and Implementation of Scenario Specifications (VISS)*, 2002.

Timed Use Case Maps

Jameleddine Hassine[1], Juergen Rilling[1], and Rachida Dssouli[2]

[1] Department of Computer Science, Concordia University, Montreal, Canada
{j_hassin, rilling}@cse.concordia.ca
[2] Concordia Institute for Information Systems Engineering, Montreal, Canada
dssouli@ece.concordia.ca

Abstract. Scenario-driven requirement specifications are widely used to capture and represent functional requirements. Use Case Maps are being standardized as part of the User Requirements Notation (URN), the most recent addition to ITU-T's family of languages. UCM models focus on the description of functional requirements and high-level designs at early stages of the development process. How a system is executed over time and how this may affect its correctness and performance, however, are introduced later in the development process which may require considerable changes in design or even worse at the requirement analysis level. We believe that timing aspects must be integrated into the system model, and this must be done already at an early stage of development. This paper introduces an approach to describe timing constraints in Use Case Maps specifications. We present a formal semantics of Timed UCM in terms of Clocked Transition Systems (CTS). We illustrate our approach using an example of a simplified wireless system.

Keywords: Use Case Maps, User Requirements Notation, timing aspects, performance, timed UCM, Clocked Transition Systems.

1 Introduction

In the early stages of common development processes, system functionalities are defined in terms of informal requirements and visual descriptions. Scenario-driven approaches, although often semiformal, are widely accepted because of their intuitive syntax and semantics. These approaches focus mainly on the description of system functionalities and little attention has been given so far to modeling time and performance aspects. These timing and performance issues are often overlooked during the initial system design. They are typically regarded as separate behaviour issues and therefore described in separate models. In recent years there has been a growing interest in integrating these aspects into a unified framework. This integration was mainly driven by the fact that time, performance, and behaviors are tightly related in embedded real-time systems, affecting directly both, functional and non-functional requirements.

Use Case Maps (UCMs) [15], a scenario based language that has gained momentum in recent years within the software requirements and specification community, has been successfully used in describing real-time systems, with a particular focus on telecommunication system and services[3,4,7,19]. Use Case Maps (UCMs), part of a new proposal to ITU-T for a User Requirements Notation (URN) [14], can be applied

R. Gotzhein and R. Reed (Eds.): SAM 2006, LNCS 4320, pp. 99–114, 2006.
© Springer-Verlag Berlin Heidelberg 2006

to capture and integrate functional requirements in terms of causal scenarios representing behavioral aspects at a higher level of abstraction, and to provide the stakeholders with guidance and reasoning about the system-wide architecture and behavior. UCM is not intended to replace UML, but rather complement it and help to bridge the modeling gap between requirements (use cases) and design (system components and behavior).

UCM abstract syntax and static semantics are informally defined in document Z.152 [15]. In a recent work, we have proposed an operational semantics for the UCM language based on Multi-Agent Abstract State Machines [10]. This ASM model provides a concise semantics of UCM functional constructs and describes precisely the control semantics. Another formalization attempt was presented in [5] where UCM constructs are translated into the formal language LOTOS.

The original UCM notation presented in [15] does not describe semantics involving time, allowing for different interpretations of timing information, such as the time needed for a transition or a responsibility to complete. To date, these issues remain unexplored.

In this work, we extend the Use Case Maps notation with timing information. We define a formal syntax and semantics of timed UCM models based on Clocked Transition Systems [18]. Clocked Transition Systems were introduced as a formal notation to model the behavior of real-time systems. Its definition provides a simple way to annotate state-transitions graphs with timing constraints using finitely many real-valued clock variables. The goal of our semantics is to support the execution and the analysis of timed UCM specifications. This paper is part of the ongoing research towards using UCM to describe, simulate, and verify real-time systems.

In an attempt to make this paper self-contained, we include some of the core background information relevant to this research. In the next section, we provide an overview of the un-timed Use Case Maps notation along with an example that is used throughout the paper. In Section 3, we present the syntax of timed UCM. Section 4 provides the formal semantics of Timed UCM in terms of Clocked Transition Systems (CTS). Section 5 presents the state of the art in describing timing semantics for modeling languages. Finally, Section 6 concludes with a brief discussion and future work.

2   Use Case Maps

The Use Case Maps notation [15] is a high level scenario based modeling technique, used to specify functional requirements and high-level designs for various reactive and distributed systems. A UCM model depicts scenarios as causal flows of responsibilities (e.g. operation, action, task, function, etc.) that can be superimposed on underlying structures of components. Components are generic and can represent software entities (objects, processes, databases, servers, etc.) as well as non-software entities (e.g. actors or hardware). These relationships are said to be causal because they involve concurrency, partial ordering of activities, and they link causes (e.g., preconditions and triggering events) to effects (e.g. post-conditions and resulting events).With the UCM notation, scenarios are expressed above the level of messages exchanged between components, hence, they are not necessarily bound to a specific underlying structure (such UCMs are called Unbound UCMs). One of the strengths of UCMs is their ability to

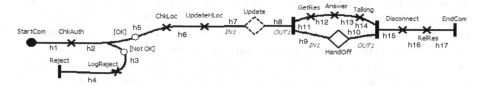

Fig. 1. Root Map for the simplified Wireless System

integrate a number of scenarios together (in a map-like diagram), and to reason about the architecture and its behavior over a set of scenarios.

Figure 1 illustrates some of the basic UCM concepts using a modified version of a simplified wireless system that was initially introduced in [2]. The root map in Figure 1 describes a scenario where a mobile station initiates a call then proceeds with a handoff. Filled circles represent start points, which capture preconditions and triggering events (for instance the start of a communication *StartCom*). End points capturing resulting events and post-conditions are illustrated with bars perpendicular to causal paths (for instance *EndCom*). Paths can fork as alternatives (OR-fork) and may also join (OR-join). Alternative branches can be guarded by conditions, shown between square brackets. A condition needs to be true for the guarded path to be followed. In Figure 2, after tuning to a new channel the signal quality might be better or worse. When it is better, the user profile is updated (*UpdProfile*) and the scenario may continue. Otherwise, the mobile station will tune to the previous channel(*TunePrevChan*). Concurrency and partial ordering of responsibilities and events are supported in UCMs through the use of AND-fork and AND-join. While an OR-join simply indicates overlapping of scenarios that share common paths, an AND-join is a synchronization between two or more paths which must all have been visited for the rest of the scenario to progress.

The diamond symbols are called stubs and are used as containers for sub-maps, which are then referred to as plug-in maps. Any map can be a plug-in. The hand-off UCM in Figure 2 is in fact a plug-in for stub Handoff. A hand-off check is triggered (*GoHO*) to determine whether a new channel would result in a better communication quality. Stubs have identifiable input and output segments (IN1, OUT1,...) connected to start points and end points in the plug-in. This binding relation is also made visual in the plug-in, where the connections to the parent stub are shown between curly brackets. Binding relationship ensure that paths flow from parent maps to sub-maps, and back to parent maps. While static stubs contain only one plug-in map (e.g *HandOff*), dynamic stubs (drawn with dashed diamonds e.g. *Update*) contain many plug-ins whose selection can be determined at run time according to a selection policy local to the stub.

Note: h_i in Figure 1 represent the hyper-edges connecting different UCM constructs (see Section 3 for more details).

After having authenticated the call originator and updated its location record in the same database (*UpdateHLoc*), the system needs also to update the visiting databases if a mobile user enters or leaves a visiting area. This can be expressed by using two alternative plug-ins for stub Update (Figure 3). The first plug-in is selected when the mobile user is in the same area as before, and the visiting profile is updated if this area is not the home area. The second plug-in is selected when the mobile user has entered a different area. Different activities (deletion and creation of visitor profiles are required to handle the various situations where the old and new areas are the home area or visiting areas (i.e. home→visiting, visiting→home, Visiting→other Visiting). After the allocation of the necessary resources (*GetRes*), the call is answered and the two parties can start communicating (*Talking*). Upon disconnection (*Disconnect*), allocated resources are released (*RelRes*) and the communication is terminated.

Fig. 2. Plug-in for the HandOff Stub

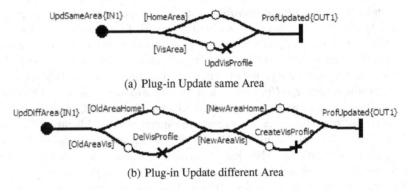

(a) Plug-in Update same Area

(b) Plug-in Update different Area

Fig. 3. Plug-ins for the Update Dynamic Stub

The set of global variables for the UCM map are: OK (call authenticated or not), Area (homeArea or VisArea), OldArea (OldAreaHome or OldAreaVis), NewArea (NewAreaHome or NewAreaVis) and Quality (better or worse). Different values of these variables are placed on the UCM guards to describe different scenarios' alternatives. A more detailed discussion on the wireless system can be found in [2].

In order to provide a formal semantics to Timed Use Case Maps, we extend the definition of Use Case Maps provided in [10] and [11] to include additional timing information.

3   Syntax of Timed Use Case Maps

We define a UCM as follows:

Definition 1 (Use Case Maps). *We assume that a timed UCM is denoted by a 8-tuple (D, H, λ, C, GVar, Bc, S, Bs) where:*

- *D is the UCM domain, composed of sets of typed elements. D= SP ∪ EP ∪ R ∪ AF ∪ AJ ∪ OF ∪ OJ ∪ Tm ∪ ST. Where SP is the set of Start Points, EP is the set of End Points, R is the set of Responsibilities, AF is the set of AND-Fork, AJ is the set of AND-Join, OF is the set of OR-Fork, OJ is the set of OR-Join, Tm is the set of Timers, and ST is the set of Stubs.*
- *H is the set of hyper-edges connecting UCM constructs to each other*
- *λ is a transition relation defined as: λ=D×H×D*
- *C is the set of components (C = ∅ for unbound UCM)*
- *GVar is the set of global variables.*
- *Bc is a component binding relation defined as Bc =D×C. Bc specifies which element of D is associated with which component of C. Bc is empty for unbound UCM.*
- *S is a plug-in binding relation defined as S = ST×RS×GVar.*
- *Bs is a stub binding relation and is defined as Bs =ST×{IN/OUT}×{SP/EP}. Bs specifies how the start and end points of the plug-in map would be connected to the path segments going into or out of the stub.*

Before defining the timed syntax of different UCM constructs, we introduce the following definitions and assumptions:

- **MClock(Master Clock).** The passing of time is modelled by a master clock that increases the global time and adjusts all local clocks accordingly. UCM constructs may be labeled with a time constraint in the following form 'MClock= τ' representing a delay in their execution. In such a case, the construct should be enabled τ time units after starting the UCM execution (i.e., MClock = 0).
- **δ.** Represents the master clock tick, which refers to the smallest time unit used to track system evolution over time. Only a tick advances time and it also defines the granularity of the master clock.
- **Duration.** Denotes the time it takes to carry out an execution of a responsibility. In general, time is only consumed by responsibilities. The absence of a duration value for a responsibility is expressed by the symbol ⊥. Control constructs, such as OR-fork, are instantaneous (Duration = 0). However, time may elapse in any UCM construct if its execution is delayed. For instance, if the master clock displays 'MClock=2δ', The execution of a UCM construct labeled with a time constraint 'MClock= 4δ' should be delayed by 2δ. Responsibility with undefined duration(i.e., Duration = ⊥) may cause a system deadlock. To avoid such situation, we assume that a responsibility with undefined duration takes one clock tick to complete.
- Time may elapse in AND-Join constructs, where incoming flows should synchronize (time passes by while waiting for all incoming hyperedges to be enabled).
- We assume that transitions are urgent and instantaneous: Transitions are processed as soon as they are enabled allowing for a maximal progress. Therefore, transitions can be considered as *eager* according to the definition of urgency introduced in [6].

Definition 2. *[Timed UCM Constructs]*

- **Start Points** are of the form *SP(PreCondition-set, TriggerringEvent-set, SPLabel, in, out, T)* where the parameter *PreConditions-set* is a list of conditions that must be satisfied in order for the scenario to be enabled (if no precondition is specified, then by default it is set to true). The parameter *TriggeringEvents-set* is a list that provides the set of events that can initiate the scenario along a path. One event is sufficient for triggering the scenario. The parameter *SPLabel* denotes the label of the start point. A start point should not have an incoming edge except when connected to an end point (called a waiting place). In such a situation, we use the parameter $in \in H$ to represent the connection with an end point. The parameter *out* $\in H$ is the (unique) outgoing hyperedge. T is optional and it introduces a delay in the start point triggering. '$T = \tau$' means that the start point is triggered at 'MClock $= \tau$'.

- **End Points** are of the form *EP(PostCondition-set, ResultingEvent-set, EPLabel, in, out)* where the parameter *PostConditions-set* is a list of conditions that must be satisfied once the scenario is completed. The parameter *ResultingEvent-set* is a list that gives the set of events that result from the completion of the scenario path. The parameter *EPLabel* denotes the label of the end point; the parameter $in \in H$ is the (unique) incoming hyperedge. End points have no target hyperedge except when connected to a start point (i.e. a waiting place). In such a case, $out \in H$ represents such connection. End points cannot be delayed.

- **Responsibilities** are of the form *Resp(in, Res, out, duration, T)* where $in \in H$ is the incoming hyperedge, *Res* is the activity to be executed, and $out \in H$ is the outgoing hyperedge. A responsibility is connected to only one source hyperedge and to one target hyperedge. 'duration' is the time taken by the responsibility to complete its execution. Similarly to the start point T is used to specify the delay before the start of execution of the responsibility.

- **OR-Forks** are of the form *OR-Fork(in, $[Cond_i]_{i \leq n}$, $[out_i]_{i \leq n}$, T)* where *in* denotes the incoming hyperedge, $[Cond_i]_{i \leq n}$ is a finite sequence of Boolean expressions, and $[out_i]_{i \leq n}$ is a sequence of outgoing hyperedges. Parameter T denotes a possible delay.

- **OR-Joins** are of the form *OR-Join($\{in_i\}_{i \leq n}$, out, T)* where $\{in_i\}_{i \leq n}$ denotes the incoming hyperedges and, *out* is the outgoing hyperedge. Parameter T denotes a possible delay.

- **AND-Forks** are of the form *AND-Fork(in, $\{out_i\}_{i \leq n}$, T)* where *in* denotes the incoming hyperedge, and $\{out_i\}_{i \leq n}$ is a sequence of outgoing hyperedges. Parameter T denotes an optional delay.

- **AND-Joins** are of the form *AND-Join($\{in_i\}_{i \leq n}$, out, T)* where $\{in_i\}_{i \leq n}$ denotes the incoming hyperedges, and *out* is the outgoing hyperedge. Parameter T denotes an optional delay.

- **Timers** are of the form *Timer(in, TriggerringEvent-set, out, out_timeout, T)*. The synchronous timer, as defined in [15], is very similar to a basic OR-Fork rule with only two disjoint branches. The parameter *TriggeringEvents-set* is the list that contains the set of events that can trigger the continuation path (i.e. represented by *out*) and the parameter *out_timeout* $\in H$ denotes the timeout path. For timers, T defines the timer's expiration time.

- **Stubs** have the form *Stub($\{entry_i\}_{i \leq n}$, $\{exit_j\}_{j \leq m}$, isDynamic, $[Cond_k]_{k \leq l}$, $[plugin_k]_{k \leq l}$)* where $\{entry_i\}_{i \leq n}$ and $\{exit_j\}_{j \leq m}$ denote respectively the set of the stub entry and exit points. *isDynamic* indicates whether the stub is dynamic or static. Dynamic stubs may contain multiple plug-ins, $[plugin_k]_{k \leq l}$ whose selection can be determined at run-time according to a selection-policy specified by the sequence of Boolean expressions $[Cond_k]_{k \leq l}$.

We have added the modelling of timing as an orthogonal feature to the untimed UCM syntax presented in [10]. The untimed syntax is restored simply by removing the duration of responsibilities and the delay of execution of different constructs.

Example: The plugin of the HandOff stub of Figure 4 can be described as follows: plug-in-HandOff=(D, H, λ, C, GVar, Bc, S, Bs).

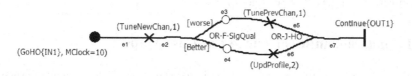

Fig. 4. Timed plug-in for stub HandOff

Where:

- D = {GoHO, TuneNewChan, OR-F-SigQual, TunePrevChan, UpdProfile, OR-J-HO, Continue}
- H = {e1, e2, e3, e4, e5, e6, e7}
- λ = {(GoHO, e1, TuneNewChan),(TuneNewChan, e2, OR-f-SigQual),(OR-F-SigQual, e3, TunePrevChan),(OR-F-SigQual, e4, UpdProfile),(TunePrevChan, e5, OR-J-HO), (UpdProfile, e6, OR-J-HO),(OR-J-HO, e7, Continue)}
- GVar = {Quality}; C = $\emptyset$; Bc = $\emptyset$; S= $\emptyset$; Bs = $\emptyset$

Start point *GoHO* in Figure 4 should be triggered at 'MClock=10'. Responsibilities *TuneNewChan* and *TunePrevChan* take 1 clock tick to complete, while *UpdProfile* takes 2 clock ticks to complete. In this example, responsibilities should start immediately without delaying. They are considered as *eager responsibilities* according to the definition of urgency introduced in [6].

Definition 3 (Access functions)

We define the following access functions:

1. **Enables:** D$\rightarrow H^n$. Given a UCM construct *Constr* $\in$ D, *enables* provides the set of hyper-edges that the construct enables after it completes its execution. For instance *enables(Resp(in, Res, out, duration, T))*={*out*}. Outgoing hyper-edges may be associated with guard conditions (i.e., OR-fork and dynamic stubs). Function *enables* evaluates the guards and chooses the outgoing hyperedge associated with the true condition.
2. **Triggered:** $\rightarrow D^n$. Gives the set of constructs that should be triggered at the present time. For instance, in Figure 4 at time *MClock=10*, start point *GoHO* may be triggered.
3. **Incoming:** D $\rightarrow H^n$. Given a UCM construct, *incoming* provides the set of hyper-edges directly leading to the construct. For instance, Incoming(OR-Join({in_i}$_{i \leq n}$, out, T))= {in_i}$_{i \leq n}$.

4. **Target:** H → D. Gives the subsequent construct directly connected to a given hyperedge.
5. **Delay:** D →ℕ. Gives the delay associated with the UCM construct. For instance *Delay(Resp(in, Res, out, duration, T))= T.*
6. **Type:** D→{SP, EP, AJ, AF, OJ, OF, Tm, ST} specifies the type of a UCM construct.

Note: For the sake of clarity, functions *enables*, *target* and *delay* could be applied to a sequence of elements of the specified types and produce a sequence of elements of the resulting types. For instance, target([h1,h2])=[d1,d2] where constructs *d1* and *d2* are respectively the targets of hyperedges *h1* and *h2*.

4   Formal Semantics of Timed Use Case Maps

Defining a solid UCM time semantics is an initial step towards defining a new version of UCM that can be used for simulation and verification of timed models. Our ultimate goal is to use UCM to build system models that combine functional, architectural and temporal aspects of real-time systems, and then apply the resulting models to check the correctness of these systems.

In this section, we define the formal semantics of timed UCM models in terms of Clocked Transition Systems (CTS) [18]. The original CTS definition introduced in [18] assumes many finitely real-valued clocks. However, models of real time have been classified in the literature as either dense time or discrete time depending on whether the time of occurrence of an event is expressed as a real number or approximated by an integer. In our proposed semantics, we consider a discrete time model to be divided into clock ticks indexed by natural numbers. The elapsed time between the events is measured in terms of ticks of a global digital clock which is increased by one with every single tick. This time model corresponds to the fictitious-clock model from [1] or the digital-clock model from [12].

Formally a Clocked Transition System (CTS): $\Phi= (V, \sigma_{init}, \rightarrow)$ consists of:

- V = (H-taken, C-active, H-enabled, C-timers, T-trigger, MClock). Where:
  - *H-Taken* represents the set of already traversed hyper-edges.
  - *C-active* represents a sequence of UCM constructs currently executing.
  - *H-enabled* represents a sequence of enabled hyper-edges (i.e. to be traversed during the next transition) associated with the sequence of active constructs in *C-active*.
  - *C-timers* represents a sequence of timers (i.e., clocks) associated with the active constructs *C-active*. *C-timers* monitor the remained executing time of active constructs. *C-timers* is initialized with the duration of execution of every construct in *C-active*.
    Note: Timers in *C-timers* cannot go below zero.
  - *T-trigger* represents the sequence of time constraints (or delays) associated with the sequence of active constructs *C-active*. *T-trigger* values correspond to the parameter *T* defined in the constructs' signatures (see Definition 2).
  - MClock is the Master Clock.

- σ_{init}: Represents the initial state. It is required that for the initial state *MClock = 0*.
- $\rightarrow$: A finite set of transitions. Each transition is a function $\rightarrow \subseteq \Sigma(V) \times \Sigma(V)$ mapping each state $s \in \Sigma$ into a set of successors states $s' \in \Sigma$. Instead of writing $(\sigma, \sigma') \in \rightarrow$, we write $\sigma \rightarrow \sigma'$. Informally, states are assignments of values to variables, called valuations. A valuation maps a variable to a value. A transition from one state to another represents that some variables are assigned a different value, i.e., the valuation changes.

A run of Φ is an infinite sequence of valuations, $\pi = \sigma_0 \sigma_1 \ldots$ satisfying:

- Initiation : $\sigma_0 \models \sigma_{init}$
- Consecution: For each i=0,1,... the valuation σ_{i+1} is a $\rightarrow$ successor of σ_i, i.e, $\sigma_i \rightarrow \sigma_{i+1}$.

A computation of Φ is a run satisfying:

- Time divergence: The sequence $\sigma_0(MClock)$ $\sigma_1(MClock)$ ... grows beyond any bound. That is, as *i* increases, the value of MClock at σ_i increases beyond any bound.

We assume that the run-to completion principle applies to the execution of a construct. The execution of a UCM construct cannot be interrupted until it is completed.

We distinguish two types of transition relations $\rightarrow$:

1. **Configuration Transitions:** When a Configuration Transitions is taken, the system configuration defined by the three sequences: *H-taken*, *C-active* and *H-enabled* is updated to indicate which transition has just been taken.
   (H-taken, C-active, H-enabled, C-timers, T-trigger, MClock)$\rightarrow$(H-taken', C-active', H-enabled', C-timers', T-trigger', MClock').
   Where(H-taken'$\neq$H-taken)$\wedge$(C-active'$\neq$C-active)$\wedge$ (H-enabled'$\neq$H-enabled)$\wedge$(C-timers'=C-timers- δ)$\wedge$(T-trigger'$\neq$T-trigger) $\wedge$ (MClock'=MClock+δ).
   A configuration transition is executed upon the expiration of one or many of elements of *C-timers* (i.e., $\exists$ t $\in$ C-timers such that, t=0) or when the delay associated with a construct elapses (i.e., MClock$\geq$T)).

2. **Time Transitions:** When a time transition is taken, then the only variables that change are the global time MClock (which is incremented by a clock tick (δ)), and the timers$\in$C-timers which are decremented by a clock tick (δ). However, the system configuration remains unchanged.
   (H-taken, C-active, H-enabled, C-timers, T-trigger, MClock)$\rightarrow$(H-taken', C-active', H-enabled', C-timers', T-trigger', MClock')
   Where (H-taken'=H-taken)$\wedge$(C-active'=C-active)$\wedge$(H-enabled'=H-enabled) $\wedge$ (T-trigger'=T-trigger) $\wedge$ (C-timers'=C-timer-δ)$\wedge$ (MClock'=MClock+δ)
   Time transitions are executed when none of the timers is about to expire (i.e., $\forall$t $\in$C-timers such that, t>0) and none of the constructs is about to start execution (i.e., MClock < T).

In order to establish binding relationship between *C-active*, *H-enabled* and *C-timers*, we define the following correspondance functions: **Atimers**:*C-timers*$\rightarrow$*C-active*; and **Htimers**: *C-timers*$\rightarrow$*H-enabled*. For instance, let *C-active*=[a1, a2, a3];*H-enabled*=[h1, h2, h3] and *C-timers*=[t1, t2, t3], **Atimers**(t1)=a1 and **Htimers**(t2)=h2.

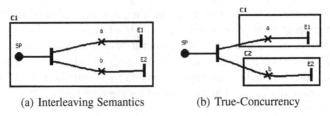

| (a) Interleaving Semantics | (b) True-Concurrency |

Fig. 5. Concurrency Semantics

4.1 Concurrency Model and Time Evolution

The UCM construct AND-Fork allows many paths to execute concurrently. Considering the assumption of run to completion introduced earlier, different scenarios may behave either in:

- **Interleaving Semantics.** At any given time t, only one responsibility may be executing.
  Or
- **True concurrency Semantics.** At any given time t, more than one responsibility may be executing.

We assume that in presence of UCM components, concurrent paths bounded to the same component are sharing also the same component resources(for instance same CPU). Therefore, these concurrent paths must behave in interleaving semantics. Figure 5(a) illustrates a UCM with two parallel paths bounded to one component. At any time, no more than one responsibility should be active. However, the choice of which responsibility goes first is non deterministic in this case. Adding timing constraints may eliminate non determinism (i.e., if responsibilities a and b have different values in *T-trigger*).

Parallel paths bounded to different components may behave either according to interleaving semantics or to true concurrency semantics. Figure 5(b) illustrates two parallel paths allocated to two different components. Responsibilities a and b can be executed in true-concurrency model, since they are enabled at the same time and they don't share the same resources. However, the decision to go with either semantics depends on the real mapping of components to different nodes on a network or to different CPUs, where true concurrency can be achieved.

Note: We assume interleaving concurrency model for unbound UCMs.

In what follows we provide the detailed semantic rules for both concurrency models. The top part of a rule is either a boolean condition that must be true or a computation of a set/subset/variable. For the sake of simplicity, we consider only unfolded UCMs, where all stubs in the root map were already replaced with their corresponding plug-in maps.

4.2 Step Semantics for Interleaving Model

The choice of an interleaving semantics reduces the size of the CTS Variables. Indeed, allowing only one construct to be executed in a given configuration, reduces the set of used variables. Therefore, sequences *C-active* and *C-timers* are reduced to one element since only one variable per sequence is necessary to track the configuration evolution.

Initial State: σ_{init} is defined with the following valuation: (H-taken=$\emptyset$, C-active =$\emptyset$, H-enabled:=enables(triggered), C-timers=0, T-trigger=$\emptyset$, MClock=0). Start points were not included in *C-active* to avoid carrying more than one active construct.

Configuration Transition. Rules 1 and 2 illustrate the configuration transition. As stated earlier in Section 3, time may elapse in AND-join constructs (waiting for all incoming hyperedges to be synchronized). To reflect this fact, we distinguish two cases: a case where no extra delay is involved (Rule 1) and a case where there is an implicit extra delay involved (Rule 2).

Rule 1. *Configuration Transition: case type(C-active)$\neq$AJ*

$$(C\text{-}timers=0) \wedge type(C\text{-}active) \neq AJ$$
$$h := \{Select\ any\ e \in H\text{-}enabled,\ such\ that,\ delay(target(e)) \leq MClock\ \}$$
$$if\ h = \emptyset\ then\ \{\ C\text{-}active' := \emptyset\ ;\ H\text{-}taken' := H\text{-}taken;\ H\text{-}enabled' := H\text{-}enabled\ \}$$
$$else\ \{C\text{-}active' := target(h)$$
$$H\text{-}enabled' := H\text{-}enabled \cup target(C\text{-}active') - \{h\}$$
$$H\text{-}taken' := H\text{-}taken \cup \{h\}\}$$
$$MClock' := MClock + \delta$$
$$C\text{-}timers' := duration(C\text{-}active')$$
$$T\text{-}trigger' := delay(C\text{-}active')$$

$$(H\text{-}taken,\ C\text{-}active,\ H\text{-}enabled,\ C\text{-}timers,\ T\text{-}trigger, MClock) \rightarrow (H\text{-}taken',\ C\text{-}active',$$
$$H\text{-}enabled', C\text{-}timers', T\text{-}trigger',\ MClock')$$

Rule 2. *Configuration Transition case type(C-active)=AJ*

$$(C\text{-}timers=0) \wedge type(C\text{-}active) = AJ$$
$$Incoming(C\text{-}active) \subseteq H\text{-}taken,\ such\ that\ h := \{any\ e \in H\text{-}enabled,\ such\ that,$$
$$delay(target(e)) \leq MClock\ \}\}$$
$$Incoming(C\text{-}active) \not\subseteq H\text{-}taken,\ such\ that,\ h := \{any\ e \in H\text{-}enabled,\ such\ that$$
$$e \notin enables(C\text{-}active)\}$$
$$if\ h = \emptyset\ then\ \{\ C\text{-}active' := \emptyset;\ H\text{-}taken' := H\text{-}taken;\ H\text{-}enabled' := H\text{-}enabled\ \}$$
$$else\ \{C\text{-}active' := target(h)$$
$$H\text{-}enabled' := H\text{-}enabled \cup target(C\text{-}active') - \{h\}$$
$$H\text{-}taken' := H\text{-}taken \cup \{h\}\}$$
$$MClock' := MClock + \delta$$
$$C\text{-}timers' := duration(C\text{-}active')$$
$$T\text{-}trigger' := delay(C\text{-}active')$$

$$(H\text{-}taken,\ C\text{-}active,\ H\text{-}enabled,\ C\text{-}timers,\ T\text{-}trigger,\ MClock) \rightarrow (H\text{-}taken',\ C\text{-}active',$$
$$H\text{-}enabled',\ C\text{-}timers',\ T\text{-}trigger',\ MClock')$$

When multiple hyperedges are enabled at a transition, one hyperedge is chosen in a non-deterministic way. Consequently, multiple runs (or timed traces) can be generated from the same UCM scenario.

Time Transition. Rule 3 shows the time transition.

Rule 3. *Time Transition*

$$(C\text{-}timers \neq 0)$$
$$MClock' := MClock + \delta \; ; \; C\text{-}timers' := C\text{-}timers - \delta$$

$$(H\text{-}taken, C\text{-}active, H\text{-}enabled, C\text{-}timers, T\text{-}trigger, MClock) \rightarrow (H\text{-}taken, C\text{-}active,$$
$$H\text{-}enabled, C\text{-}timers', T\text{-}trigger, MClock')$$

4.3   Step Semantics for True Concurrency Model

Contrary to the interleaving semantics, *C-active*, *C-timers* and *T-trigger* may have more than one element in presence of concurrent paths. Indeed, *C-active* contains UCM constructs that are being executed concurrently. *C-timers* and *T-trigger* contain their respective sequence of timers and sequence of time delays.

Initial State: σ_{init} is defined with the following valuation: (H-taken=$\emptyset$, C-active =$\emptyset$, H-enabled:=enables(triggered), C-timers=$\emptyset$, T-trigger=$\emptyset$, MClock=0).

Configuration Transition. Rules 4 and 5 show the configuration transition. As stated in the previous section we devise a special rule for AND-join.

Rule 4. *Configuration Transition: case* $\forall constr \in C\text{-}active, type(constr) \neq AJ$

$$let \; expire \subseteq C\text{-}timers \; such \; that \; expire \neq \emptyset \; and \; \forall t \in expire, t=0$$
$$\exists constr \in C\text{-}active \; such \; that \; delay(constr) \leq MClock$$
$$C\text{-}active' := C\text{-}active - Atimers(expire) \cup target(Htimers(expire))$$
$$H\text{-}enabled' := H\text{-}enabled - Htimers(expire) \cup enables(target(Htimers(expire)))$$
$$H\text{-}taken' := H\text{-}taken \cup Htimers(expire)$$
$$MClock' := MClock + \delta$$
$$\forall t \in C\text{-}timers \; such \; that \; t>0, C\text{-}timers' := (C\text{-}timers - \delta) - expire \cup$$
$$duration(target(Htimers(expire)))$$
$$T\text{-}trigger' := delay(C\text{-}active')$$

$$(H\text{-}taken, C\text{-}active, H\text{-}enabled, C\text{-}timers, T\text{-}trigger, MClock) \rightarrow (H\text{-}taken', C\text{-}active',$$
$$H\text{-}enabled', C\text{-}timers', T\text{-}trigger', MClock')$$

Rule 5. *Configuration Transition case* $\exists constr \in C\text{-}active, type(constr)=AJ$

$$let \; expire \subseteq C\text{-}timers \; such \; that \; expire \neq \emptyset \; and \; \forall t \in expire, t=0$$
$$let \; AJ\text{-}active \subseteq C\text{-}active \; / \; \forall \; aj \in AJ\text{-}active, type(aj)=AJ \; and \; Incoming(aj) \subseteq H\text{-}taken$$
$$C\text{-}active' := C\text{-}active - Atimers(expire) \cup target(Htimers(expire))$$
$$\cup target(enables(AJ\text{-}active))$$
$$H\text{-}enabled' := H\text{-}enabled - Htimers(expire) \cup enables(target(Htimers(expire))) \cup$$
$$enables(target(enables(AJ\text{-}active)))$$
$$H\text{-}taken' := H\text{-}taken \cup Htimers(expire) \cup enables(AJ\text{-}active)$$
$$MClock' := MClock + \delta$$

$\forall t \in$ C-timers such that t>0, C-timers':= (C-timers- δ)- expire $\cup$
duration(target(Htimers(expire)))$\cup$ duration(target(enables(AJ-active)))
T-trigger':= delay(C-active')

(H-taken, C-active, H-enabled, C-timers, T-trigger, MClock)→(H-taken', C-active',
H-enabled', C-timers', T-trigger', MClock')

Time Transition. Rule 6 shows the time transition.

Rule 6. *Time Transition*

$$\forall t \in \text{C-timers} \ / \ t \neq 0$$
$$MClock':=MClock+\delta \ ; \ \text{C-timers}':=\text{C-timers-}\delta$$

(H-taken, C-active, H-enabled, C-timers, T-trigger, MClock)→(H-taken, C-active,
H-enabled, C-timers', T-trigger, MClock')

Note that the runs in the true concurrency semantics model have less states compared
to the same runs in the interleaving semantics.

4.4 Applying Timed Semantics to the Simplified Wireless System

Due to space constraints, we limit ourselves to a partial run of the UCM introduced in
Figure 1.

$H-taken$	$C-active$	$H-enables$	$C-timers$	$T-trigger$	$MClock$
{}	[]	[h1]	[]	[]	0
{h1}	[ChkAuth]	[h2]	[1]	[⊥]	1
{h1}	[ChkAuth]	[h2]	[0]	[⊥]	2
{h1, h2}	[OR-F-Auth]	[h3]	[0]	[⊥]	3
{h1, h2, h3}	[LogReject]	[h4]	[2]	[⊥]	4
{h1, h2, h3}	[LogReject]	[h4]	[1]	[⊥]	5
{h1, h2, h3}	[LogReject]	[h4]	[0]	[⊥]	6
{h1, h2, h3, h4}	[Reject]	[]	[0]	[⊥]	7

Fig. 6. Partial Execution

We have chosen a scenario, where the call originator is not authenticated, resulting
in a call rejection (i.e., OK=false). We assume also *duration(ChkAuth)=1* while *dura-
tion(LogReject)=2* and δ=1. Figure 6 illustrates the corresponding run.

To illustrate the concurrency model semantics, we present another partial run of
the UCM of Figure 1 starting from the AND-Fork construct. The scenario starts at
MClock=9 to allow the start point *GoHO* to be enabled at MClock=10. Variable *Quality* is initialized to *better* and responsibilities *talking* and *UpdProfile* have respectively
5 and 2 as durations. The duration of the remaining responsibilities is fixed to 1. Only
new elements of *H-taken* are shown in Figure 7.

$H - taken$	$C - active$	$H - enables$	$C - timers$	$T - trigger$	$MClock$
$\{h1..h8\}$	[AF-Root]	[h9,h11]	[]	[⊥]	9
$\{h9, h11\}$	[GoHO, GetRes]	[e1,h12]	[0,1]	[10,⊥]	10
$\{e1\}$	[tuneNewChan,GetRes]	[e2,h12]	[1,0]	[⊥,⊥]	11
$\{h12\}$	[tuneNewChan,Answer]	[e2,h13]	[0,1]	[⊥,⊥]	12
$\{e2\}$	[OR-F-SigQual,Answer]	[e4,h13]	[0,0]	[⊥,⊥]	13
$\{h13, e4\}$	[UpdProfile,talking]	[e6,h14]	[2,5]	[⊥,⊥]	14
$\{\}$	[UpdProfile,talking]	[e6,h14]	[1,4]	[⊥,⊥]	15
$\{\}$	[UpdProfile,talking]	[e6,h14]	[0,3]	[⊥,⊥]	16
$\{e6\}$	[OR-J-HO,talking]	[e7,h14]	[0,2]	[⊥,⊥]	17
$\{e7\}$	[Continue,talking]	[h10,h14]	[0,1]	[⊥,⊥]	18
$\{h10\}$	[AJ-Root,talking]	[h15,h14]	[0,0]	[⊥,⊥]	19
$\{h14\}$	[AJ-Root]	[h15]	[0]	[⊥]	20
$\{h15\}$	[Disconnect]	[h16]	[1]	[⊥]	21
$\{\}$	[Disconnect]	[h16]	[0]	[⊥]	22
$\{h16\}$	[RelRes]	[h17]	[1]	[⊥]	23
$\{\}$	[RelRes]	[h17]	[0]	[⊥]	24
$\{h17\}$	[EndCom]	[]	[0]	[⊥]	25

Fig. 7. Partial Execution: True Concurrency

5   Related Work

In this section, we discuss work related to the notion of time and its support in other modeling languages. The research in this area has taken several directions. One direction consists on focusing on the enhancement of current modeling languages by adding new constructs. UML Real-Time profile [20] uses this approach and adds features for describing a variety of aspects used to model real-time systems, such as timing, resources, performance, schedulability, etc. The current standard UML 2.0 [22] pays more attention to time related aspects than the previous UML version [21]. Indeed, timers and time related types, are present in UML 2.0. In the context of SDL [13], an ITU standard formal description language described in Z.100 document, each action takes an indeterminate time to execute, and that a process stays an unfixed amount of time in a certain state before taking the next fireable transition. This choice may be practical for code generation, in the sense that actual implementations of the system conform to it. However, for simulation purposes, it might be unreasonable since we need to consider all possible combinations of execution times, timer expirations and timers consumptions. Existing simulation tools consider that actions take 0 time to execute allowing for a high degree of determinism. Our timed UCM semantics, primarily used for simulation purposes, provide a fixed duration to actions (may be relaxed in the future by providing only an upper bound). A valid model of the interpretation of an SDL system is a complete interleaving of different processes at the level of all actions that cannot be transformed into a list of actions (possibly containing implicit states). While using this notion of atomic actions, our proposed semantics consider both concurrency modes: interleaving and true concurrency. The selection of either mode is based on architectural choices.

Another research direction is the combination of an existing modeling notation with another formal description technique to provide better handling of timing aspects. The semantics presented in this paper is comparable to the one presented in [8] where Eshuis presented a formal semantics of UML activity diagrams in terms of clocked transition systems (CTS). However, no distinction between concurrency modes is discusses. The authors in [17] translated UML models with timed properties (e.g. guarded timeouts, transitions dependent on other transition times, etc.) into first-order temporal logic with time support. Knapp et al. [16] used timed state machines for describing a model, and collaboration diagrams with time constraints to describe system properties. In [9] the authors used OCL 2.0 [23] to describe real-time constraints specifications.

6   Conclusion

In this paper, we have presented an extension to the Use Case Maps language that introduces timing information for modeling real-time systems. We have provided a concise formal operational semantics for timed UCM based on Clocked Transition Systems. However, our approach does not consider checking the consistency of the time constraints in the model. In fact, when using true concurrency semantics, one has to ensure that concurrent responsibilities are not updating the same global variables. This can be achieved through a data flow analysis.

As part of our ongoing work, we are investigating the possible extension of our timed UCM syntax and semantics by adding new timed UCM constructs such as *asynchronous timers*, as well as offering the possibility to describe new time constraints.

As part of our future work, we will investigate the possible use of our timed semantics to check the correctness and the consistency of timed UCM specifications.

References

1. Alur, R., Dill, D.L., A Theory of Timed Automata, Theoretical Computer Science, 126, pp.183-235, 1994.
2. Amyot D., Introduction to the user requirements notation: learning by example, Computer Networks: The International Journal of Computer and Telecommunications Networking, Vol. 42, No. 3, pp. 285-301, 2003.
3. Amyot D. and Andrade R., Description of wireless intelligent network services with Use Case Maps, SBRC'99, 17th Simposio Brasileiro de Redes de Computadores, Salvador, Brazil, May 1999, pp. 418-433.
4. Amyot D., Buhr R.J.A., Gray T. and Logrippo L., Use Case Maps for the Capture and Validation of Distributed Systems Requirements. RE'99, Fourth IEEE International Symposium on Requirements Engineering, Limerick, Ireland, June 1999,44-53. http://www.UseCaseMaps.org/pub/re99.pdf
5. Amyot D., Formalization of Time threads Using LOTOS. Master Thesis, Department of Computer Science, University of Ottawa, Canada, 1994.
6. Bornot S., Sifakis J., and Tripakis S., Modeling urgency in timed systems. In International Symposium: Compositionality - The Significant Difference, LNCS 1536, 1998.
7. Buhr R. J. A., Elammari M., Gray T. and Mankovski S., Applying Use Case Maps to multiagent systems: A feature interaction example. In 31st Annual Hawaii International Conference on System Sciences, 1998.

8. Eshuis R., Semantics and Verification of UML Activity Diagrams for Workflow Modelling, Ph.D. Thesis, University of Twente, 2002.
9. Flake S. and Mueller W., A UML Profile for Real-Time Constraints with the OCL. In S. Cook J. M. Jezequel, H. Hussmann, editor, UML2002, Dresden, Germany, number 2460 in LNCS. Springer Verlag, 2002.
10. Hassine, J., Rilling, J., and Dssouli, R. (2005) An Abstract Operational Semantics for Use Case Maps. In: Farn Wang (Ed.): Formal Techniques for Networked and Distributed Systems - FORTE 2005, 25th IFIP WG 6.1 International Conference, Taipei, Taiwan, October, 2005. LNCS 3731 Springer 2005, 366-380
11. Hassine, J., Dssouli, R., and Rilling, J. (2004) Applying Reduction Techniques to Software Functional Requirement Specifications. In Amyot, D. and Williams, A.W. (Eds) System Analysis and Modeling - Fourth International SDL and MSC Workshop, SAM 2004, Ottawa, Canada, June 2-4, 2004, LNCS, Volume 3319, Springer, 2005, 138-153
12. Henzinger, T. A., Manna, Z., Pnueli, A., What good are digital clocks?, Proceedings of the ICALP92, LNCS 623, pp.545-558, Spriger-Verlag,1992.
13. ITU-T Recommendation Z.100: Specification and Description Language (SDL). (2002)
14. ITU-T - International Telecommunications Union (2003). Recommendation Z.150 (02/03), User Requirements Notation (URN) - Language Requirements and Framework. Geneva, Switzerland.
15. ITU-T, URN Focus Group (2003), Draft Rec. Z.152 - UCM: Use Case Map Notation (UCM). Geneva. Switzerland, Sept. 2003
16. Knapp A., Merz S., and Rauh C., Model Checking - Timed UML State Machines and Collaborations. In Formal Techniques in Real-Time and Fault-Tolerant Systems, 7th International Symposium, FTRTFT 2002, Oldenburg, Germany, September 9- 12, 2002, volume 2469 of Lecture Notes in Computer Science, pages 395-416. Springer, 2002.
17. Lavazza L., Quaroni G., and Venturelli M., Combining uml and formal notions for modelling real-time systems. In Joint 8th European Software Engineering Conference, 9th ACM SIGSOFT. ACM SIGSOFT, 2001.
18. Manna Z. and Pnueli A., Clocked transition systems. In A. Pnueli and H. Lin, editors, Logic and Software Engineering, pages 3-42. World Scientific, 1996.
19. Nakamura N., Kikuno T., Hassine J., and Logrippo L., Feature Interaction Filtering with Use Case Maps at Requirements Stage. In: Sixth International Workshop on Feature Interactions in Telecommunications and Software Systems (FIW'00), Glasgow, Scotland, UK, May 2000.
20. OMG. Response to the OMG RFP for Schedulability, Performance and Time, v. 2.0. OMG document ad/2002-03-04, March 2002.
21. OMG Unified Modeling Language Specification, Version 1.5, June 2002.
22. Object Management Group: UML 2.0 Superstructure Specification. (2004)
23. OMG Unified Modeling Language Specification - Object Constraint Language Version 2.0, 2003.

Application of Stuck-Free Conformance to Service-Role Composition

Fritjof Boger Engelhardtsen[1,2] and Andreas Prinz[1]

[1] Agder University College, Faculty of Engineering and Science, Dep. of Information and Communication Technology, Grimstad, Norway
{Fritjof.B.Engelhardtsen, Andreas.Prinz}@hia.no
[2] Norwegian University of science and technology, Faculty of Information Technology, Mathematics and Electrical Engineering, Dep. of Telematics, Trondheim, Norway

Abstract. We use SDL and UML 2.0 state machines for behavior modeling of communication control software for telecommunication services. To ensure consistent designs we want to identify when a signal sent is not consumed and when a state machine waits indefinitely for a signal that never arrives. One approach to ensure such consistency is to derive interface contracts for each port from the properties of the state machine and use the contracts to check consistency. In this paper we describe how Calculus for Communicating Systems (CCS) [1] and stuck-free conformance [2] can be used as a formal fundament for this consistency checking. Interface descriptions should be comprehensible without having to learn process algebra. Therefore we introduce a graphical notation for both the port contracts and for the interaction made possible across the interface of two state machines.

1   Introduction

Our approach to incremental development and analysis is based on the concept of interface projections [3]. Interface projections are used to derive behavioral contracts for the ports from the state machines and their properties. In this process we hide as much as possible of the internals of the state machine (timers, save, choice and data) and the effects of communication on *hidden interfaces*. By hiding we mean that we abstract from the details of the state machine implementation in a way that preserves a description of the behavior that must be exercised at each port of the state machine in order for every transition to have a possibility of triggering. This description also states which signals the environment must be ready to receive at the same port. To understand the concept of hidden interfaces, consider a state machine with multiple ports allowing it to communicate with multiple other state machines. If we consider the behavioral properties of one port at a time, the remaining ports will be considered as hidden interfaces. These hidden interfaces may or may not affect the behavioral properties of the interface currently visible.

As an example, consider the state machines A, B, C and D in Fig. 1 (their exact behavior is given in Sect. 4.1). Analyzing the interface that state machine

R. Gotzhein and R. Reed (Eds.): SAM 2006, LNCS 4320, pp. 115–132, 2006.
© Springer-Verlag Berlin Heidelberg 2006

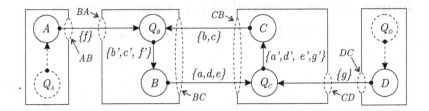

Fig. 1. State machines, queues and interface contracts given per-port

B has towards C, that is BC, the communication between B and A occurring across the interfaces BA and AB will be considered hidden. In this example we want to check that the interaction between B and C is consistent by checking the interface contracts BC and CB alone. The challenge is then to ensure that BC and CB correctly encompass the effects of dependencies on the hidden interfaces and the crossing of signals due to concurrent initiatives. A concurrent initiative occurs when A and C concurrently can send a signal to B. In order to model this situation the queue Q_B must be sufficiently long so that neither A nor C blocks while trying to send a signal to B. Note that we use the port concept to encompass SDL gates and that SDL channels may have delay. In the examples given in this paper we assume that one queue is sufficient to correctly represent the interleaving made possible by both the input queues and the channels.

To make these interface contracts we build on the results from [4]. We seek to define an underlying formal basis for the existing results based on process algebra. By doing so we hope to build confidence in the correctness of the existing consistency checking algorithms and enhance our understanding of interface behavior. We use the concept of stuck-free CCS processes as presented in [2] that formalizes the property that a process is stuck waiting for a message that never arrives or that a process attempts to send a message that is never consumed. To our knowledge stuck-free conformance has not been applied specifically to analysis of SDL models or models using UML 2.0 "in the SDL tradition".

The interface contracts we describe in this paper are currently derived from existing state machine designs and may not be suitable for an early phase of the collaboration design. For this we recommend an approach such as the CoSDL [5] collaboration specification language. Later in the design process, contracts with stuck-free semantics could possibly be derived from the collaborations, that each state machine participating in the collaboration must adhere to.

We begin this paper by giving a short introduction to the concepts of role-based service modeling in Sect. 2. Sect. 3 proceeds with a short introduction to CCS and stuck-free conformance adapted to an SDL-like context. In Sect. 4 we present our approach to translate SDL or (restricted) UML 2.0 state machine models into process algebraic agent expressions that are used to create the interface contracts. Sect. 5 presents a hypothetical service example and shows its derived interface contracts. In Sect. 6 we introduce a graphical representation for the interface contracts where CCS internal execution steps (τ) giving rise to nondeterminism in the collaboration are depicted using the SDL signal *none*. By attempting to compose two such contracts we check if two state machines can communicate without signal discarding and identify when a state machine may wait indefinitely for a signal that never arrive.

2   Role-Based Service Modeling

Development of control logic for advanced telecom services puts challenges on the developer in handling complex behavior and interactions. Making this process as manageable as possible we apply the principles of role-based modeling [6]. In this methodology we typically represent external entities in the environment of the system as active objects (agents) inside the system (called *environment mirroring*). This simplifies comprehension of system structure. We want these active objects, whose behavior is modeled using state machines to be as independent as possible, having manageable dependencies thereby supporting incremental development.

Service execution is typically performed by a collaboration among active objects or agents that are dynamically linked. *"... the same system agent often participates in several collaborations. Thus, the state machine of an agent needs to be split off between these different collaborations, which leads us to the concept of collaboration roles."* [7]. In an open service system, new service agents may be added and removed from a system dynamically. It is therefore essential that validation can be performed incrementally and to some extent dynamically. This paper explores how stuck-free conformance can be used to analyze the interaction between these collaboration roles.

Our system components are typically modeled as SDL composite states or as UML 2.0 submachines. The examples given in this paper assume that these principles are applied, allowing the validation to be restricted to structures of state machines participating in a collaboration rather than the entire system. To achieve such manageable dependencies between the state machines we must adhere to certain design constraints. To be able to apply stuck-free conformance to consistency checking of our components we require the following design constraint to be followed.

Design Constraint: For the parts of the state machine encompassed by the interface contract we require that: Every signal sent must always eventually be consumed and not be discarded. No transition can deterministically stay untriggered.

3   CCS and Stuck-Free Conformance Applied to SDL

3.1   Short Introduction to CCS

CCS is a process algebra developed by Robin Milner [1]. It allows modeling of interacting processes and reasoning about their behavior and structural composition using a small but expressive set of operators. Concurrency in standard

CCS has interleaving semantics in that actions performed in parallel will inter-leave in multiple ways. The act of communication between two agents is modeled as a synchronous handshake where both the sender and receiver must be ready to synchronize for the communication to take place. This means that CCS ab-stracts away from the fact that there may be an "active" sender-part and a "passive" receiver-part. However, in the application of CCS $\overline{co\text{-}label}$ is normally used to denote sending actions and *label* (no "overline") to denote receiving actions. It is also common to denote sending by " ! " and reception by " ? ".

Communication between two processes can only occur on oppositely labeled action pairs (label and co-label). If one process is ready to communicate on action "a" then it may communicate with some other process that is ready to synchronize on " $\overline{a}$ ". This is quite different from the semantics of SDL, but we shall later see that despite this difference it allows us to analyze interesting aspects of SDL models. Indeed, because of this difference we are able to precisely capture interleaving and its effect on the interface contracts.

Behavior and structural composition is modeled in CCS using the operators prefix " . ", choice " $+$ ", parallel composition " $|$ "and restriction " $\backslash$ ". Using the prefix operator an action can be bound to a process. $P \stackrel{\Delta}{=} a.Q$ means that process P is defined by a process that can perform an action a and continue by the definition of process Q. $P \stackrel{\Delta}{=} a.Q + b.R$ means that P may either perform an a action and proceed as Q or perform a b action and proceed as R. The operator " $|$ " allows for composition of multiple parallel processes. Composition $P \mid Q$ enables communication between P and Q (and with their environment). Restricting some actions to only allow internal communication (and not with the environment of the processes) is achieved using the " $\backslash$ " operator. For example, processes $(a.b.0 \mid \overline{a}.c.0)\backslash a$ can only proceed by first performing an internal syn-chronization on a. This is called a τ-transition: $(a.b.0 \mid \overline{a}.c.0)\backslash a \stackrel{\tau}{\longrightarrow} (b.0 \mid c.0)\backslash a$.

3.2 Applying the Theory to SDL State Machines and Port Contracts

This section will be weak in formal definitions so the reader must refer to the original papers for details. At the heart of stuck-free conformance theory [2] lies the distinction between *external* and *internal choice*. This distinction allows us to conceptually differentiate between the actions under control of a component from the actions under control of the component's environment. We want to make this distinction in the port contracts outlined in the introduction. By doing so we can express what acts of communication the component internally chooses to perform with the consequence that the environment must be ready to handle the effect of the choice. This internal choice may be dependent on communication on hidden interfaces. The same contracts must also express what actions the component allows the environment to decide.

This difference is expressed in CCS by τ-transitions. Given CCS processes P and Q, then $\tau.P + \tau.Q$ denotes internal choice. The difference between $a.P + b.Q$ and $\tau.a.P+\tau.b.Q$ is fundamental. For $a.P+b.Q$ it is the environment of the process that chooses to synchronize on a or b whereas for $\tau.a.P + \tau.b.Q$ the process makes

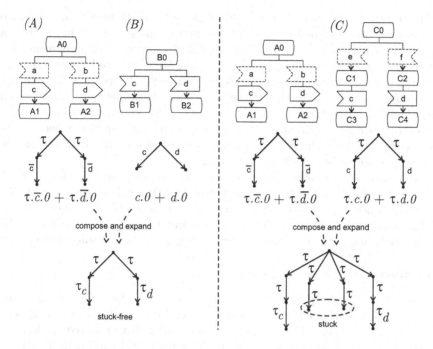

Fig. 2. External versus internal choice and interface contracts

an internal choice, not under control of the environment, to transition to either $a.P$ or $b.Q$. When composing two processes it is a possibility that the composite system gets stuck on an action. Assume a composition $P \mid Q$ having an action a restricted in scope to only allow communication between P and Q. Informally, the system $P \mid Q$ can then get stuck on a if a is a residual action that one of the processes wants to synchronize on but cannot do so because the connected process never becomes ready to synchronize on an oppositely labeled action.

Consider Fig. 2. Starting with the two leftmost state machines A and B we assume that they communicate using the signal set $\{c, d\}$ and that A receives the signals $\{a, b\}$ on a distinct port from some other state machine. From the perspective of B, A will receive $\{a, b\}$ on a hidden interface and B will have no control over whether A chooses to send c or d. B will regard this as an internal choice of A and be ready to "handle" both eventualities.

The rightmost composition in Fig. 2 is different in that C may receive the signals $\{e, f\}$ on yet another distinct interface towards some other state machine. In this case the reception of $\{e, f\}$ will occur on an interface hidden to A. E.g. if C receives e only c will allow it to make progress to state $C3$. We can see that B in the leftmost composition will never discard signal c or d while C in the rightmost composition, from the perspective of A, nondeterministically chooses to consume or discard c and d.

The transition graphs and agent definitions underneath the state machines do not directly represent the behavior of the state machines. Instead they represent the interface between the state machines detailing how the environment of a specific port must behave in order for the composite system to behave according to the design constraint in Sect. 2. We can immediately see that C, from the perspective of A, is erroneous because it presents the reception of c or d as an internal choice. A on the other hand, is allowed to present the sending of c or d as an internal choice. This is in line with our understanding that when a state machine is in a state where it can receive two different signals it will allow the environment to choose which signal to send.

Performing a reachability analysis on the composition of the left and right interface definitions in Fig. 2 we can see that the leftmost is stuck-free while the rightmost is not. It is important to understand that we would detect that the rightmost system is erroneous before we attempt to compose the contracts by the fact that one of the contracts presents reception as an internal choice.

3.3   Stuck-Free Conformance

A number of process equivalences have been introduced for CCS. Yet, it is the authors' impression that the novel results of stuck-free conformance in [2] adds another level of practical applicability, making CCS better suited to describe interfaces and their properties. People familiar with CCS will know the theory of observational equivalence (bisimulation) and the initially somewhat confusing concept of the ability of an experimenter to "observe" certain τ-transitions. Stuck-free conformance is a novel refinement relation making the comprehension of τ-transitions easier from a practical point of view. With stuck-free conformance we think of the τ-transitions in an interface description as information conveying how a component may fail to promise to be able to synchronize on a specific action. If this failure to promise to always be able to synchronize on a specific action is unacceptable by the environment of the component, we know that the composition is erroneous.

Consider an environment E, a contract C and an implementation I. Stuck-free conformance ensures that if $E \mid C$ is stuck-free and $I \leq C$ (I is a stuck-free conformance preserving refinement of C) then $E \mid I$ is also stuck-free. Stuck-free conformance is proven to be a precongruence relation. That is $I \leq S$ *implies* $C[I] \leq C[S]$, where C ranges over all CCS contexts. This property may be utilized in multiple ways. First, we may be given some contract and the task to make a conformant implementation that does not get stuck in a specific environment. Secondly, we may derive a contract from some implementation we have, using the contract to find out if our implementation is stuck-free in a given environment. Or equally useful, we may have an implementation I_1, add some new functionality (e.g. communication on a new interface) and get I_2. Having made sure that the changes made to I_1 preserves conformance, we can be sure that I_2 can replace I_1.

4   Making and Composing Interface Contracts

4.1   An Example with Concurrent Initiatives

The complexity in utilizing stuck-free conformance for consistency analysis of SDL models appears to be mostly related to the queued communication in SDL and the fact that the state machines may have multiple interfaces. In order to incrementally analyze composition, we typically do not want to make an interface contract for the complete state machine but rather for each of its interfaces. The examples presented here will therefore mostly focus on conflicting initiatives and signal interleaving. A short overview of how other SDL state machine constructs can be mapped to process algebra is given in Sect. 4.4.

Assume an agent having one input queue concurrently receiving inputs from two other agents. Then the receiving agent cannot know in which order the signals will arrive (that is, be ready for consumption from the input queue). We call call this *concurrent initiatives* and it typically occur in systems where active objects communicate asynchronously. Here "*Initiatives may be taken independently and simultaneously and lead to conflicts that must be resolved.*" [8].

Given a system designed to handle each opportunity for interleaving, its execution may still present nondeterminism on a specific interface. The reason being that the environment of a specific port has no control over how its inputs interleave with inputs received on the hidden interfaces. Seeking robust designs, we typically want to handle this nondeterminism and that the interface contracts reflect this uncertainty correctly. Interface contracts in the presence of queues are hard to understand because the environment of a specific port is not only the adjacent state machine but also the adjacent state machine's input queue. In this situation we must make sure that the interface contracts can capture how the messages are allowed to interleave across the interface of one port when each side concurrently can make an output.

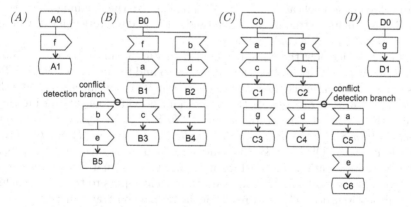

Fig. 3. State machines allowing concurrent initiatives to occur

Consider the state machines in Fig. 3 being connected as defined in Fig. 1. This example is given because it shows how concurrent initiatives are reflected in the interface contracts. By taking the queues into consideration we are able to model how inputs to the state machine may interleave and the situation that signal a from B is en route to C while signal b from C is en route to B. Recall from Fig. 1 that AB, BA, BC, CB, CD and DC are interface contracts and that Q_B and Q_C are input queues. Seen from C the inputs from A to Q_B will occur on a hidden interface. From the perspective of A and C the consumption B performs from its input queue Q_B (that is the reading actions $\{b', c', f'\}$) is hidden (see Fig. 1). That is, A and C cannot interrupt B's consumption from its input queue.

4.2   Translating the State Machine Model to CCS

Recall that the interface contracts should detail how the environment of a specific port must behave in order for the state machine owning the port to execute according to the design constraint in Sect. 2. In this description a distinction is made between the acts of communication the environment can decide and what actions the component internally decides to perform. The internal choices may be dependent on communication on a hidden interface. Interleaving of inputs may result in internal nondeterminism in the component because the environment of a port cannot control if its input signal is consumed before or after a signal received on a hidden interface.

In order to identify this internal nondeterminism arising from the interleaving we translate the state machines from our models into CCS agents that perform reading actions on the input queues (and outputs to the input queues of other state machines). Given the input signal set of the state machines and assuming that we can determine the queue length required for nonblocking operation we automatically generate CCS queue agents (Q_B and Q_C in Fig. 1). The following approach is not very optimal nor universally applicable to include designs where delaying channels adds additional complexity to the handling of interleaving. This is our first attempt to understand and handle interleaving within the framework of stuck-free conformance.

Let us consider how the state machine B in Fig. 3 can be translated into a process algebraic representation that allows us to find the interface contract BC. This representation reflects how B consumes from its input queue Q_B and either triggers a transition or discards the inputs and provides outputs on interfaces towards the queues of other state machines. "*In SDL input signals which are not expected at an SDL-state are discarded implicitly. In process algebra this has to be made explicit.*" [9]. We take the same approach in order to make a process algebraic representation of the state machine where signal discarding can be detected. The reason being that we want to prevent inputs to the state machine that will be discarded. This is a result of the design constraint in Sect. 2.

In the examples given in this paper we have used Concurrency Work Bench [10] to apply the CCS expansion law (Proposition 5, chapter 3.3 in [1]) to the agent definitions. Fig. 4 shows the agent definitions given to CWB for state

```
agent B0 = f'.'a.B1 + b'.'d.B2 + c'.DI;            agent B3 = 0;
agent B1 = f'.DI + b'.'e.B5 + c'.B3;               agent B4 = 0;
agent B2 = f'.B4 + b'.DI + c'.DI;                  agent B5 = 0;
agent DI = 0;                                      agent QB_ff = 'f'.QB_f;
agent Always_f = 'f.Always_f;                      agent QB_bf = 'b'.QB_f;
                                                   agent QB_cf = 'c'.QB_f;
agent BC = ((B0 | QB)\{f',b',c'} | Always_f)\{f};  agent QB_fb = 'f'.QB_b;
                                                   agent QB_bb = 'b'.QB_b;
agent QB = f.QB_f + b.QB_b + c.QB_c;               agent QB_cb = 'c'.QB_b;
agent QB_f = 'f'.QB + f.QB_ff + b.QB_fb + c.QB_fc; agent QB_fc = 'f'.QB_c;
agent QB_b = 'b'.QB + f.QB_bf + b.QB_bb + c.QB_bc; agent QB_bc = 'b'.QB_c;
agent QB_c = 'c'.QB + f.QB_cf + b.QB_cb + c.QB_cc; agent QB_cc = 'c'.QB_c;
```

Fig. 4. CWB representation of state machine and queue

machine B and its input queue. Here $\{b', c', f'\}$ represent reading operations on the queue while $\{\bar{a}, \bar{d}, \bar{e}\}$ represent sending actions. Notice that a sending action in the textual format in Fig. 4 is denoted 'a. What we want to identify is the queue states allowed if the state machine shall execute without discarding inputs and have a possibility of reaching every exit point. The allowed interleaving of input signals is found by identifying the queue contents and the input and output operations allowed on the queue in each of these states. It is important to understand that by modeling a queue of length two, we do not restrict one of the actual queues in the execution platform to have the exact same length. We only model the queue length required to ensure nonblocking operation of the state machines assuming that the execution platform has equal or longer queues. This simplification cannot in general be made for any SDL system but appears to be sound for the design of our service roles.

For the interface contract BC the collaboration between B and A is considered hidden. In fact, when making the contract BC we may not know the exact implementation of A. The only thing we know about A is that it should have the properties allowing the A-B collaboration to be stuck-free. Indeed, before any A implementation is allowed to be connected to B we assume that the AB and BA contracts are validated to be stuck-free. In order to ensure that B does not get stuck waiting for a message that never arrives from A without knowing the specific implementation of A, we use the agent $Always\_f$. This agent is always ready to provide inputs to Q_B from the input signal set of the BA interface (here that is $\{f\}$). Some of these input signals will be discarded by B. However, the resulting "undesirable" buffer states can be identified.

Our initial approach to identify the "allowed" states of the input queue is to recursively apply the CCS expansion law to the state machine representation and its queue. The resulting transition graph will represent both desirable and undesirable queue states. By traversing this transition graph we are able to identify the inputs that will be discarded. Having identified the inputs that will be discarded, we can remove the input from the agent representing desired interface behavior. Applying the expansion law to an agent representing all possible queue states also has the effect that the resulting transition graph has inputs that could not have been made because they can only occur *after* specific outputs. By looking at Fig. 3 we can see that input of c can only occur after an output of $\bar{a}$. This property can be determined by examining state machine B alone. These illegal inputs must also be removed from the transition graph in order to find desired queue states. We also assume that the input queues are initially empty and that no more inputs will be accepted once an exit point is reached.

For large input sets and long queue lengths we obviously get a large state space and are therefore looking for more efficient algorithms. We are working on a more efficient algorithm that directly from the SDL or UML model can determine the allowed contents of the input queue when the state machines execute according to the design constraint in Sect. 2.

4.3   Reducing and Composing the Interface Agents

Fig. 5 shows a visualization in (1) and (2) of the result from having identified what states the input queues can have as input signals interleave. The directed transition graphs (1) and (2) have nodes representing different combinations of state machine and queue states. For each node the contents of the input queue is given in the brackets. The edges identify both internal (τ) and external visible actions. The τ-actions represents communication on the hidden interfaces and non-discarded consumption from the queue. For each τ-transition where the action pair responsible for the synchronization can be identified we write τ_a, where a identifies the action pair. The visible actions are the actions defined by the input and output set of the interface.

The transition graphs (1) and (2) contain more information than needed to describe the difference between actions under the control of the component from actions under the control of the environment. A reduction preserving stuck-free conformance preserves this information and allows (1) to be reduced to (3) and (2) to be reduced to (4). In the transition graphs (3) and (4) we have abstracted away a lot of details about the reading actions on the queues and communication on the hidden interfaces. We are left with two transition graphs explicitly showing input-output interleaving and the component's internal nondeterminism from the perspective of the port's environment.

To check that B and C can collaborate according to the design constraint in Sect. 2, we compose the contracts BC_0 (3) and CB_0 (4) and internalize all their actions before applying the expansion law to get the transition graph (5). This transition graph represents the stuck-free collaboration across the BC-CB interface.

Some may desire an informal argument why the remaining τ-transition in (3) and (4) cannot be reduced. Considered from CB, BC will never refuse to receive an input b. However, due to uncontrollable interleaving of input b with input f, BC may nondeterministically refuse to give the output $\overline{d}$. In BC we can also see how input b interleaves with output $\overline{a}$. Informally we can think of the remaining τ-transitions as information that cannot be reduced. This information is needed to convey how the component may fail to promise to always be able to synchronize on a specific action.

The same approach can be applied to find BA and CD. The BA contract has a single f transition while CD has a single g transition. Because we require the state machine to be stuck-free on each of its interfaces there will be

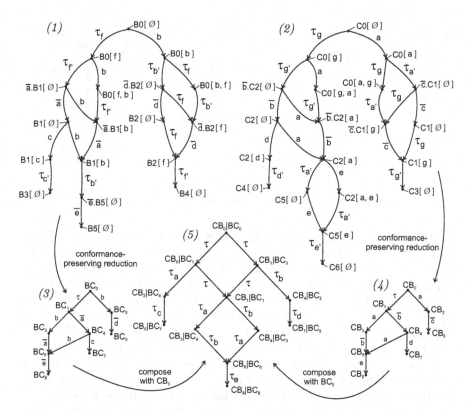

Fig. 5. Reduction of interface agents and creation of a collaboration agent

dependencies between the collaborations on the different ports. E.g. B cannot be stuck-free towards C if it is stuck towards A. This allow us to analyze dependencies among the collaborations on multiple ports and how multiple state machines have interdependencies in order for the design constraint in Sect. 2 to be fulfilled.

4.4   SDL State Machine Constructs

So far we have focused on concurrent initiatives and signal interleaving considering only a very limited subset of SDL. In this section we will therefore give a short overview on how we intend to utilize already existing results in order to make interface contracts for state machines with save, choice and timers.

In order to make a contract for a state machine that can save signals on the input port we require that every signal saved is always eventually consumed and not discarded. The requirements for when an SDL state machine with save can be transformed into an equivalent FSM without save is given a formal treatment in [11]. Fig. 6 (a) from [11] shows an example where this transformation is straight forward.

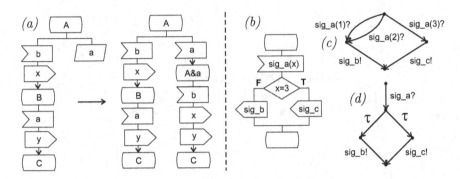

Fig. 6. SDL-save (from [11]) and choice (from [9])

In the interface contracts we intend to abstract data-values and consider decisions as nondeterministic. This is the same approach as taken in [9] (Fig. 6 (b) and (d)). However, when there are dependencies between choices and the environment can observe that there are dependencies between certain outputs we cannot consider a choice as nondeterministic. This will need further investigation. By modeling a choice as nondeterministic the intent is to force the design of the connected state machine not make assumptions about which signal it will receive based on signal parameters in messages it sends.

Timers are treated similar to communication on hidden interfaces. They represent hidden signals not under control of the environment of a specific port. We intend to take the same approach to handling models with timers as presented in [12]: "*The timers can be abstracted away after a simple check that each set timer has a "timer expired" event associated with it. [...] We abstract from the value of the timer, replacing it by a CWB action tau which can be non-deterministically chosen as an input.*" From our perspective a timer is only different from an input signal from a state machine connected to a hidden interface in that a timeout signal from a stopped timer is removed from the input queue.

5   Application of the Theory to an Example Service

Let us apply the theory to a simplified telecom service design. Fig. 7 shows four collaborating agents where the state machine design is given for two of them. This is similar to the design provided in [13]. The sensible usage scenarios for the two agents have been identified and marked by the dashed lines. We can see that they may provide messaging functionality, calling functionality or both features. We do allow an *initiator*-agent without or not utilizing its messaging functionality to be connected to a *contacted*-agent having messaging functionality. What we do not want is incompatible agents being connected. The result may be that one agent sends a message the other agent cannot consume or that two agents wait indefinitely for the other to send a message. In this situation we would want to differentiate between the features of the agents because the different features have different dependencies across the interfaces of the agent.

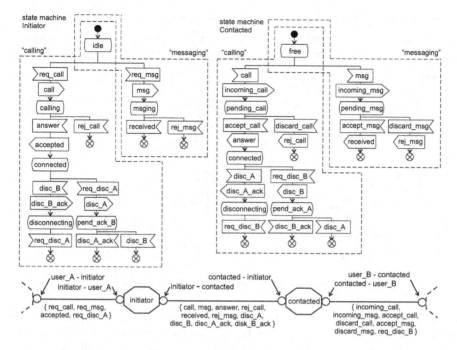

Fig. 7. Example service state machines

Assume that *user_A* is capable of requesting the messaging functionality but not the calling functionality of *initiator*. Then *initiator* would not request the calling functionality of *contacted*. In order to identify such dependencies we make multiple contracts for the interfaces, one for each feature or sensible usage scenario. Fig. 8 shows the different interface contracts for each port of the example service in Fig. 7. Each of these transition graphs represent behavior that must be stuck-free executable on a specific interface in order for the parts of the state machine encompassed by the contract to behave according to the design constraint in Sect. 2.

Start by considering the contract *initiator-contacted* produced for the messaging feature. Our informal understanding of this contract should be as follows. If only the messaging feature is invoked in *initiator* then the environment of the *initiator-contacted* port should be able to receive and consume a *msg* signal. Thereafter the contract allows for the input of signals *received* or *rej_msg* to be an external choice. By external choice we do not mean that the environment is free to never send the signal *rej_msg*. Indeed, if the environment is not capable of sending *rej_msg* we would want to detect this inconsistency. Instead the contract conveys the information that the environment may nondeterministically choose between sending *received* and *rej_msg*. Indeed, contract *contacted-initiator* has this selection as an internal choice and the composition of these two contracts is stuck-free.

The reader may wonder whether the τ-transitions in the contracts are somewhat redundant because sending actions will always be internal choices and receiving actions will always be external choices. This observation is correct for

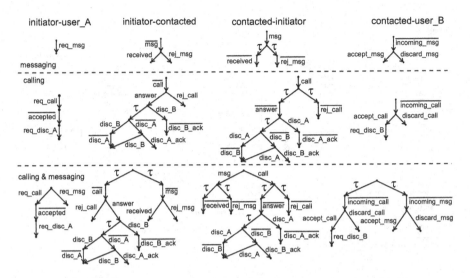

Fig. 8. Multiple interface contracts for the different features

collaborations without inconsistencies and interleaving. However, because we want to detect design errors by analyzing the contracts and correctly capture interleaving we cannot ignore the τ-transitions. Indeed, they will allow us to detect errors. If a contract presents the reception of two signals as an internal choice we know that the component owning the contract is erroneous. No environment of such a port will be able to provide inputs without the receiving component nondeterministically discarding the input signals. The only exception to this rule would be if the environment has a second path via another port to the component presenting the "receiving nondeterminism". If the environment via the second path either could observe or control the outcome of the internal choice it would be able to give input signals on a port having "receiving nondeterminism" and still avoid nondeterministic discarding. This is called *second order errors* in [4].

6   A Graphical Notation for Contracts and Their Composition

The transition graphs in Fig. 8 depicting CCS agents may not be very visually appealing to a designer accustomed to SDL or UML. Also, we cannot require that developers must comprehend the concept of τ-transitions in CCS in order to analyze the composition of state machines. We are therefore experimenting with a more SDL-like notation for such interface contracts where the nondeterminism captured by τ in CCS is depicted using the nondeterministic SDL signal *none*. The designer should be able to check that two adversary contracts are stuck-free by mere visual inspection. In order to present an example of the graphical notation depicting signal interleaving we have chosen the two contracts in the center of Fig. 8.

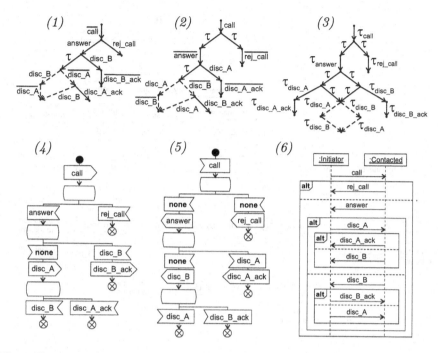

Fig. 9. Port contracts, a stuck-free collaboration agent and a message sequence chart

In Fig. 9 we have repeated the contracts *initiator-contacted* and *contacted-initiator* for the calling feature as (1) and (2). To check that the two contracts are stuck-free we can perform a reachability analysis resulting in the transition graph (3). This transition graph represents the stuck-free collaboration across the contacted-initiator interface. In making an SDL-like notation for the interface agents we have to take into account that the interleaving explicit in CCS is "invisible" in SDL. The reason is that when we consider an SDL state machine we imagine that it has a sufficiently large input buffer such that inputs provided to the state machine are not blocked. In the transition graphs (1) and (2) we can see that the interleaving of *disc_A* and *disc_B* is explicit (marked by dashed transitions). In the SDL-like notation (4) and (5) this interleaving is implicit and presented in a more intuitive way. For example, in (4) it is implicit that the state machine can receive and consume *disc_B* despite the sending of *disc_A*. Also, keep in mind that because the communication is queued, a reception symbol in the contract does not represent immediate consumption but rather an "ability to consume".

In Fig. 10 we have given a more comprehensible representation of the collaboration agent. This is made by matching the sending and receiving actions of the two interface contracts. Because a consistent communication across an interface involves a sending action and a receiving action we have represented the synchronization as a combined sending and receiving symbol. If we cannot match a sending action to a corresponding receiving action it indicates that a signal may be discarded. On the other hand, if a receiving action cannot be matched

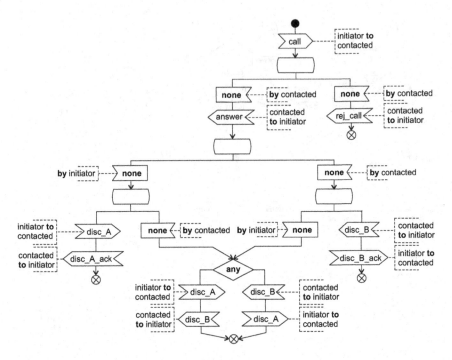

Fig. 10. A more visual representation of the collaboration agent

to a sending action it means that the state machine may wait for an input signal that never arrives. The reception of signal *none* in the collaboration agent means that some internal steps are taken by one of the agents (e.g. communication on a hidden interface) resulting in nondeterministic branching in the collaboration agent. Keep in mind that communication on a hidden interface does not always gives rise to nondeterminism in the collaboration (such communication is hidden in the interface contract). Also, take notice of the fact that the entry and exit points in this specific collaboration agent represent pairs of entry and exit points in the interface agents. The choice symbol with *any* as argument is used to attempt to capture the nondeterministic aspect of signal interleaving. This usage of a choice symbol does not have SDL semantics, it is merely added as "syntactic sugar" to make comprehension of the collaboration easier.

7   Related Work

Interface contracts as presented in this paper is related to the work on using collaborations for compositional service specification of reactive systems. For SDL systems we can use the CoSDL [5] language to specify the all possible interaction scenarios between collaborating agents. How UML 2.0 collaborations and collaboration uses can model feature composition for the type of systems addressed by this paper is explored in [14].

8   Further Work

We will continue work on the application of stuck-free conformance and especially how it practically can be used to guide refinement. We are typically
interested in how we can add communication on a new interface without affecting the existing interfaces and dependencies. Another challenge is to examine
existing approaches to collaboration design and how interface contracts based
on stuck-free semantics can be derived from the collaboration specifications.

A number of algorithms and optimizations are required for the ideas presented
to be applicable in practice. First we need more efficient ways to identify signal
interleaving and the queues effect on the interface contracts. Secondly we need
an algorithm that can determine if a contract presents reception nondeterminism
(e.g. the reception of two signals is an internal choice). To identify such nondeterminism in input queued agents we may be able build on the results in [15].
This includes testing for *input-confluence* in the interface contracts to ensure
that an output never precludes an input action (but merely allow various inter-
leavings of input and output to occur). We also want to use the identification
of stuckness in the collaboration to automatically pinpoint the inconsistency in
the model.

9   Conclusions

In this paper we have given an outline of how stuck-free conformance for CCS can
be applied to consistency analysis of service components modeled as SDL-like
state machines. Specifically we have considered state machines allowing input
interleaving on multiple interfaces where the interface contracts are given on a
per-port basis. By explicitly modeling the queues we are able to incrementally
analyze dependencies between pairs of state machines. Further we have given a
graphical representation of these interface contracts using an SDL-like notation.
Ideas have been presented on how to deal with multiple features and how theses
features or usage scenarios may have dependencies across several interfaces. A
graphical representation of interface collaboration agents based on the transition
graph resulting from applying the CCS expansion law to two adversary interface
contracts has been presented.

References

1. Robin Milner. *Communication and Concurrency.* Prentice-Hall, Inc., Upper Saddle
   River, NJ, USA, 1989.
2. Cédric Fournet, C. A. R. Hoare, Sriram K. Rajamani, and Jakob Rehof. Stuck-
   Free Conformance. In *Computer Aided Verification, 16th International Conference,
   CAV 2004, Boston, MA, USA, July 13-17, 2004*, volume 3114 of *LNCS*, pages 242–
   254, 2004.
3. Jacqueline Floch and Rolv Bræk. Using Projections for the Detection of Anomalous
   Behaviors. In *Proceedings of the 11th International SDL Forum, Stuttgart 2003,
   Springer LNCS*, 2003.

4. Jacqueline Floch. *Towards Plug-and-Play Services: Design and Validation using Roles*. Doctoral dissertation, Norwegian University of Science and Technology, Faculty of Physics, Informatics and Mathematics, Department of Telematics, Trondheim, February 2003.
5. F. Rößler, B. Geppert, and R. Gotzhein. CoSDL - An Experimental Language for Collaboration Specification. In *Proceedings the 3rd SAM (SDL And MSC) Workshop, Aberystwyth 24th-26th June 2002, Revised Papers, LNCS, Springer*, 2002.
6. Rolv Bræk. Using Roles with Types and Objects for Service Development. In *Proceedings of the IFIP International Conference on Intelligence in Networks (Smartnet '99), November 1999, Bangkok*. Kluver Academic Publishers, 1999.
7. F. Rößler, B. Geppert, and R. Gotzhein. Collaboration-Based Design of SDL Systems. In *Proceedings of the 10th International SDL Forum, Copenhagen, Denmark, June 27-29, 2001, LNCS, Springer*, 2001.
8. Rolv Bræk and Jacqueline Floch. ICT Convergence: Modeling Issues. In *System Analysis and Modeling, 4th International SDL and MSC Workshop, SAM 2004, Ottawa, Canada, June 1-4, 2004, Revised Selected Papers*, volume 3319 of *LNCS*, pages 237–256. Springer, 2004.
9. H.-A. Schneider and D. Taubner. Process Algebra Techniques for Verification of SDL-Diagrams. In *Proceedings of the 8th International Conference on Software Engineering for Telecommunication Systems and Services, March/April 1992, Florence, Italy*, pages 107–111, 1992.
10. Faron Moller and Perdita Stevens. Edinburgh Concurrency Workbench user manual (version 7.1). Available from http://homepages.inf.ed.ac.uk/perdita/cwb/.
11. G. Luo, A. Das, and G. V. Bochmann. Software Testing Based on SDL Specifications with Save. *IEEE Trans. Softw. Eng.*, 20(1):72–87, 1994.
12. Marsha Chechik and Hai Wang. Bisimulation Analysis of SDL-Expressed Protocols: a Case Study. In *CASCON '00: Proceedings of the 2000 conference of the Centre for Advanced Studies on Collaborative research*, page 2. IBM Press, 2000.
13. Richard Torbjørn Sanders, Jacqueline Floch, and Rolv Bræk. Dynamic Behaviour Arbitration using Role Negotiation. In *Proceedings of the 9th Open European Summer School and IFIP WG6.3 Workshop on Next Generation Networks (EUNICE 2003), 8th-10th November 2003, Balatonfred, Hungary*, 2003.
14. Richard Torbjørn Sanders, Humberto Nicolás Castejón Martínez, Frank Alexander Kraemer, and Rolv Bræk. Using UML 2.0 Collaborations for Compositional Service Specification. In *ACM/IEEE 8th International Conference on Model Driven Engineering Languages and Systems. (MoDELS 2005) Jamaica October 2005*, 2005.
15. Peter Selinger. First-Order Axioms for Asynchrony. In *Proceedings of the 8th International Conference on Concurrency Theory (CONCUR '97)*, volume 1243 of *LNCS*, pages 376–390, London, UK, 1997. Springer.

A Simulator Interconnection Framework for the Accurate Performance Simulation of SDL Models

Thomas Kuhn and Philipp Becker

Networked Systems Group, University of Kaiserslautern, Germany
{kuhn, becker}@informatik.uni-kl.de

Abstract. To produce accurate performance assessments of SDL models by simulation, all resources influencing system performance must be simulated together. Existing performance simulators usually support the simulation of a single resource only. One way to achieve support of multiple resources is the extension of existing simulators. In this paper, we present a different solution that can be realized with a relatively small effort. The core of the solution is a simulator interconnection framework for the performance simulation of SDL models. With this framework, existing simulators for different resources can be integrated. We show how the framework has been used to integrate *ns-2* (network simulation), Avrora (hardware simulation), and a simulator extension for SDL models. Several performance simulations of a Mica network scenario provide evidence for the additional accuracy achieved with the integrated simulator.

1 Introduction

Model-Driven Development (MDD) approaches [1] enable developers to specify systems on an abstract level, thus facilitating reuse of models across multiple platforms. While this is very convenient for the developer, there is a considerable risk that a model does not behave as expected on the target platform due to resource constraints. To reduce this risk, we propose performance simulations that predict the performance of the system in execution to identify these resource constraints.

In this paper, we focus on communication systems, and on SDL, the Specification and Description Language [2], as design language for specifying models of communication systems. Our objective is to identify resource bottlenecks that may affect the behavior of SDL models when deployed on real hardware, and to also identify resource bottlenecks that interact and, resulting from this, affect each other. To capture all of these effects during simulations, it is necessary to simulate all relevant resources together, and with a sufficient level of accuracy.

While simulators for certain individual resources are available, it turns out that there is a lack of simulators that are able of simulating several resources together. Especially with increasing system complexity and increasing heterogeneity, a need for the joint simulation of several different aspects becomes

R. Gotzhein and R. Reed (Eds.): SAM 2006, LNCS 4320, pp. 133–147, 2006.

apparent. This is especially true when simulating mobile ad-hoc networks, which are affected by various resource bottlenecks, e.g. processing power, bandwidth and energy.

For the accurate simulation of resource bottlenecks that affect each other, it is essential to simulate them together, i.e. in one simulation scenario. Our solution to this problem is a framework for simulator interconnection supporting the performance simulation of SDL systems. By interconnecting specialized simulators, it is possible to create system simulators out of simulator components with a well defined interface.

In this paper, we present such a framework, its instantiation and results of performance simulations thus providing evidence for the feasibility of our approach.

The remaining part of this paper is structured as follows: Section 2 gives an overview of related work on performance simulations, with a focus on of SDL systems. Section 3 presents our simulator interconnection framework. Section 4 describes PartsSim, an instantiation of the simulator interconnection framework. Section 5 presents simulation results that prove the feasibility of our approach. Section 6 draws conclusions and points out areas of future research.

2   Related Work

There is a large body of work on performance simulation in general. In this section, we first survey a selection of simulators for single resources and SDL models. Then, we summarize previous work on simulator interconnection.

2.1   Performance Simulators for Single Resources

To assess the performance of communication networks, the following specialized simulators are available:

- The network simulator *ns-2* [7] is a widely known simulator in the network research community. Its widespread use and the large number of available components originate from the fact that this simulator is publicly available. The simulation model of *ns-2* is an event-driven model, networks are simulated on packet level. Being a specialized network simulator, *ns-2* accurately simulates protocols, MAC layers, mobility, and propagation models.
- Like *ns-2*, GloMoSim [10] uses an event-driven model and simulates a network on packet level. All simulated application functionality must be implemented within the GloMoSim library. There is no support for resource bottlenecks other than the network.
- While using a simulation model similar to *ns-2* and GloMoSim, OpNet [9] uses a slightly different methodology for specifying the behavior of simulated nodes. OpNet specifies the network nodes as a set of hierarchical state machines that make up the simulated behavior of a network node.

GloMoSim, *ns-2* and OpNet have the same basic characteristics: They concentrate on the accurate performance simulation of networks by simulating network propagation, MAC layers, protocols, and the timing of the network. They also have the same main shortcomings. First, the application and protocol behavior must be implemented directly in the simulator by using a simulator specific methodology. Second, they simulate network resources only; i.e. they do not take other resources such as a node's processing power or energy resources into account. Having to implement the simulated code in the simulator is problematic because code must be developed twice, once for simulation and once for the target platform. This lowers the credibility of simulations significantly, because the two code bases may contain different defects and shortcomings.

Another class of specialized simulators is the class of platform simulators. Platform simulators provide an accurate model of a given hardware platform. They support loading the same binaries that are loaded on real hardware. To assess the performance of a program running on this platform, the binaries are executed under the control of the simulator, yielding an accurate timing behavior.

- The atemu simulator [11] simulates the Mica platform, which is based on the AVR microcontroller. Its goal is to simulate the complete hardware including radio transmissions. However, only one type of radio transmitter is implemented, and there are no studies concerning the accuracy of the simulation of radio transmissions available. Also, there is only one radio propagation model, and no mobility models are implemented.
- Avrora [5] is a Java-based simulator of the Mica2 platform. Its main concerns are simulation of a program's behavior including the accurate simulation of a node's hardware and timing as well as the energy consumption by network nodes. The simulation of radio transmissions is implemented, but compared to specialized network simulators its simulation capabilities are severely limited, especially with respect to the simulation of different communication hardware, propagation and mobility models.

Both platform simulators have significant shortcomings: They are able to simulate one or a small set of platforms accurately, but the simulation of radio transmissions lacks the accuracy and flexibility of specialized network simulators. Additionally, to extend them with new simulated hardware, like new transceiver chips, an enormous effort is necessary, because the complete hardware interface of the added hardware must be recreated. Since hardware is normally accessed through a hardware abstraction layer, a more abstract interface would be sufficient for most simulations, especially for the simulation of models.

2.2   Performance Simulators for SDL Models

The following simulators are capable of simulating the performance of SDL models:

- ns+SDL, the network simulator for SDL systems [3], is an extension to the *ns-2* [7] that added the capability of loading SDL models as nodes into the simulated network. Thus, it is possible to directly simulate SDL models without having to re-implement them as *ns-2* classes in C++. It has been shown that simulation accuracy is increased compared to a pure SDL simulation, because of the added network simulator. However, ns+SDL is not able to simulate accurate processor timing or memory constraints.

- The University of Aachen developed a tool environment for performance simulations of SDL systems [8]. SDL systems are compiled to C++ code which can then be linked with the performance evaluation class library SPEETCL. SPEETCL contains components that support basic network simulations like several error models, traffic generators and components for random number generation.
- Telelogic TAU [13] supports only rudimentary performance simulations. Although closed SDL systems can be simulated by using SDL modeled media, the simulation of advanced network and platform resources like network bandwidth, radio propagation or processor and interrupt timing is not supported.

2.3   Performance Simulator Interconnection

Simulator interconnection has been addressed in the following work:

- The Fraunhofer Institute for integrated circuits has created a simulator coupling infrastructure for a different application domain that aims at connecting User Mode Linux systems and VHDL simulations to the *ns-2* [4]. This simulator facilitates using external behavior in *ns-2* simulations, by loading native applications into a User Mode Linux process, and by using ModelSim or Mathlab/Simulink for simulating the application behavior.
- UMLSim [12] is a simulator that uses User Mode Linux to load simulated applications. One User Mode Linux is loaded per simulated node. Being restricted to TCP/IP, and due to the huge memory footprint that every User Mode Linux task requires, this approach is not feasible for simulations with a large number of simulated nodes. An interesting fact is, although the User Mode Linux kernels are not connected to a network simulator, that this approach theoretically enables a stepwise execution of applications within the simulator, so processor timing could be simulated to some extent. However, only the simulation of Linux nodes, with the simulated platform being the same as the host platform, is possible with UMLSim.

3   The Interconnection Framework

The accurate performance simulation of a specific scenario requires the joint simulation of different resources. To solve this problem, we have decided to create a simulator interconnection framework for the systematic interconnection of specialized, event-driven simulator components. Each simulation component is simulating one specific aspect of the simulated system. By turning already existing simulators that concentrate on specific aspects of the simulated system into simulation components, it is possible to reuse these simulators. Our framework ensures that the simulation components interoperate in a defined manner and produce credible simulation results.

3.1 Resource Bottlenecks and Further Influencing Factors

For the simulation of distributed embedded systems, we identified the following resource bottlenecks that may affect the outcome of simulations:

- Peripheral devices
  All peripheral devices may affect the timing of the simulated model - the most evident resource bottlenecks are communication links and networks. The impact of simulated communication networks as a resource bottleneck to simulations has already been addressed in [3]. In that paper, we have shown the increased simulation accuracy when a network simulator was added to the simulation of a SDL model.
- Hardware platform
  Another constraint that becomes evident is the hardware platform, the simulated SDL system and its runtime environment will run on. Depending on the resource requirements of the simulated system, memory constraints or the hardware timing will affect system performance.
- Energy
  Mobile nodes are usually affected by energy constraints as they are battery powered. Especially when communication layers that adapt to energy resources are developed, an accurate simulation of spent and remaining energy is important.

Furthermore, there are additional influencing factors that also affect the outcome of performance simulations significantly:

- Network topology and mobility
  The network topology affects network connectivity. The position of every node determines the number of hops that is required for reaching a node, and whether the node can be used as a router or not.
- Simulated SDL model
  The objective of simulation is to evaluate the performance of a given SDL model (and probably its runtime environment) in a particular resource situation. This can be done either with the goal of creating an SDL model that provides good performance with a given hardware, or with the goal of finding hardware that performs well with a given SDL model. For creating credible simulation results, it is important to execute the same SDL models in simulations that will be executed in real systems after deployment. So re-implementing systems into network simulators is out of question.

3.2 Framework Structure

For the development of the simulator interconnection framework, it is crucial to have all simulators working together in the same simulation scenario. Since resource bottlenecks like hardware timing and the network may interact with each other, it is important to capture these interactions also in simulations. This requires the specialized simulators to interact with each other during the

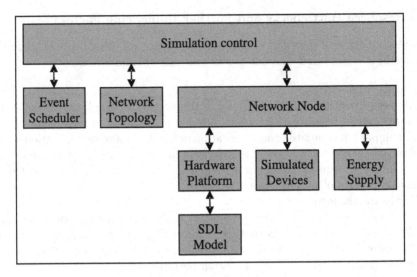

Fig. 1. Structure of the simulator interconnection framework

simulation. The interfaces between the simulator components are language independent and message based, so that simulators, which are implemented in different programming languages or that are running on different machines can also be integrated.

The simulator interconnection framework consists of three groups of logical components that serve different purposes: Simulating resource bottlenecks, simulating other influencing factors, and core simulator components. The structure of the framework is shown in Fig. 1. The following core components are part of the framework:

- Simulation control
  The control component is the core component of the simulation that creates all other simulator components and triggers their simulation steps.
- Event scheduler
  The scheduler component ensures that all simulation events are being processed in the correct order.
- Network node
  The network node component represents one simulated node, consisting of platform resources and SDL system. Different nodes can have different resources, so it is possible to have multiple specialized simulators, for example for peripheral devices (i.e. the simulated network) or for the hardware platform in one simulation scenario that are connected to the node component.

All specification components can be realized by different simulators, however, it is also possible to have multiple components realized by the same simulator. The realizations should be independent of each other and should only communicate by using the defined interfaces between the specification components. This

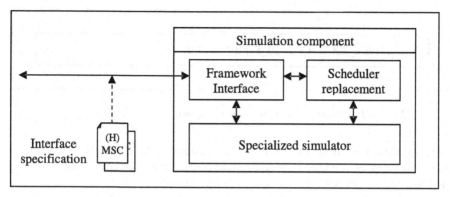

Fig. 2. Artifacts that make up a simulation component

is important in scenarios where multiple specialized simulators should be used together to simulate multiple node types with different hardware.

3.3   Integration of Simulator Components

Simulator components consist of the simulator itself and on a well defined interface. To convert a specialized simulator into a simulation component, the following main steps are performed: First, the scheduler of the specialized simulator must be replaced to use an external scheduler. Second, an interface to the simulation framework must be developed. Therefore, the relevant well defined interfaces must be implemented. Fig. 2 shows the artifacts that make up a simulation component, whose are, besides the specialized simulator, the interface of the component and a replacement of the components scheduler.

A set of Message Sequence Charts (MSC's) and High-Level Message Sequence Charts (HMSC's) define one interface. The use of HMSC's enables us to specify interface semantics while MSC's specify always one message scenario.

Interfaces of the simulation framework can be grouped into specialized interfaces and generic interfaces. Specialized interfaces are only relevant for one type of simulation components while generic interfaces are relevant for all simulation components. Specialized interfaces exist currently for simulation components that simulate energy supplies, network platforms and hardware platforms. Generic interfaces handle the scheduling of simulation timers, the simulation time and generic acknowledgments and error messages.

Integrating specialized hardware into the simulation. Depending on the type of simulated hardware, the predefined interfaces have to be enriched by specialized coordination messages. For example, while the NodeDevice_TX and NodeDevice_RX messages are sufficient for a basic network interface, the integration of specialized transceiver chip simulator components requires a more sophisticated interface. This can be achieved by using the generic messages as frames for more specific messages, as illustrated in Fig. 3. Here, the specific message for a transceiver chip is encapsulated in a generic NodeDevice_TX message. This

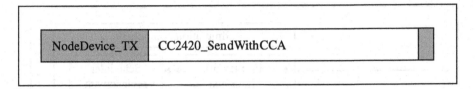

Fig. 3. Hardware specific message encapsulated in a basic message

way, simulation components that simulate complex hardware like transceiver chips can be integrated into the simulation framework without having to extend the framework API with device-specific messages.

Integrating specialized hardware. In Section 2, we have addressed two different methodologies for integrating simulated applications into simulations. Either this is done by re-implementing the simulated application into the simulators, or by loading binaries for the real platform into the simulator. To fulfill our requirements, we require a hybrid approach.

On the one hand, it is imperative that the simulated SDL models are not changed for simulations, so the interface between the models and the hardware must not be changed to support simulations. This also holds for the simulation of specific hardware, whose messages are framed within the defined generic messages between simulators. On the other hand, it is not feasible to simulate the complete interface for every simulated piece of hardware. Doing so would lead to an enormous effort when new platform simulators are developed or when new hardware devices should be integrated into the simulation, because the interface to a simulated hardware has to be provided by the platform simulator that executes the model while the implementation of the simulated hardware would be provided by a specialized simulator. This would result in unwanted dependencies between platform simulators and specialized simulators, for example simulators for network devices.

Our solution to this problem is to integrate the simulator support in the runtime platform SEnF (SDL Environment Framework) for SDL systems. This way, the SDL system can use the same interface to the runtime platform for interacting with hardware, regardless of whether it is being executed on real or on simulated hardware. It is straightforward to integrate new hardware and platforms into simulations, because only the platform dependent SEnF drivers must be developed. The simulator is supported as a target platform in SEnF, such as any other target platform (see Fig. 4).

The simulated platform is integrated as a new hardware platform, so only a part of the hardware abstraction layer of SEnF for the simulated platform(s) needs to be changed. The platform simulator uses a virtual device for connecting the simulated peripheral devices to the hardware abstraction layer of the SEnF.

The hardware dependent timing of the drivers for the original hardware can be added to the simulation by the drivers for the simulated hardware, depending on the simulated platform. This way, the simulation of hardware-dependent timing can be preserved. Additionally, creating hardware devices that exist only in

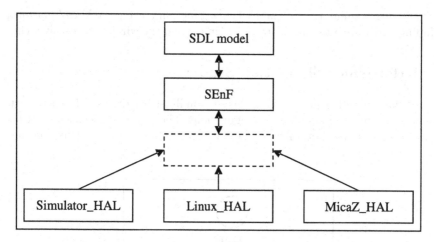

Fig. 4. Hardware Abstraction Layers (HAL)

simulations like a comprehensive logging device is much more simple when a simulator specific hardware abstraction layer is used, since no low-level interface to the simulated hardware must be developed in that case.

4   Instantiation of the Interconnection Framework

We have instantiated the interconnection framework to create PartsSim. The core components EventScheduler and SimulationControl have been created out of *ns-2* components and are part of the simulator interconnection framework, as well as the NetworkNode component. These components form the basic structure of every interconnected simulator.

Other simulators are integrated as simulation components. Currently, as shown in Fig. 1, the following types of simulation components are supported: Network-Topology, HardwarePlatform, SimulatedDevices and EnergySupply.

In PartsSim, a topology simulation component that is based on the network topology of *ns-2* is used. PartsSim simulates two types of nodes, the MicaZ nodes that are manufactured by Crossbow Industries [6] and generic nodes who do not have any computational resources. All types of nodes may be mixed within the same simulation scenario. In simulations, where only generic nodes are simulated, the simulation results are comparable to the results from ns+SDL.

The simulation component that simulates the MicaZ hardware platform is the Avrora simulation component, a simulation component that was created out of the Avrora simulator. One of the simulated devices is the CC2420 wireless transceiver chip. In this instantiation, the component that simulates the CC2420 transceiver chip is a simulation component that has been created out of an *ns-2* component - however, it is also possible to implement simulated devices independent from *ns-2*. The simulation of an energy supply is currently not implemented in PartsSim, so there are no limitations with respect to available energy.

The resulting simulator is capable of accurately simulating the MicaZ platform, including hardware interrupts, processor timing and the wireless transceiver chip.

5   Performance Simulation Studies

The simulation studies presented in this section illustrate different levels of accuracy between different simulator configurations. The simulated scenario captures a number of resource bottlenecks like platform timing, network delay, and network collisions.

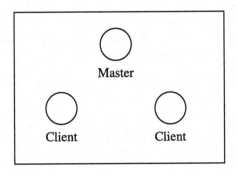

Fig. 5. Basic simulation scenario

The simulation scenario consists of three nodes (see Fig. 5). All nodes use wireless transmissions and are in transmitting range of each other. The master node is responsible for synchronizing the client nodes, using a beacon frame sent every 8ms. Transmission slots of the two clients start 2 ms and 4 ms after the beacon was received, respectively. The two clients resume listening for the beacon 4 ms and 3 ms after their own transmission, respectively. The simulation of this simple scenario is performed using three different simulators: TAU as a pure SDL simulator, ns+SDL that additionally simulates network performance, and PartsSim, the simulator that was created out of simulation components, namely ns+SDL and Avrora by instantiating the simulator interconnection framework. The simulation results of ns+SDL and PartsSim are compared to real measurements.

5.1   Simulation Results with the TAU SDL Simulator

For the simulation with the TAU SDL simulator, we have specified a global SDL model by instantiating nodes and connecting them by SDL channels. As the TAU SDL simulator does not consider resource bottlenecks, the SDL timers are the only sources of delays. The delay between transmission start of the master node's beacon frame and the transmission start of corresponding data frames is 2 ms and 4 ms, respectively, depending on the slot used by the client node (See Fig. 6). This means that in the simulation, packets are transmitted on schedule, with no further propagation or reception delays. With no resources being simulated, this is the expected timing behavior.

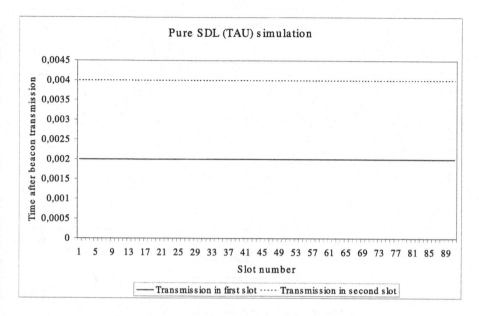

Fig. 6. Time between beacon transmission and reception of data packets with SDL simulator

5.2   Simulation Results with ns+SDL

For the simulation with the ns+SDL simulator, we have instantiated a distributed simulation scenario, consisting of three nodes, each simulating an SDL model. In this configuration, the network characteristics including transmission ranges, network delay, and frame collisions are incorporated. Due to the synchronized medium access in the given scenario, no collisions can occur. Also, all nodes are within range of each other. Thus, the additional effect that shows up in the simulation is the (constant) transmission delay, which is about 0.45 ms per frame. This is also the only additional source of delay to the SDL timers, since no platform delays are simulated by ns+SDL. Fig. 7 shows that the simulated network delay is very accurate, compared to real measurements.

In Fig. 7, there is a small jitter visible in the measured network delay that cannot be seen in the simulated network delay. This results from the measurements being taken from a real platform that has a limited timer resolution and suffers also from platform jitter. The simulator, in this configuration, is not capable of simulating this jitter. The network delay originates from the radio propagation, from the time required for transmitting the data with a given network bandwidth, and from delays within the transceiver chip.

Fig. 8 shows the delays between beacon transmission and reception of the client's data packets in the simulated scenario. As expected, the additional effect of the simulated transmission delay shows up in the simulation, delaying the transmission of data frames by 0.45 ms. The same results can be obtained by running this simulation scenario in PartsSim when using the generic node platform.

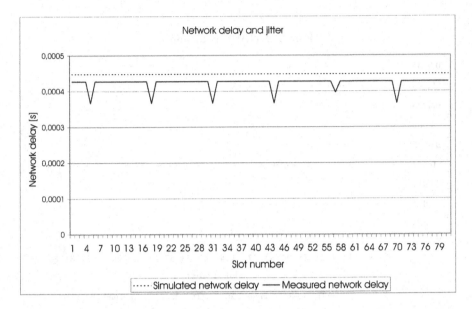

Fig. 7. Sources of delay with ns+SDL

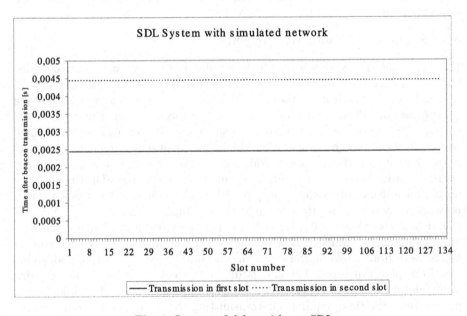

Fig. 8. Sources of delay with ns+SDL

5.3 Simulation Results with PartsSim

The third simulation is run using PartsSim, with the same scenario as before. In addition to ns+SDL, PartsSim considers the MicaZ hardware platform. The

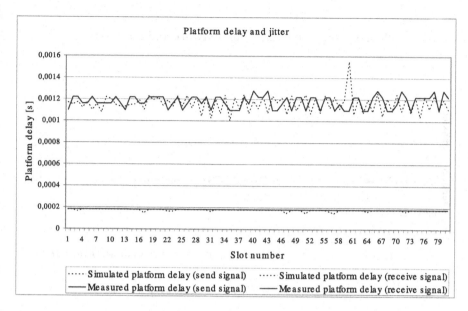

Fig. 9. Sources of delay with partssim

binary code generated from the SDL model is now executed under timing control of the simulator, which produces additional delays for reacting to hardware interrupts and for processing sending and reception of frames. Although this is a very complex simulation, its results are still very comparable to real world measurements. Fig. 9 shows a comparison of the time required for sending SDL-Signals from and to the SDL-Environment on a single network node. The measured time is the time that is required for sending a SDL-Signal from within the SDL-System to a device driver in the SDL-Environment, or for sending a SDL-Signal from the device driver to the SDL-System, respectively. As it can be seen, both values are almost identical, with the exception of jitter. It can also be seen, that it takes much more time to receive a SDL-Signal from the SDL-Environment than it takes to send a signal to the SDL-Environment.

As it can be seen, PartsSim is not able to only simulate platform delay, but it provides also an accurate simulation of the delay jitter. The timing behavior of this scenario is shown in Fig. 10. In addition to the network delay, there is a platform delay of about 1.5 ms per frame as well as a considerable jitter. Fig. 10 reveals timing problems that can only be detected if all resource bottlenecks are simulated together. First, transmission is delayed by about 2 ms w. r. t. to the assigned data slot. Second, due to internal jitter, the second client does not always receive the beacon frame while listening. In these cases, it interprets the data frame of the first client as beacon frame, and synchronizes to this event. This causes an additional transmission delay of 4 ms w. r. t. the corresponding beacon transmission. When missing the next data frame of the first client, the second client is resynchronized to the beacon period, however, by losing one data slot.

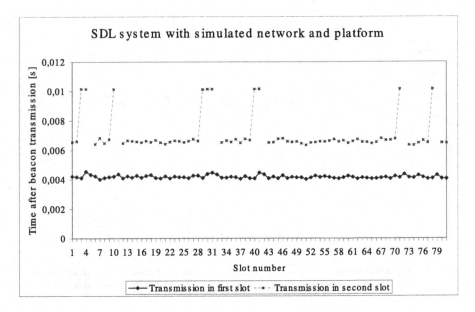

Fig. 10. Sources of delay with partssim2

With more simulated resources, the simulation time in the above simple scenario increases substantially. The simulation with TAU runs for about 2 sec, the ns+SDL simulation takes about 10 sec, and the simulation time with PartsSim is 2:07 min. As already pointed out, the purpose of the above simulations is to show the additional accuracy that is gained by simulating several resources together. From the results of the simulation with PartsSim, we can conclude that there are timing problems caused by resource bottlenecks. From the scenario, it is obvious how these problems can be avoided. However, without an accurate performance simulation, it would be difficult to predict this timing behavior even for this simple scenario.

6   Conclusion and Future Work

In this paper, we have presented a simulator interconnection framework. With this framework, existing simulators for different resources can be interconnected with a modest effort. Simulators obtained by applying the framework consist of simulation components, which can be created from scratch, or by modifying already existing simulators to provide the necessary interfaces. This enables developers to interconnect simulators by combining existing simulator components to simulate models with the level of accuracy that is necessary to produce credible simulation results.

By applying the framework, we have obtained PartsSim, which integrates *ns-2* (main control and network simulation), Avrora (hardware simulation) and a simulator extension for SDL models. The simulations with PartsSim produced accurate results. All relevant factors of the simulated scenario were captured and the increased accuracy over existing simulators has been shown.

Although our focus was on simulating SDL models, some platform simulation components are able to simulate other native software systems. Integrating the support for miscellaneous software systems is an interesting area for future work. Future work also includes the integration of mechanisms that speed up simulations, especially when realistic platforms and native software systems are included in simulation scenarios.

References

[1] M. Book, S. Beydeda, and V. Gruhn: *Model-driven Software Development*. Springer, 2005

[2] International Telecommunications Union: *Specification and Description Language (SDL)*. ITU-T Recommendation Z.100, August 2002.

[3] T. Kuhn, A. Geraldy, R. Gotzhein, and F. Rothländer: *ns+SDL - The Network Simulator for SDL Systems*. In A. Prinz, R. Reed, and J. Reed, editors, SDL 2005, Lecture Notes in Computer Science (LNCS) 3530, pages 103-116. Springer, 2005.

[4] U. Hatnik, and S. Altmann: *Using ModelSim, Matlab/Simulink and NS for Simulation of Distributed Systems*. IEEE PARELEC 2004, Dresden, September 7-10, 2004, ISBN 0-7695-2080-4, 114 - 119

[5] B. L. Titzer, D. K. Lee, and J. Palsberg: *Avrora: Scalable Sensor Network Simulation with Precise Timing*. Proceedings of the Fourth International Symposium on Information Processing in Sensor Networks, IPSN 2005, April 25-27, 2005, UCLA, Los Angeles, California, USA

[6] Crossbow: *Micaz wireless measurement system*. http://www.xbow.com/Products/ Product_pdf_files/Wireless_pdf/MICAz_Datasheet.pdf.

[7] Information Sciences Institute, University of Southern California: *The Network Simulator ns-2*, http://www.isi.edu/nsnam/ns/

[8] AixCom GmbH: *SPEETCL*, http://www.aixcom.com/Produkte/Speet/ Produkt_e.php

[9] X. Chang: *Network Simulations with OPNET*. In: P.A. Farrington, H.B. Nembhard, D.T. Sturrock and G.W. Evans, Eds., Proc. of WSC '99, vol. 1, pp. 307–314. Piscataway, New Jersey (U.S.A.): IEEE, 1999.

[10] X. Zeng, R. Bagrodia, and M. Gerla: *GloMoSim: a library for parallel simulation of large-scale wireless networks*. Proceedings. Twelfth Workshop on Parallel and Distributed Simulation PADS '98: IEEE Comput. Soc, 1998. p.154-61. xii+197

[11] J. Polley, D. Blazakis, J. McGee, D. Rusk, and J. Baras: *Atemu: A fine-grained sensor network simulator*. In Sensor and Ad Hoc Communications and Networks, pages 145–152, 2004.

[12] W. Almesberger: *umlsim - A UML-based simulator*. Proceedings of the 10th International Linux System Technology Conference (Linux-Kongress 2003), pp. 202-213, October 2003

[13] Telelogic AB: *Telelogic Tau Generation 1*, http://www.telelogic.com/products/ tau/index.cfm

Refactoring and Metrics for TTCN-3 Test Suites

Benjamin Zeiss[1], Helmut Neukirchen[1], Jens Grabowski[1],
Dominic Evans[2], and Paul Baker[2]

[1] Software Engineering for Distributed Systems Group,
Institute for Informatics, University of Göttingen,
Lotzestr. 16-18, D-37083 Göttingen, Germany
{zeiss, neukirchen, grabowski}@cs.uni-goettingen.de
[2] Motorola Labs, Jays Close, Viables Industrial Estate, Basingstoke, RG22 4PD, UK
{vnsd001, Paul.Baker}@motorola.com

Abstract. Experience with the development and maintenance of test suites has shown that the *Testing and Test Control Notation* (TTCN-3) provides very good concepts for adequate test specification. However, experience has also demonstrated that during either the migration of legacy test suites to TTCN-3, or the development of large TTCN-3 test specifications, users have found it is difficult to construct TTCN-3 tests that are concise with respect to readability, usability, and maintainability. To address these issues, this paper investigates refactoring and metrics for TTCN-3. Refactoring restructures a test suite systematically without changing its behaviour. Complementary metrics are used to assess the quality of TTCN-3 test suites. For automation, a tool called TRex has been developed that supports refactoring and metrics for TTCN-3.

1 Introduction

The maintenance and migration of legacy test suites is an important issue for industry. For example, within Motorola test suites developed with a high coupling between value and behaviour specification can lead to a large maintenance burden [1]. A single change to a data type can result in the need to change many tests. The *Testing and Test Control Notation* (TTCN-3) [2,3] contains concepts that can alleviate such issues, such as *templates*. However, experience has demonstrated that it is not always obvious how to use such concepts in a manner that can maximise the readability, usability, and maintainability of TTCN-3. In addition, Motorola teams have encountered problems migrating their test suites to TTCN-3. In doing so, they develop tools that perform simple translations of legacy test suites to TTCN-3. This can often result in non-optimal TTCN-3 code. For example, the conversion of a legacy test suite for a UMTS based component to TTCN-3 resulted in 60,000 lines of code, which then leads to another maintenance burden.

To this end, Motorola has collaborated with the University of Göttingen to develop a tool, called *TRex*, for assessing attributes and subsequent restructuring of a TTCN-3 test suite. The current aims for TRex are to: (1) enable the assessment of a TTCN-3 test suite with respect to lessons learnt from experience, (2) provide a means of detecting opportunities to avoid any issues, and (3) a means for

R. Gotzhein and R. Reed (Eds.): SAM 2006, LNCS 4320, pp. 148–165, 2006.

restructuring TTCN-3 test suites to improve them with respect to any existing issues. The actual restructuring is performed by applying *refactorings*. For software development, refactoring [4] is a proven means to restructure software with the aim of improving its quality. We suggest to apply refactoring also to TTCN-3 test suites.

This paper is structured as follows: In the next chapter, foundations on refactoring and a survey on related work are presented. Chapter 3 contains the main contribution of this paper; our catalogue of 49 refactorings for TTCN-3. In Chapter 4 we give an overview of our activities into automating the application of these refactorings using our TRex tool; making an assessment of TTCN-3 test suites based on metrics we have defined and employing a rule based approach to derive applicable refactorings. Finally, we conclude with a summary and outlook.

2   Foundations

Refactoring is defined as *"a change made to the internal structure of software to make it easier to understand and cheaper to modify without changing its observable behavior"* [5]. This means refactoring is a remedy against software ageing [6]. While refactoring can be regarded as "cleaning up source code", it is more systematical and thus less error prone than arbitrary code clean-up, because each refactoring provides a checklist of small and simple transformation steps. Due to the simplicity of the steps, the effects of the changes are predictable. Sometimes, steps even appear to be awkward, but in fact such steps help to figure out the consequences of a refactoring as soon as possible and maintain the correctness of software not only before and after, but even within a refactoring.

The essence of most refactorings is independent from a specific programming language. However, a number of refactorings make use of particular constructs of a programming language, or of a programming paradigm in general, and are thus only applicable to source code written in this language.

Examples for simple refactorings are: renaming a variable to give it a more meaningful name, encapsulating fields of a class by replacing direct field accesses by calls to corresponding getter and setter accessor methods, or extracting a group of statements and moving it into a separate function. More complex refactorings are often based on simpler refactorings. For example, converting a procedural design into an object-oriented design requires to convert record types into data classes, to encapsulate the public fields of the data classes, and to extract and move statements from procedures into methods of the data classes.

Even though refactoring has a long tradition in the evolutionary software development community around *Smalltalk*, the first detailed written work on refactoring was the PhD thesis of Opdyke [7] who treats refactoring of *C++* source code. Refactoring has finally been popularised by Fowler and his book *"Refactoring"* [5] which contains a catalogue of 72 refactorings which are applicable to *Java* source code.

2.1 Related Work

Existing work on refactoring deals mainly with the refactoring of source code and little is known on the refactoring of test specifications. Probably the most frequent refactoring of tests occurs in agile software development processes: for example, in the *Extreme Programming* approach [8], the implementation and the unit test suite, which is realised using the same programming language as the implementation (e.g. the *JUnit* framework [9] for unit testing Java implementations), are both subject of refactoring. However, only one publication is known which treats refactoring of unit tests on their own: van Deursen et al. [10] suggest to automate also the creation of external resources, to check equality of two Java objects not by comparing the results of their toString() methods, but to implement and use the more robust equals() method instead, and to provide an explanatory message when a test fails. While the latter refactoring is also applicable to TTCN-3, the other refactorings are specific to unit testing which is not the primary target of TTCN-3.

Concerning TTCN-3 and its predecessor, the *Tree and Tabular Combined Notation* (TTCN-2) [11], three publications [12,13,14] deal with transformations which can be regarded as refactoring. Schmitt [12] and Wu-Hen-Chang et al. [13] propose solutions for the automatic restructuring of test data descriptions. Even though different approaches are chosen and Schmitt treats the *constraints* of TTCN-2, whereas Wu-Hen-Chang et al. deal with TTCN-3 *templates*, both apply semantics preserving operations to the test data description. In fact, these operations are refactorings. They are based on the concepts which are available in both test languages to specialise, parametrise, and reference test data descriptions. Deiß [14] improves the TTCN-3 code generated by an automated conversion of a TTCN-2 test suite by applying some refactoring-like transformations. For example, TTCN-3 altsteps which only contain an else branch starting with a send statement, are transformed into a more appropriate TTCN-3 function.

2.2 Validating the Equivalence of Tests

Opdyke [7] and Fowler [5] address the problem of how to ensure that a refactoring does not change the observable behaviour of the modified software. While Opdyke assumes that an automated tool performs the actual refactoring by applying transformation steps which are proven to be behaviour preserving, Fowler suggests a manual approach which is applicable if no such tool exists. Each entry in his refactoring catalogue provides so called *mechanics*: concise, systematic step-by-step instructions for humans of how to carry out the refactoring. To validate that refactoring did not change the observable behaviour, Fowler presumes that an adequate suite of automated tests exists. If the implementation passes that test suite before and after the refactoring, it is assumed that its observable behaviour was not affected by the refactoring.

When refactoring tests manually, van Deursen et al. [10] suggest running the test suite which is subject of a refactoring against the same implementation before and after the refactoring; checking that the same verdict is returned in both cases. However, this is not sufficient since not all paths of the test suite may be executed. Instead, *bisimulation* [15] of both the original and refactored test suites is required to validate their equivalence, i.e. that they yield the same verdict for the same behaviours of an implementation.

3   A Refactoring Catalogue for TTCN-3

The presentation of our refactorings for TTCN-3 is inspired by Fowler's refactoring catalogue for Java [5]. Hence, we use the same fixed format for describing our refactorings: each refactoring is described by its *name*, a *summary*, a *motivation*, *mechanics*, and an *example*. The name of a refactoring is always written in *slanted* type. The mechanics section contains systematic checklist-like instructions of how to perform the refactoring. In that section, we use the term "source" to refer to the code which is addressed by a refactoring and thus usually removed or simplified and the term "target" to refer to code which is created as a result of a refactoring. The example section illustrates the refactoring by showing TTCN-3 core notation excerpts before and after the refactoring is applied.

The mechanics sections provided in this refactoring catalogue can be exploited in two ways: the refactorings can be applied manually or automated by building a tool based on the experience distilled in the step-by-step instructions. Since manual refactoring is error prone, the mechanics also contain the "compile" and "validate" instructions. The compile step is used to check whether syntax and static semantics of the test case are still valid. The validate step means to start the bisimulation process to validate that the original and refactored test suite still behave equivalently. To detect possible mistakes during refactoring as soon as possible, compile and validate steps are suggested as soon and as often as they are applicable. As discussed in Section 2.2, we suggest to automate the application of refactorings using our TRex tool which is described in Section 4.

We have divided our refactoring catalogue into refactorings for test behaviour, refactorings for data descriptions, and refactorings which improve the overall structure of a test suite. This classification is used in sections 3.1 and 3.2.

3.1   Language Independent Refactorings Applicable to TTCN-3

We investigated which of the 72 refactorings from Fowler [5] are also relevant for TTCN-3. Even though these refactorings were intended for Java, some of them are language independent or can be reinterpreted in a way that they are applicable to TTCN-3. For their reinterpretation, it is necessary to replace the notion of Java *methods* by TTCN-3 *functions* or *testcases*. While TTCN-3 is not an object-oriented language, some of the Java refactorings are nevertheless applicable if the notion of Java *classes* and *fields* is replaced by TTCN-3 *component types* and *variables*, *constants*, *timer*, and *ports* local to a component respectively. Furthermore, whenever Fowler's mechanics instruct to "test" the refactored implementation, the refactored test suite needs to be validated.

Under these circumstances, we found that 28 refactorings are applicable to TTCN-3. Where necessary, we have changed the name of these refactorings to reflect their reinterpretation for TTCN-3. In this case, the original name used by Fowler is given in square brackets. The list of these refactorings is as follows:

Refactorings for Test Behaviour

- *Consolidate Conditional Expression,*
- *Consolidate Duplicate Conditional Fragments,*
- *Decompose Conditional,*
- *Extract Function [Extract Method],*
- *Introduce Assertion,*
- *Introduce Explaining Variable,*
- *Inline Function [Inline Method],*
- *Inline Temp,*
- *Remove Assignments to Parameters,*
- *Remove Control Flag,*
- *Replace Nested Conditional with Guard Clauses,*
- *Replace Temp with Query,*
- *Separate Query From Modifier,*
- *Split Temporary Variable,*
- *Substitute Algorithm.*

Refactorings for Improving the Overall Structure of a Test Suite

- *Add Parameter,*
- *Extract Extended Component [Extract Subclass],*
- *Extract Parent Component [Extract Superclass],*
- *Introduce Local Port/Variable/Constant/Timer [Introduce Local Extension],*
- *Introduce Record Type Parameter [Introduce Parameter Object],*
- *Parametrise Testcase/Function/Altstep [Parameterize Method],*
- *Pull Up Port/Variable/Constant/Timer [Pull Up Field],*
- *Push Down Port/Variable/Constant/Timer [Push Down Field],*
- *Replace Magic Number with Symbolic Constant,*
- *Remove Parameter,*
- *Rename [Rename Method][1],*
- *Replace Parameter with Explicit Functions [Replace Parameter with Explicit Methods],*
- *Replace Parameter with Function [Replace Parameter with Method].*

No refactorings which are solely suitable for data description can be obtained by reinterpreting Fowler's refactorings, since data description relates mainly to the notion of TTCN-3 *templates* which do not exist in Java. However, some of Fowler's refactorings like *Inline Method* or *Add* and *Remove Parameter* are quite generic and may also be reinterpreted for TTCN-3 templates. Where the mechanics of these refactorings differs significantly when applied to templates, we have considered them as TTCN-3 specific refactorings and describe them in the next section.

---

[1] Note that while Fowler refers only to renaming a method, not only the corresponding TTCN-3 constructs **testcase** and **function** qualify for renaming, but also variables, types, templates, constants, ports, timer, components, modules, groups and altsteps are reasonable subjects of the *Rename* refactoring.

3.2 TTCN-3 Specific Refactorings

In addition to the language independent refactorings, restructuring of TTCN-3 test suites can be leveraged by considering language constructs which are specific to TTCN-3. Currently, our refactorings take advantage of TTCN-3 altsteps, templates, grouping, modules and importing from modules, components, restricted sub-types, logging, and creating concurrent test cases.

Those refactorings which refer to templates and to adding an explanatory log message include some of the known transformations surveyed in Section 2.1. However, we go beyond the existing work by being more extensive and by providing for each refactoring detailed step-by-step instructions and examples for their application.

Until now, we identified 21 TTCN-3 specific refactorings. The summaries of these refactorings are as follows:

Refactorings for Test Behaviour

- *Extract Altstep:* One or more alternative branches of an **alt** statement occur several times in a test suite and are thus moved into an altstep on its own.
- *Split Altstep:* Altsteps that contain branches which are not closely related to each other are split to maximise reuse potential.
- *Replace Altstep with Default:* Altsteps that are referenced in more than one **alt** statement are removed from the **alt** statements and activated as default altsteps.
- *Add Explanatory Log:* Add a **log** statement to explain why a testcase aborted or a non-**pass** verdict was assigned.
- *Distribute Test:* Transform a non-concurrent test case into a distributed concurrent test case.

Refactorings for Improving the Overall Structure of a Test Suite

- *Extract Module / Move Declarations to Another Module:* Move parts of a module into a newly created module or into another existing module to improve structure and reusability.
- *Group Fragments:* Add additional structure to a module by putting code fragments into groups.
- *Restrict Imports:* Restrict **import** statements to obtain smaller inter-module interfaces and less processing load for TTCN-3 tools.
- *Prefix Imported Declarations:* Prefix imported declarations to avoid possible name clashes.
- *Parametrise Module:* Parametrise modules to specify environment specific parameters at tool level.
- *Move Module Constant to Component:* A declaration of a constant at module level used exclusively in the context of a single component is moved into the component declaration.
- *Move Local Variable/Constant/Timer to Component:* A local variable, constant, or timer is moved to a component when used in different functions, testcases, or altsteps which run on the same component.

- *Move Component Variable/Constant/Timer to Local Scope:* A component variable, constant, or timer is moved to a local scope when only used in a single function, testcase, or altstep.
- *Generalise Runs On:* Relax **runs on** specification by using a more general component type.

Refactorings for Data Descriptions

- *Inline Template:* A template that is used only once is inlined.
- *Extract Template:* Inlined templates that are used more than once are extracted into a template definition and referenced.
- *Replace Template with Modified Template:* Templates of structured or list type with similar content values that differ only by a few fields are simplified by using modified templates.
- *Parametrise Template:* Several templates of the same type, which merely use different field values, are replaced by a single parametrised template.
- *Inline Template Parameter:* A formal parameter of a template which is always given the same actual value is inlined.
- *Decompose Template:* Complex template declarations are decomposed into smaller templates using references.
- *Subtype Basic Types:* Range constrained subtypes are used instead of basic types in order to more easily detect code flaws.

In the following, we will focus on refactorings for data descriptions, since most of the maintenance problems at Motorola were related to the use of templates. To give an impression of how our TTCN-3 refactoring catalogue looks, we present two refactorings in detail: *Inline Template Parameter* and *Parametrise Template*. Please refer to our complete TTCN-3 refactoring catalogue [16] for a detailed description of all refactorings.

3.2.1   Parametrise Template

Summary: Several templates of the same type, which merely use different field values, are replaced by a single parametrised template.

Motivation: Occasionally, there are several template declarations of the same type which are basically similar, but vary in values at the same fields. These template declarations are candidates for parametrisation. Instead of keeping all of them, they are replaced with a single template declaration where the variations are handled by template parameters. Such a change removes code duplication, improves reusability, and increases flexibility. If the template declarations are similar, but the values vary in different fields, the *Replace Template with Modified Template* refactoring may be a better choice.

Mechanics
- Create the parametrised target template signature. It is of the same type as the source templates. Introduce a parameter for each field in which the source template values differ. The target template declaration's name should reflect the meaning of the non-parametrised values.

- Copy one source template body to the parametrised target template declaration and replace the varying parts with their newly introduced template parameters.
- Compile.
- Repeat the following steps for all references to the source template declarations:
    • Replace the source template reference with a reference to the parametrised target template. As parameter values, use the field values from the originally referenced template declaration corresponding to the parametrised values in the target template.
    • Compile and validate.
- Remove the source template declarations from the code. They should not be referenced anymore.
- Compile and validate.

Example: Listing 1.1 shows the unrefactored example. The source template declarations firstTemplate (lines 6–9) and secondTemplate (lines 11–14) differ only in the values of ipAddress.

Listing 1.1. Parametrise Template (Unrefactored)

```
1  type record ExampleType {
2    boolean ipv6,
3    charstring ipAddress
4  }
5
6  template ExampleType firstTemplate := {
7    ipv6 := false,
8    ipAddress := "127.0.0.1"
9  }
10
11 template ExampleType secondTemplate := {
12   ipv6 := false,
13   ipAddress := "134.72.13.2"
14 }
15
16 testcase exampleTestCase() runs on ExampleComponent {
17   pt.send( firstTemplate );
18   pt.receive( secondTemplate );
19 }
```

Listing 1.2. Parametrise Template (Refactored)

```
1  type record ExampleType {
2    boolean ipv6,
3    charstring ipAddress
4  }
5
6  template ExampleType parametrisedTemplate( charstring addressParameter ) := {
7    ipv6 := false,
8    ipAddress := addressParameter
9  }
10
11 testcase exampleTestCase() runs on ExampleComponent {
12   pt.send( parametrisedTemplate( "127.0.0.1" ) );
13   pt.receive( parametrisedTemplate( "134.72.13.2" ) );
14 }
```

The resulting code after applying *Parametrise Template* is shown in Listing 1.2. A new target template declaration parametrisedTemplate (lines 6–9) is created which has a parameter for the varying ipAddress field in the source template declarations. The references to firstTemplate (Line 12) and secondTemplate (Line 13) are replaced with parametrisedTemplate and their corresponding IP addresses as parameters.

3.2.2   Inline Template Parameter
Summary: A formal parameter of a template which is always given the same actual value is inlined.

Motivation: Templates are typically parametrised to avoid multiple template declarations that differ only in a few values. However, as test suites grow and change over time, the usage of its templates may change as well. As a result, there may be situations when all references to a parametrised template have one or more actual parameters with the same values. This can also happen when the test engineer is overly eager: he parametrises templates as he thinks it might be useful, but it later turns out to be unnecessary. In any case, there are template references with unneeded parameters creating code clutter and more complexity than useful. Thus, the template parameter should be inlined and removed from all references.

Mechanics

- Verify that all template references to the parametrised source template declaration have a common actual parameter value. The parameter with the common actual parameter values is the source parameter. Record the common value.
  - If you have more than one common actual parameter value in all references, it is easier to inline them together. Therefore, perform each step that concerns the source parameters for each source parameter at once.
- Copy the source template declaration and give the copied declaration a temporary name. It is the target template declaration.
- In the target template declaration body, replace each reference to the source parameter with the value noted in the first step. In the target template declaration signature, remove the parameter corresponding to the source parameter.
- Compile.
- Rename the name of the target template declaration using the name of the source template declaration.
- Find all references to the target template declaration. Remove the source parameter from the actual parameter list of each reference.
- Remove the source template declaration.
- Compile and validate.
- Consider usage of the *Rename* refactoring to improve the target template declaration name.

Example: Listing 1.3 contains the parametrised template exampleTemplate in lines 6–9. All references to this template use the same actual parameter value (lines 12 and 13). Hence, the corresponding parameter addressParameter in Line 6 is inlined.

Listing 1.3. Inline Template Parameter (Unrefactored)

```
1  type record ExampleType {
2     boolean ipv6,
3     charstring ipAddress
4  }
5
6  template ExampleType exampleTemplate( charstring addressParameter ) := {
7     ipv6 := false,
8     ipAddress := addressParameter
9  }
10
11 testcase exampleTestCase() runs on ExampleComponent {
12    pt.send( exampleTemplate( "127.0.0.1" ) );
13    pt.receive( exampleTemplate( "127.0.0.1" ) );
14 }
```

After applying the *Inline Template Parameter* refactoring (Listing 1.4), the string value "127.0.0.1" is inlined into the template body of exampleTemplate (Line 8), the corresponding formal parameter of the template (Line 6) and the corresponding actual parameter of each reference to exampleTemplate (lines 12 and 13) are removed.

Listing 1.4. Inline Template Parameter (Refactored)

```
1  type record ExampleType {
2     boolean ipv6,
3     charstring ipAddress
4  }
5
6  template ExampleType exampleTemplate := {
7     ipv6 := false,
8     ipAddress := "127.0.0.1"
9  }
10
11 testcase exampleTestCase() runs on ExampleComponent {
12    pt.send( exampleTemplate );
13    pt.receive( exampleTemplate );
14 }
```

4   Automation of TTCN-3 Refactoring

In the following we describe how the restructuring of TTCN-3 test suites can be automated. To locate inappropriate usage of TTCN-3 we use so called *bad smells* or *code smells*, a kind of anti-pattern [17]. Examples for code smells include duplicated code, overly long testcases, or templates which are never referenced. Some of them can only be detected by pattern recognition, but some of them may also be detected by calculating metrics. We have started with a metrics-based approach (Section 4.1) which is also suitable for a general assessment of

TTCN-3 test suites. Based on these metrics we provide rules of when to apply which refactoring. Our TRex tool (Section 4.2) calculates these metrics, applies the rules to suggest appropriate refactorings, and automatically performs the individual steps of a refactoring.

4.1   TTCN-3 Metrics

According to Fenton et al. [18], the term *software metrics* embraces all activities which involve software measurement. Software measurement can be classified into measures for properties or attributes of *processes*, *resources*, and *products*. For each class, internal and external attributes can be distinguished. *External attributes* refer to how a process, resource, or product relates to its environment; *internal attributes* are properties of a process, resource, or product on its own, i.e. separate from any interactions with its environment. Hence, to measure external attributes of a product, execution of the product is required, whereas for measuring internal attributes, static analysis is sufficient. Since we are interested in properties like readability or maintainability of a TTCN-3 specification, we consider only internal product metrics in the remainder.

Internal product metrics can be structured into *size* and *structural* metrics. Size metrics measure properties of the number of usage of programming or specification language constructs. Well-known size metrics are the Halstead metrics [19], e.g. *number of operators*, *number of operands*, or *program volume*. Structural metrics analyse the structure of a program or specification. The most popular examples are the McCabe complexity metrics [20]. They are based on the control flow graph of a program and measure properties of this graph, such as the *cyclomatic number*. Object-oriented metrics [21] are also structural since they measure relationships between classes or methods. A popular example of such metrics is the Chidamber & Kemerer metrics suite [22] which measures properties of inheritance relationships like *depth of inheritance tree*, or coupling properties like *coupling between objects* or *lack of cohesion in methods*.

Vega et al. [23] list some metrics which they suggest to apply to TTCN-3 tests suites. However, it is not clear how these metrics can be interpreted to assess the actual quality of test suites. To avoid this problem, our development of TTCN-3 metrics was guided by the *Goal Question Metric* (GQM) approach from Basili et al. [24]: First the goals to achieve were specified (e.g. Goal 1: "Improve maintainability of TTCN-3 source code"; Goal 2: "Improve readability of TTCN-3 source code"). Then, for each goal a set of meaningful questions was derived that characterises it (e.g. for Goal 1: "Are many changes to test behaviour required if values inside of test data change?"; for Goal 2: "Are unnecessary indirections used?" and "Are there any unused definitions?"). Finally, one or more metrics were defined to gather quantitative data which gives answers to each question (e.g. some coupling metrics for answering the question of Goal 1; counting the number of references for answering the questions of Goal 2).

Based on the above goals and questions, we started to investigate metrics to assess the quality of TTCN-3 test suites in terms of maintainability and readability. For this, we want to use (and possibly adapt) the well-known previously mentioned metrics, but also define new TTCN-3 specific metrics. In a first step, we implemented some basic size metrics and one coupling metric in the TRex tool. These are:

- *Number of non-comment lines of TTCN-3 source code.*
- *Number of test cases*, including *Number of references[2] to each test case.*
- *Number of functions*, including *Number of references to each function.*
- *Number of altsteps*, including *Number of references to each altstep.*
- *Number of port types*, including *Number of references to each port type.*
- *Number of component types*, including *Number of references to each component type.*
- *Number of data type definitions*, including *Number of references to each data type.*
- *Number of template definitions*, including *Number of references to each template* and *Number of parametrised templates.*
- *Template coupling*, which will be computed as follows:

$$Template\ coupling := \frac{\sum\limits_{i=1}^{n} score(stmt(i))}{n}$$

Where *stmt* is the sequence of behaviour statements referencing templates in a test suite, n is the number of statements in *stmt*, and *stmt(i)* denotes the ith statement in *stmt*. *score(stmt(i))* is defined as follows[3]:

$$score(stmt(i)) := \begin{cases} 1, & \text{if } stmt(i) \text{ references a template without parameters,} \\ & \text{e.g. MyPort.\textbf{send}(MyTemplateRef)} \\ & \text{or uses wildcards only, e.g. MyPort.\textbf{send}(MyType:?)} \\ 2, & \text{if } stmt(i) \text{ references a template with parameters,} \\ & \text{e.g. MyPort.\textbf{send}(MyTemplateRef(1, "a"))} \\ 3, & \text{if } stmt(i) \text{ uses an inline template,} \\ & \text{e.g. MyPort.\textbf{receive}(MyType:\{n:=1, s:="a"\})} \end{cases}$$

Template coupling measures the dependence of test behaviour and test data in the form of template definitions, i.e. whether a change of test data requires changing test behaviour and vice versa. The value range is between 1 (i.e. behaviour statements refer only to template definitions or use wildcards) and 3 (i.e. behaviour statements only use inline templates). For the interpretation of such a coupling score appropriate boundary values are required. These may depend on the actual usage of the test suite. For example, for good maintainability a decoupling of test data and test behaviour (i.e. the template coupling score is close to 1) might be advantageous and for optimal readability most templates may be inline templates (i.e. the template coupling score will be close to 3).

---

[2] Since we consider only internal product metrics, we only measure the number of references obtained by static analysis. In contrast, the dynamic number of references would count how often a definition is actually referenced during test execution.

[3] Non-equidistant values might be used to give different weights to the different cases.

With appropriate boundary values for the different metrics, we want to identify places in TTCN-3 specifications which need refactoring. At the moment we have a rough idea of suitable values and have started to analyse real-world test suites to further improve our estimates. Some metrics may even allow an entirely automatic refactoring to take place.

We have found some rules that obviously help to improve the quality of TTCN-3 test suites with respect to template definitions. Most of these rules can be directly related to metrics and refactorings:

Rule 1: A template definition which is not referenced (Metric value: *Number of References to the Template = 0*) should be removed.

Rule 2: A template definition which is only referenced once (Metric value: *Number of References to the Template = 1*) should be inlined and its definition should be removed (Application of *Inline Template* refactoring which, for parametrised templates, includes the inlining of parameters.)

Rule 3: If a user wants to achieve "optimal readability" (i.e. maximise the *Template Coupling Score*), a template definition which is referenced multiple times (Metric value: *Number of References to the Template > 1*) should be inlined and its definition should be removed (Application of *Inline Template* refactoring).

Rule 4: If a user wants to achieve "good maintainability" (i.e. a *Template Coupling Score* close to 1), a template definition without parameters which is referenced multiple times (Metric value: *Number of References to the Template > 1*) should not be altered.

Rule 5: A template definition in which all fields receive their values by means of parameters should be inlined and its definition removed (Application of *Inline Template* refactoring).

Rule 6: Unused parameters of a template definition (e.g. parameters which are not used in assignments) should be removed altering the template definition (Application of *Remove Parameter* refactoring).

Rule 7: For a template definition which is referenced multiple times and which has formal parameters that do not adhere to Rules 5 or 6 the following rules apply:

(a) If all instantiations of a template are the same, i.e. all formal parameters are given the same values, then the formal parameters are removed and the assigned elements are defined explicitly (Application of *Inline Template Parameter* refactoring).

(b) If instantiations of a template vary, i.e. all formal parameters are given different values, formal parameters account for the values of 50% or more of the fields within the template definition and the user wants "optimal readability", then the template shall be inlined and its definition be removed (Application of *Inline Template* refactoring).

Rule 8: If the user aims for "good maintainability" and two or more template definitions exist for the same type, then the following rules could apply:

(a) If template values only differ for the same template fields and these differing fields account for a certain percentage (assume 30%) of the overall fields for the template definition then the templates can be reduced to a single parametrised definition (Application of *Parametrise Template* refactoring).

(b) If template values differ for different template fields, then we currently do nothing as the user would have to choose which field to parametrise upon.

The rules presented above can only give an impression of how metrics can steer the refactoring process. We are currently refining the rules and defining new rules for the refactoring of test behaviour and the TTCN-3 module structure. This includes the definition of further metrics to underpin the rules, analysis of the influence of the rule ordering, and the investigation of options such as "good maintainability or "optimal readability" which are informally mentioned above. (E.g. using inline templates optimises readability only up to a certain size of template, or the fact that parametrised templates promote reuse, but not necessarily maintainability or readability.)

4.2   Tool Support

We have implemented a first version of *TRex*, the *TTCN-3 Refactoring and Metrics* tool. Based on the rules defined in the previous section, refactorings are suggested automatically by TRex and the user is given the option to apply them to one or more template or reference. Otherwise the user needs to identify the places where a refactoring is to be applied. In some cases, additional information needs to be provided, e.g. the desired new name for the *Rename* refactoring. In any case, all further steps are then performed automatically. This significantly reduces the risk of changing the behaviour of a test suite. Automated refactoring has been successfully applied to source code of implementation languages, e.g. using the Java Development Tools of the Eclipse platform [25].

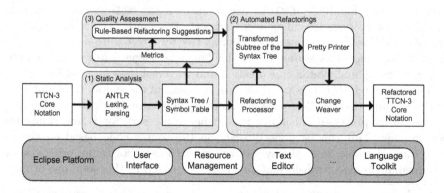

Fig. 1. The TRex Tool Chain

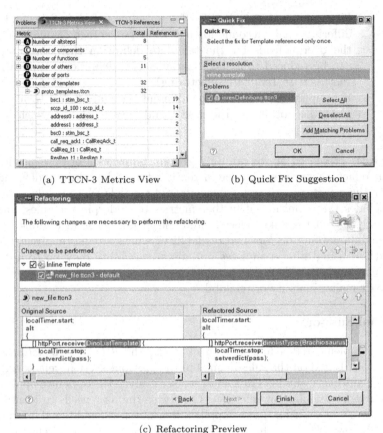

(a) TTCN-3 Metrics View   (b) Quick Fix Suggestion

(c) Refactoring Preview

Fig. 2. TRex Screenshots

The TRex tool analyses data flow and inspects declarations, references, and scopes of TTCN-3 language constructs. As shown in Figure 1, TRex is implemented as a plug-in for the Eclipse platform which provides infrastructure for user interfaces, handling of workspace resources, text editing, and a language toolkit for basic language independent support of semantic preserving workspace transformations. For building up the syntax tree for a test suite we use *'ANother Tool for Language Recognition'* (ANTLR) [26], a parser generator which supports lexing, parsing, and syntax tree creation and traversal (Block (1) of Figure 1).

The actual refactoring is performed on the basis of the syntax tree[4], the symbol table, and the TTCN-3 core notation. As shown in Block (2) of Figure 1, a refactoring processor calculates the changes necessary for transforming the source code. This can be done directly on the source code based on the information obtained from the syntax tree and the symbol table, otherwise an intermediate subtree transformation step is necessary. In this step, one or more

---

[4] An alternative approach is to build up a TTCN-3 meta model [27] representation of a TTCN-3 test suite and to use this representation instead of the syntax tree.

syntax subtrees are transformed and the corresponding core notation is obtained by a TTCN-3 pretty printer. These changes are weaved into the original TTCN-3 core notation using a programmatic text editor (which is provided by the Eclipse platform). The original formatting is therefore mostly preserved.

In Block (3) of Figure 1, the metrics are built up, based on the list in Section 4.1, by traversing the syntax tree and counting the number of basic elements and their references, whilst also processing each communication statement to generate the Template Coupling score. During this traversal we also apply the rules for detecting suitable areas for refactorisation to every template. From this we generate a table for the 'Problems' view of TRex, listing each detection as a warning, with one or more appropriate refactorings supplied as 'Quick Fix' options for the user to apply automatically.

Figure 2 shows screenshots of the metrics view, an automatic metrics-based 'Quick Fix' refactoring suggestion, and a refactoring wizard providing a preview of a refactoring. Currently, TRex supports those refactorings which we consider most important to improve the quality of Motorola's test suites: *Inline Template*, *Inline Template Parameter*, *Parametrise Template*, and *Rename*. In addition to refactoring and metrics, TRex provides state of the art editing functionality for TTCN-3 test suites. TRex is released as open source software under the *Eclipse Public License* (EPL). More detailed information on TRex is available at its website [28] and in further publications [29].

5   Summary and Outlook

We presented a catalogue of 49 refactorings which can be used to restructure existing TTCN-3 test suites without changing their observable behaviour. The aim of our refactorings is to improve readability, extensibility, modularity, reusability, complexity, maintainability, and efficiency of test suites. Each of our refactorings provides detailed step-by-step instructions on how to perform the actual transformations and is accompanied by TTCN-3 examples which illustrate their application. In this paper, we gave an overview of our TTCN-3 refactoring catalogue and presented some examples from the full version [16]. Furthermore, we outlined an initial set of metrics to assess the quality of test suites and described how they can be used to automate the refactoring process.

We implemented the TRex tool, which calculates metrics, makes suggestions for applying refactorings, and automatically performs the specific steps of a refactoring. TRex is already proving to be a very useful environment for the editing, assessment, and restructuring of TTCN-3 test suites.

Currently we are working on a case study to obtain boundary values for our metrics and to demonstrate the benefits of our refactorings on a large scale. We already applied TRex to a test suite for the *Session Initiation Protocol* (SIP) [30] and TRex automatically identified 10 unused definitions and 22 templates which could be parametrised and merged. By applying only a few related automatically suggested refactorings, TRex was able to reduce the size of the data description module of this test suite by about 7% in terms of lines of code.

We have just started to study complexity metrics [31] and pattern-based code smells. Future research aims at extending our rules of when to apply which refactoring. We also plan to implement tool support for the validation of manual refactoring by providing a TTCN-3 bisimulation tool which allows the equivalence of TTCN-3 test suites to be checked.

Finally, we believe that refactoring would also be beneficial for e.g. *UML 2.0 Testing Profile* (U2TP) [32] test specifications or *Specification and Description Language* (SDL) [33] specifications, as well as for language migration, e.g. between different versions of TTCN-3.

References

1. Baker, P., Loh, S., Weil, F.: Model-Driven Engineering in a Large Industrial Context – Motorola Case Study. In Briand, L., Williams, C., eds.: Model Driven Engineering Languages and Systems: 8th International Conference, MoDELS 2005, Montego Bay, Jamaica, October 2–7, 2005. Volume 3713 of Lecture Notes in Computer Science (LNCS)., Springer (2005) 476–491
2. ETSI: European Standard (ES) 201 873-1 V3.1.1 (2005-06): The Testing and Test Control Notation version 3; Part 1: TTCN-3 Core Language. European Telecommunications Standards Institute (ETSI), Sophia-Antipolis, France, also published as ITU-T Recommendation Z.140 (2005)
3. Grabowski, J., Hogrefe, D., Réthy, G., Schieferdecker, I., Wiles, A., Willcock, C.: An Introduction into the Testing and Test Control Notation (TTCN-3). Computer Networks **42**(3) (2003) 375–403
4. Mens, T., Tourwe, T.: A Survey of Software Refactoring. IEEE Transactions on Software Engineering **30**(2) (2004) 126–139
5. Fowler, M.: Refactoring. Addison-Wesley (1999)
6. Parnas, D.L.: Software Aging. In: Proceedings of the 16th International Conference on Software Engineering (ICSE), May 16–21, 1994, Sorrento, Italy., IEEE Computer Society/ACM Press (1994) 279–287
7. Opdyke, W.F.: Refactoring Object-Oriented Frameworks. PhD thesis, University of Illinois at Urbana-Champaign, USA (1992)
8. Beck, K.: Extreme Programming Explained. Addison Wesley (2000)
9. Gamma, E., Beck, K.: JUnit. http://junit.sourceforge.net (2006)
10. v. Deursen, A., Moonen, L., v. d. Bergh, A., Kok, G.: Refactoring Test Code. In Marchesi, M., Succi, G., eds.: Proceedings of the 2nd International Conference on Extreme Programming and Flexible Processes in Software Engineering. (2001)
11. ETSI: Technical Report (TR) 101 666 (1999-05): Information technology – Open Systems Interconnection Conformance testing methodology and framework; The Tree and Tabular Combined Notation (TTCN) (Ed. 2++). European Telecommunications Standards Institute (ETSI), Sophia-Antipolis, France (1999)
12. Schmitt, M.: Automatic Test Generation Based on Formal Specifications – Practical Procedures for Efficient State Space Exploration and Improved Representation of Test Cases. PhD thesis, University of Göttingen, Germany (2003)
13. Wu-Hen-Chang, A., Viet, D.L., Batori, G., Gecse, R., Csopaki, G.: High-Level Restructuring of TTCN-3 Test Data. In Grabowski, J., Nielsen, B., eds.: Formal Approaches to Software Testing: 4th International Workshop, FATES 2004, Linz, Austria, September 21, 2004, Revised Selected Papers. Volume 3395 of Lecture Notes in Computer Science (LNCS)., Springer (2005) 180–194

14. Deiß, T.: Refactoring and Converting a TTCN-2 Test Suite. Presentation at the TTCN-3 User Conference 2005, June 6–8, 2005, Sophia-Antipolis, France (2005)
15. Milner, R.: A Calculus of Communicating Systems. Volume 92 of Lecture Notes in Computer Science (LNCS). Springer (1980)
16. Zeiss, B.: A Refactoring Tool for TTCN-3. Master's thesis, Institute for Informatics, University of Göttingen, Germany, ZFI-BM-2006-05 (2006)
17. Brown, W.J., Malveau, R.C., McCormick, H.: Anti-Patterns. Wiley (1998)
18. Fenton, N.E., Pfleeger, S.L.: Software Metrics. PWS Publishing Company (1997)
19. Halstead, M.H.: Elements of Software Science. Elsevier (1977)
20. Watson, A.H., McCabe, T.J.: Structured Testing: A Testing Methodology Using the Cyclomatic Complexity Metric. NIST Special Publication 500-235, National Institute of Standards and Technology, Gaithersburg, MD, USA (1996)
21. Henderson-Sellers, B.: Object-Oriented Metrics. Prentice Hall (1996)
22. Chidamber, S.R., Kemerer, C.: A Metric Suite for Object-Oriented Design. IEEE Transactions of Software Engineering 20(6) (1994) 476–493
23. Vega, D.E., Schieferdecker, I.: Towards Quality of TTCN-3 Tests. In: Proceedings of SAM'06: Fifth Workshop on System Analysis and Modelling, May 31–June 2, 2006, University of Kaiserslautern, Germany. (2006)
24. Basili, V.R., Weiss, D.M.: A Methodology for Collecting Valid Software Engineering Data. IEEE Transactions on Software Engineering SE-10(6) (1984) 728–738
25. Eclipse Foundation: Eclipse. http://www.eclipse.org (2006)
26. Parr, T.: ANTLR parser generator. http://www.antlr.org (2006)
27. Schieferdecker, I., Din, G.: A Meta-model for TTCN-3. In Núñez, M., Maamar, Z., Pelayo, F., Pousttchi, K., Rubio, F., eds.: Applying Formal Methods: Testing, Performance and M/ECommerce, FORTE 2004 Workshops, Toledo, Spain, October 1–2, 2004. Volume 3236 of Lecture Notes in Computer Science (LNCS)., Springer (2004)
28. TRex Website: http://www.trex.informatik.uni-goettingen.de (2006)
29. Baker, P., Evans, D., Grabowski, J., Neukirchen, H., Zeiss, B.: TRex – The Refactoring and Metrics Tool for TTCN-3 Test Specifications. In: Proceedings of TAIC PART 2006 (Testing: Academic & Industrial Conference – Practice And Research Techniques), Windsor, UK, 29th–31st August 2006, IEEE Computer Society (2006)
30. ETSI: TS 102 027-3: SIP ATS & PIXIT; Part 3: Abstract Test Suite (ATS) and partial Protocol Implementation eXtra Information for Testing (PIXIT). European Telecommunications Standards Institute (ETSI), Sophia-Antipolis, France (2005)
31. Zeiss, B., Neukirchen, H., Grabowski, J., Evans, D., Baker, P.: TRex – An Open-Source Tool for Quality Assurance of TTCN-3 Test Suites. In: Proceeedings of CONQUEST 2006 – 9th International Conference on Quality Engineering in Software Technology, September 27–29, Berlin, Germany, dpunkt.Verlag (2006)
32. OMG: UML Testing Profile (Version 1.0 formal/05-07-07). Object Management Group (OMG) (2005)
33. ITU-T: Recommendation Z.100 (08/02): Specification and Description Language (SDL). International Telecommunication Union (ITU-T), Geneve (2002)

SDL Design of a Radio Resource Control Protocol for 3G Evolution Systems with Two Different Approaches

Tae-Hyong Kim[1], Jae-Woo Kim[1], Qi-Ping Yang[1], Jae-Hyoung Lee[1], Soon-Gi Park[2], and Yeun-Seung Shin[2]

[1] School of Computer and Software Engineering,
Kumoh National Institute of Technology, Gumi, Gyeongbuk 730-701 Korea
{taehyong, eva0191, saintwind, zzeng09}@kumoh.ac.kr
[2] Mobile Telecommunication Research Laboratory,
Electronics and Telecommunications Research Institute, Daejeon, 305-350 Korea
{yoyo, shinys}@etri.re.kr

Abstract. Despite the increasing need of formal methods, people in the industry still hesitate to use them for product development because they are not sure of success with that novel approach in their own situation. In order to encourage those people we show our experience of designing a radio resource control protocol for ETRI's 3G evolution systems in SDL with two different approaches: pure-SDL and hybrid-SDL approaches. From our design and verification results, we make an empirical evaluation of those two approaches in several aspects and suggest a simple guideline for selecting an appropriate approach according to the situation.

1 Introduction

Since several formal description techniques were developed and standardized to help developing a reliable network system, a lot of work has been done to design, implement, and verify communication protocols with formal methods[1,2,3]. Among those languages the Specification and Description Language (SDL)[4] showed a remarkable success owing to the continual refinement of its syntax and powerful development tools such as Telelogic Tau[5]. Those tools provide integrated environments for the design and implementation of a distributed system with automated verification features such as trigger-based simulation and reachability-analysis-based validation. The reliability of a product is a major goal of the industry however it normally costs very much. Therefore the existence of powerful SDL tools encouraged the industry to use formal methods for the development of network products.

However, a lot of system development engineers still stick to traditional development methods with general programming languages such as C language because most of them are afraid that formal development methods will greatly increase their works in developing a real-world large and complex network system. In addition the development of current large network systems generally involves many working groups of cooperating engineers, each of which is in charge

R. Gotzhein and R. Reed (Eds.): SAM 2006, LNCS 4320, pp. 166–182, 2006.

of developing a part of the whole system. Therefore, the decision to change the development method usually requires the agreement of all those engineers. That can be a practical barrier for a formal method to become popular in the industry.

Cellular communication systems evolved from the present third generation (3G) system, usually called the third generation evolution (3GE) or the long-term evolution (LTE) cellular systems, may be a good example of such a real-world large and complex system. Such a new communication system, however, is based on the previous system so usually uses quite a few features of the previous system. This means there are many of the existing components or libraries can be used in a new system with a little modification. Naturally they want to use them to reduce the cost and the risk of developing a whole system newly. Hence it may be very difficult to design such a system with a new language and a new tool.

We designed a radio resource control protocol between the User Equipment (UE) and the Universal Mobile Telecommunications System (UMTS) Terrestrial Radio Access Network (UTRAN) for a 3GE cellular system of Electronics and Telecommunications Research Institute (ETRI) with an SDL and C combined approach, which we call *hybrid-SDL* approach. This work was done as a collaborative project with ETRI in order to construct a prototype UTRAN for a 3GE system with other protocol implementations. The protocol was named Radio Resource Control Plus (RRCP) and is based on the specification of the third Generation Partnership Project (3GPP) release 6[6]. RRCP is the core protocol of UTRAN and is the most complex so we used SDL for producing a functionally correct implementation. Actually the hybrid-SDL approach was a reasonable solution because all the other protocols of that prototype UTRAN were decided to be implemented in C and the data structure and libraries constructed in C must be shared with all the protocols.

In this paper we describe design issues in modeling RRCP with the hybrid-SDL approach. In order to evaluate that design we modeled the same protocol again mostly in the SDL world. This approach we call *pure-SDL* approach. We evaluate those approaches by comparing the two designs and their verification results. After identifying the strength and weakness of those approaches, we present a simple guideline for selecting an appropriate design approach to develop real-world network systems for various situations.

Section 2 summarizes several related works that designed UMTS protocols in SDL. The target system, ETRI's 3GE-2005 system and the motivation of this work are briefly explained in section 3. In section 4 we explain two design approaches, pure-SDL and hybrid-SDL approaches, in detail. Section 5 explains overall design issues and some design details of our SDL system. Then the process and results of verification and target porting are presented in section 6. Section 7 evaluates those design approaches and suggests a simple guideline to decide an appropriate one in a certain situation. Finally we conclude this paper in section 8.

2 Related Works: Designing UMTS Protocols in SDL

The UMTS is the 3G cellular communication system that is currently serviced mostly in European countries. The 3GPP generally updates standard documents several times every year. So the UMTS protocols are good targets for the implementation with formal languages for automatic verification. There have been a couple of case studies that designed UMTS protocols in SDL, some of which we briefly introduce as follows.

P.J. Song *et al.* designed Wide-band Code Division Multiple Access (WCDMA) radio interface protocols based on the 3GPP Release 99 specification in SDL[7]. The design goal was to verify UE protocols with Tau Simulator in the SDL environment. Hence the design of WCDMA protocols focused on the UE side of the system. Modeling each block in SDL did not follow the standard structure of its corresponding protocol specified in the 3GPP requirements. The UE side protocols were designed fully in SDL including the Abstract Syntax Notation One (ASN.1) encoding and decoding. But that SDL design had not been ported to a specific target system. It could be free from additional C coding because it is a stand-alone system in the SDL environment only and the performance was not the main design issue. The functional behavior of the SDL design was verified successfully by simulating that design with Tau Simulator. Afterwards another team of ETRI designed a beyond-3G (B3G) system based on the 3GPP Release 5 specification[8]. They implemented a radio control protocol for the access network side, which is called 'RC', and it corresponds to Radio Resource Control (RRC) in the 3GPP specification. They used SDL for modeling the system but most of the functional behaviors were implemented in inline C-code and external C libraries because one of the main goals was a porting of the system to a real platform, the VxWorks system[9]. Accordingly not much effort had been done in the SDL design and its verification.

R.J. Skehill *et al.* at the University of Limerick developed distributed UMTS signalling layers in SDL to construct a testbed for the Information Technologies Programme (IST) Advanced Radio Resource management fOr Wireless Service (ARROWS) project[10]. They used the so-called SDL Object Modeling Techniques (SOMT) for the effective system design, which is now a general formal design technique using SDL and its tool. Two UMTS signalling protocols, RRC and Radio Access Network Application Part (RANAP), and Non-Access Stratum (NAS) drivers for UE and the Core Network (CN) were designed together in an SDL system for the verification of UMTS upper signalling layers. After the simulation and reachability analysis for the whole system with Tau, each protocol was integrated independently into Linux. They focused on signalling functions when modeling each protocol in SDL but technical solutions for fast implementation or good performance seem to be not considered seriously.

J. Colás *et al.* at the University of Málaga designed UMTS protocol layers for the radio access interface in SDL with object oriented design techniques supported by SDL-2000[11]. They wanted to follow the structure division suggested by the specifications unless they found more appropriate solutions. They especially tried to make the design have a good reusability because communication protocols maintain many similarities along the evolution path of the systems. They were interested in the quality of SDL design and used various object oriented syntax of SDL-2000. As a consequence, their design seems to be structured

well: very refined and optimized. Such a sophisticated design, meanwhile, may
have low readability due to its unfamiliar syntax especially to novices of the
language. In [12] they ported the layer 2 protocols to Windows 2000 and Linux
to measure their efficiency with regard to the data transmission rate.

3   ETRI's 3GE-2005 System

In order to develop a reliable and ultimate 3GE system with an incremental
approach, each year ETRI makes an interim design for the final system, implements, and verifies with in-house testing. The 3GE system developed in 2005
is called 3GE-2005 system and it is based on the specification of 3GPP release
6 as indicated before. This system is composed of three subsystems: the access system subsystem (ASS), the UE subsystem (UES), and the CN subsystem
(CNS). Figure 1 shows the structure of ETRI's 3GE-2005 system focusing on
the ASS.

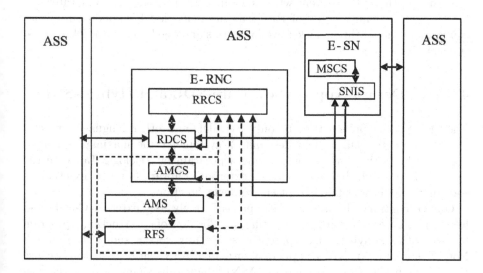

Fig. 1. The structure of ETRI's 3GE-2005 system emphasizing the ASS

The ASS contains the Evolved Radio Network Controller (E-RNC), the
Evolved Serving Node (E-SN), the Access system Modem baseband Subsystem
(AMS), and the Radio Frequency Subsystem (RFS). The target protocol of this
paper, RRCP is for both the RRC subsystem (RRCS) in E-RNC and the peer
part in the UES. The RRCS in E-RNC provides the functions and services of the
existing RRC and RANAP including MBMS services, such as signalling for call
processing, the radio resources management in the ASS, the radio resource control of a UE, the coordination between the E-RNC and the E-SN, and the message
routing between the E-SN NAS and the UE NAS.

The 3GE-2005 system was designed with a general top-down approach. The team designed the structure of ASS by analyzing the requirements of that system, decided the order of message exchanges between modules in the subsystems with Message Sequence Charts (MSC) for each functional process, designed the data structures for messages, local databases, and interfaces, and finally implemented functions of each module. When implementing and verifying modules of the system they used a traditional implementation method with C language except one module, RRCS. Because RRCS is the most complex part in the system, they wanted to use SDL in designing RRCS for obtaining a functionally correct implementation with formal verification techniques supported by SDL tools. In order to make the most use of powerful verification techniques of an SDL tool, however, not only RRCS but other modules in ASS and in UES must be included in the SDL world. For this reason they designed an SDL system for the whole system including both ASS and UES. Design issues of those additional modules are discussed in section 5.1. Note that the main goal of that SDL system is to make a functionally correct RRCS implementation. Figure 2 shows the top-level structure of that SDL system which contains a UTRAN block and three UE blocks for functional testing of RRCS at the multiple-UE's condition. It also contains additional three blocks: two for testers and one for emulating broadcast transmission by air.

4   Two Design Approaches: Pure-SDL and Hybrid-SDL

The pure-SDL approach tries to only use SDL and other languages directly supported by an SDL tool in designing a system for the maximal formality. Figure 3 shows the flow of constructing a program by Telelogic Tau with the pure-SDL approach. It tries to use no external C libraries and no external C-code including header files except environment functions.

On the contrary the hybrid-SDL approach freely uses external C-code and header files according to the given situation. The flow of constructing a program by Tau with the hybrid-SDL approach used in our work is shown in Figure 4. Note that we used ASN1C compiler[13] instead of ASN.1 utilities of Tau because the data structure in C produced by ASN1C had to be shared with developers in charge of other parts of ASS. The source code produced by ASN1C consist of type definitions and encode/decode functions. ASN1C also provides a run-time library required to use those encode/decode functions.

As described in the introduction, the hybrid-SDL approach is a reasonable solution in the situation such that data structures or libraries written in C are used in common. In addition, system developers that are not used to designing in SDL are likely to give a preference to this approach when he has to use SDL. In this situation this approach will probably take less time in designing than the pure-SDL approach. Furthermore they need not stick to SDL tools; they can use other tools or libraries freely for better performance. However we can expect that the power of the SDL tool in use may be limited and that there may be some potential problems in the implementation due to the integration

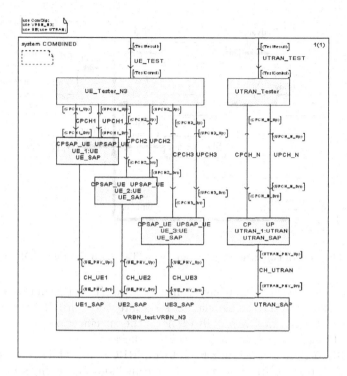

Fig. 2. The top-level structure of the SDL system designed

of heterogeneous modules. We examine the strong and weak points of those two approaches in detail from the results of design and verification in Section 7.

5   Designing the SDL System

This section describes design issues of the SDL system shown in Figure 2. Some points for the overall design are explained and then a part of design details follows with the hybrid-SDL and pure-SDL approaches.

5.1   Overall Design

Recall that the design goal of our SDL system is to build a functionally correct RRCS implementation. In order to satisfy that goal we drew up the global design as follows. First, block division and channel structure of the system were designed according to the specification suggested by the 3GPP standards for the sake of high readability and reliability. We modified the structure division only we identified where it was really necessary to make changes for better performance. Figure 5 shows the top-level design of block type UTRAN. Block RRCP is for the target protocol that corresponds to RRCS, and block HMAC stands for higher Medium Access Control (MAC) and includes the protocols, Radio Link

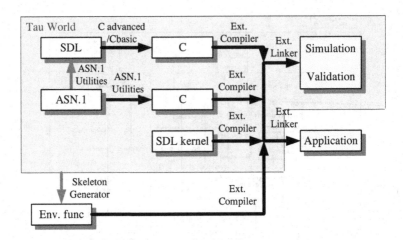

Fig. 3. The flow of constructing a program by Tau with the pure-SDL approach

Control (RLC), Packet Data Convergence Protocol (PDCP), and Radio Packet Tunneling Block (RPTB). The channel structure between RRCP and HMAC, and between HMAC and MAC also follows the specification of service access points (SAP) and logical channels of the standards.

The SDL design of the target protocol, RRCP in UTRAN is shown in Figure 6. According to the standards, RRCP includes four entities for its functional behavior, Dedicated Control Function Entity (DCFE), Broadcast Control Function Entity (BCFE), Paging and notification Control Function Entity (PNFE), and Shared Control Function Entity (SCFE). Transfer Mode Entity (TME) and Routing Function Entity (RFE) handles the mapping and routing of messages between different entities respectively. We added Control Routing Function Entity (CRFE) for the routing of lower layer configuration messages between some function entities in RRCP, DCFE, BCFE, and PNFE, and lower layer protocols because those functional entities exchange several pairs of those configuration messages with each of low layers.

The second point of the overall design is for the lower layers, HMAC, MAC, and PHY. Actually the porting of those protocols to a real platform is the work of other team who did not use SDL so we did not have to implement complete functions of those layers. For protocols inside HMAC: RLC, PDCP, and RTB, we designed their structure according to the standard specifications. Those protocols manage messages with a separate process for each connection according to the transmission mode, e.g. acknowledged mode (AM) or unacknowledged mode (UM). However we left out detailed massage manipulation functions such as segmentation and reassembly, or ciphering for their future completion for direct targeting from SDL designs. For the remaining lower layers, MAC and PHY, we implemented the minimum functions required to pass messages correctly and to exchange controlling messages with RRCP according to the specifications. The modeling effort of those additional blocks took much less time, compared with that of RRCP, because they don't have much detailed processing to do.

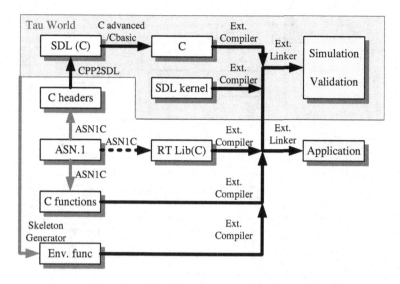

Fig. 4. The flow of constructing a program by Tau with the hybrid-SDL approach

The SDL system shown in Figure 2 contains two tester blocks for UE's and UTRAN respectively. The main goal of these tester blocks is to send appropriate triggering or response messages for testing UE's and UTRAN. Block UTRAN_Tester also includes a NAS simulator for UTRAN because NAS exists not in UTRAN but in CN. It exchanges RANAP and MBMS session management messages with RRCP according to the specification. Block VRBN indicating virtual radio broadcast network is used to broadcast messages from UTRAN to all UE entities because Tau does not support broadcast transmission with the phrase 'VIA ALL'.

Finally, we tried to use simple syntax instead of complex object-oriented features supported by SDL-2000 for simplicity and reliability except some block types for increasing reusability. Note that a major advantage of SDL is that it is easy to learn, read and write, especially for beginners, owing to its intuitive diagram and simple grammar. At first we wanted to use some object-oriented syntax for reusability and systematization such as state aggregation but we had to tiresomely check if Tau supports those syntax. The available version of Tau, 4.6.3, unfortunately, did not support many of SDL-2000 features. For the features that are required but not supported by SDL such as pointers we could use the special packages or libraries offered by Tau. Those were very useful for complicated function implementation but their incompleteness also became the problems for modeling.

5.2   Design Details for Message Handling

We skip the detailed design of each block and process on account of the limited space. Note that we tried to increase the readability and scalability of our design

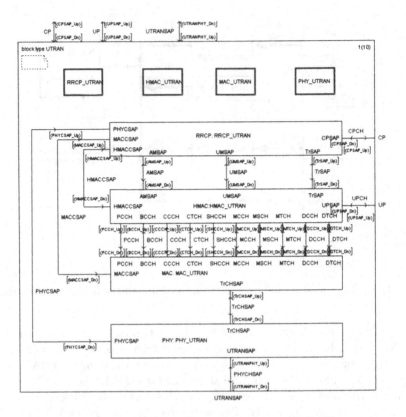

Fig. 5. The top-level design of block type UTRAN

and we regretted that we could not use composite states in our design because they are not supported by Tau. In this section we describe only a part of design for RRCS message handling with the hybrid-SDL and pure-SDL approaches.

With the hybrid-SDL approach, we used the ASN1C compiler to handle the RRCP definition in ASN.1 which was obtained from a slight modification of the standard RRC definition[6]. ASN1C generated some C header files for the data structure and some C functions for encoding and decoding of the data in class definition, protocol data unit (PDU) definition, and information elements from the RRCP definition. These functions provide application programming interfaces (API) to handle RRCP messages. Figure 7 shows how RRCP handles a message for radio resource management when it sends and receives that message respectively. When sending such a message, RRCP initializes the message contents, encodes them in ASN.1, constructs the message, and finally sends it. Receiving process of a radio resource management message is in the opposite order; RRCP decodes the ASN.1-encoded part, extracts the message type, controls radio control procedure, and finally stores the message contents in its local database.

In order to process messages efficiently, we created C libraries, 'make', 'pack', 'unpack', and 'store' for making message contents out of information elements

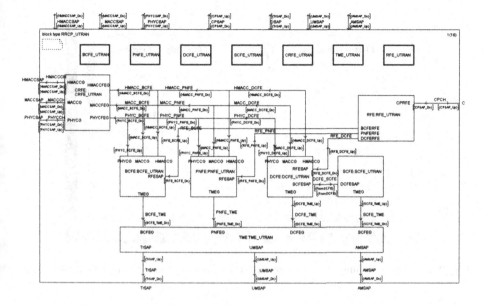

Fig. 6. The top-level design of block type RRCP

stored in the local database, for encoding them in ASN.1, for decoding the message contents encoded in ASN.1, and finally for storing information elements required for call and MBMS processing in the local databases. For example, the function fnRrcp_make_msgInitialDirectTransfer() fills up the contents of 'Initial Direct Transfer' message with appropriate values and the data from information elements stored in the database named 'callInfo' for the given condition. In addition, we created another C library, 'utility' for extra functions to process some miscellaneous work, e.g. fnRrcp_initialize_mbmsInfo() to initialize the database named 'mbmsInfo'.

With the pure-SDL approach, the built-in ASN.1 utilities of Tau are used to handle the data in ASN.1. The data structures in the RRCP specification in ASN.1 were transformed automatically in SDL by those utilities. Local databases were also transformed in SDL. Instead of C libraries we created the corresponding SDL procedure for each function included in those libraries. We also used inline C coding supported by Tau where the modeling is difficult with SDL syntax only.

6   Verification of the Design

In order to verify the design of RRCP, we used simulation, validation with reachability analysis, and testing on target. We used both SDL models designed with the hybrid-SDL and the pure-SDL approaches. Figure 8 shows the verification process we used.

First, we checked the functional consistency of the design with the test scenario in MSC by Simulator UI of Tau at both single-UE and multiple-UE's con-

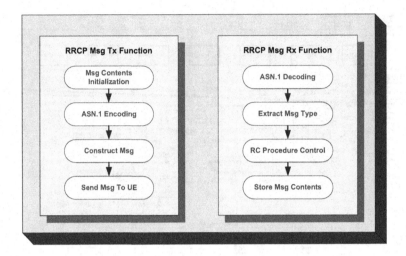

Fig. 7. Message handling procedure of RRCP for radio resource management messages

ditions. That test scenario was designed to check if the functional behavior of the SDL model matches the design requirements of RRCS in normal situations. During the simulation at the single-UE condition, there was neither mismatching of logic flows nor semantic errors in SDL design for either model. Verification of the design at multiple-UE's condition is necessary to check if the resource management functions of RRCP in UTRAN handle each of the UE's without any problem. In addition, the system may do wrong actions due to some signal racing problems caused by the messages sent by multiple UE's. Those errors are usually due to the incorrectness or incompleteness of the design that cannot be easily identified during the simulation at the single-UE condition. Fortunately there was no error found during that simulation for either SDL model.

Next, we made a couple of reachability analyses of the design with Validator UI of Tau for the multiple-UE's condition. We skipped validation for single-UE condition from the experience with simulation. Validation of the whole system requires a lot of time and memory due to its huge size and high complexity so we decided to decrease the scope of validation to the 'attach' process only. We used two reachability analysis techniques supported by Validator UI, bit-state and tree walk explorations. In case of the model designed with the hybrid-SDL approach, we unfortunately failed to obtain the result due to unexpected run-time errors. Those errors say that the program failed to read the value at a specific location of system memory. From several experiments to clear the cause, we found they are related to the libraries generated by ASN1C compiler. Thorough exploration of the global state of the system might cause a memory crash due to imperfect integration with C libraries that cannot be found in ordinary situation. With the model designed with the pure-SDL approach, we had not experienced any run-time errors. During that validation, we found some weaknesses of the design that can produce errors in very exceptional situations

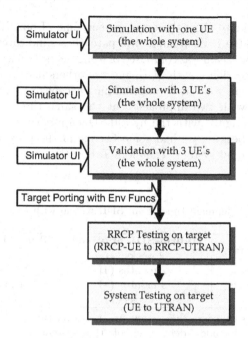

Fig. 8. The verification process

such as extremely long transmission delay of a specific message which may cause the signal racing problem. Owing to that validation we could obtain a more reliable implementation by eliminating those weaknesses.

After verifying the design by simulation and validation, we ported each RRCP module in UE and in UTRAN to the Linux platform by completing the environment functions required for the target integration. The socket interface was used for the communication with other modules. Before system testing between UE and UTRAN, preliminary testing between two Linux-ported RRCP modules was performed to increase the possibility of its successful operation during the final system testing. In system testing, only the RRCP module for UTRAN was used to generate a UTRAN instance; UE instances were created from the SDL model designed by other team. The goal of this testing was to verify the inter-operability of UE entities and the UTRAN implementation developed by different teams; the efficiency of implementations was out of interest this time. Fortunately the testing on target was successful; there were no particular errors except a couple of trivial ones due to some configuration problems. We note that the testing on target was performed entirely by ETRI.

7   Comparative Evaluation of Two Approaches

From the result of design and verification, we evaluate the two design approaches in various aspects and suggest a simple guideline for selecting an appropriate one according to specific conditions.

First, we would like to show the development time of our SDL system with two approaches in Table 1. Each number in parentheses indicates the number of members involved. Our team was composed of 6 engineers; two were SDL experts, another had some experience with SDL, and the others had no experience with SDL. All members were good at C programming except one. Actually we could not start designing with two approaches at the same time due to our tight schedule. First we designed with the hybrid-SDL approach and then with the pure-SDL approach because we had some C-code of the previous system that was a basis for the target system. Therefore Table 1 is not a fair comparison; it just shows our result.

Table 1. The development time of our SDL system with two approaches

	Hybrid-SDL approach	**Pure-SDL approach**
Training	2 weeks (4)	1 week (3)
Implementing libraries	2 months (4)	1.5 month[1] (3)
Modeling SDL system[2]	3 months (4)	1 month[3] (3)
Verification	2 weeks (1)	3 weeks[4] (1)

Notes 1. We could save some time owing to the experience with the hybrid-SDL approach. 2. This includes debugging of the system. 3. We could use a lot of SDL-code written by the hybrid-SDL approach. 4. This includes validation time as well as simulation time.

After the development we discussed the strong and weak points of two approaches. We agreed that those points depend on the technical experience and expertness of an engineer. Also the development condition is a significant factor to give preference to one approach. Our members who were C experts but SDL novices said they preferred the hybrid-SDL approach because they could use C-code in complex functions of the system. To the other members, however, the pure-SDL approach was easier because they can use ASN.1 data structures directly in the SDL system without troublesome conversion. According to the time for learning design skills related to SDL and Tau, two approaches have both pros and cons. The hybrid-SDL approach required some time for learning how to connect the SDL system to external libraries, while it took some time to learn SDL syntax and Tau-specific features with the pure-SDL approach. The modeling speed of two approaches, according to our experience, depends on the engineers; the hybrid-SDL approach would be faster for engineers who are C experts but SDL novices, and the pure-SDL approach faster for others. As for the frequency of errors made in design and the time for correcting them, we agreed the pure-SDL approach is much better thanks to its integrated development environment. Table 2 summarizes differences between them noticed from our experiences.

According to the time required for verification and the application execution time, comparing with the pure-SDL approach, the hybrid-SDL approach took less time in performing 'analysis 'and 'make'. That was mainly because the source

Table 2. Noticeable differences between two approaches related to the development

	Hybrid-SDL approach	Pure-SDL approach
Learning issues	connecting SDL to C	Tau-specific functions
Modeling speed	faster to C experts/SDL novices	faster to the others[1]
Frequency of errors	more	fewer
Debugging time	longer	shorter

Note 1. the engineers who are C novices or SDL experts

Table 3. The strength and weakness of two approaches

	Hybrid-SDL approach	Pure-SDL approach
Strength	· can use the exiting libraries · may be easier to C experts · can easily collaborate with other team using data structures in C	· efficient/integrated design environment · higher readability and manageability · larger verification scope · higher reliability of the implementation · direct use of ASN.1 data structures
Weakness	· extra source management required · some coding may be overlapped · careful integration required · external tools may be used	· higher dependency of SDL tools · expertise on SDL/tools required · SDL-only coding can be difficult occasionally

Table 4. A simple guideline for selecting an appropriate design approach

Situation	Recommendation
· when a lot of existing C-code and libraries can be used · when collaborating with other team using C is required · when most members are SDL beginners and time is limited · when complicated data processing is often required[1]	Hybrid-SDL approach
· when a new system is entirely designed · when readability and reusability of code is important · when reliability of the implementation is the first priority · when there is enough time for learning SDL and its tools	Pure-SDL approach

Note 1. C coding is easier for complicated data processing such as complex pointer manipulations.

conversion from ASN.1 to SDL is performed each time in analysis with the pure-SDL approach. With respect to the simulation time the pure-SDL approach took more time because the simulator shows more detailed simulation results with the pure-SDL approach. In validation, as we described before, we could not compare two approaches due to the failures happened during validation with the hybrid-SDL approach. Fortunately no errors happened during execution of the implementations. The execution time will depend on the optimization of the code and the characteristics of libraries used in each approach. We narrowed down the scope of comparison to the execution time of the attach process in order to find out the cause of difference. In several experiments, two approaches did not show a significant difference in execution time. This result show that the performance of Tau with its built-in functionalities is good enough to be used in the development of real-world network systems. In order to evaluate the performance of the generated software exactly, however, more detailed analysis and experiments are required.

According to our discussion, we draw the strength and weakness of the two approaches as shown in Table 3. Table 4 is a simple guideline to developers in the industry for the selection of an appropriate design approach. We note that it was generated from our experiences and accepting this guideline as a general one requires more experiments and experience. In addition, actually our division of the design approach is rather idealistic because the pure-SDL approach is very strict and difficult to follow completely. With a right understanding of the two approaches, however, you can find a good compromise between them appropriate for your situation.

8   Conclusions

Lately the industry has taken a great interest in the reliability of products to win in the fiercely competitive market and formal approaches to the development of a product are now coming into their sight. Especially in the telecommunication area, more and more successful stories have been reported enough to encourage the industry. However people in the industry still seem to hesitate to apply formal methods in development because they usually don't know well how to start with a new approach and how to migrate from the existing approach. Sometimes they want to use a formal approach partly in a specific condition as a trial. But they usually don't have enough information that will be direct help to their development.

This paper showed an experience in the development of a network proto-col, RRCP for ETRI's 3GE systems, with two different design approaches: the hybrid-SDL and the pure-SDL approaches. We also draw the strength and weak-ness of those two approaches in several aspects from our experience and present a simple guideline for the selection. Actually the hybrid-SDL approach can be a practical solution when you migrate from the traditional approach with C lan-guage or when you have to share the data structure or C libraries with other team. But you should be careful in using external tools or writing external C-code to obtain a reliable implementation because imperfect integration of SDL and C code may cause unexpected run-time errors. The pure-SDL approach gives higher readability, reliability, manageability, and verification capability than the hybrid-SDL approach in general and you can easily handle all sources in the inte-grated environment provided by the SDL tool. Hence the pure-SDL approach is recommended when you start to design a new system entirely. You can also find a good compromise between the two approaches which is appropriate for your situation. To derive detailed criteria to decide design methods for various situa-tions, further systematical analysis of design approaches should be performed.

The International Telecommunication Union (ITU) Telecommunication standardization sector (ITU-T) now has an objective to integrate its standard languages such as SDL, MSC, and ASN.1 using Unified Modeling Language (UML) 2[14] as a framework and defining UML 2 profiles for those languages[15]. Owing to the enhanced features of version 2 such as formal syntax added and powerful commercial tools supporting UML 2, UML seems ready to be an excellent tool in the formal development of a general system. In order to encourage the industry to come into this formal world, we hope for a lot of practical experiences in various situations with UML also.

Acknowledgements

This paper was supported in 2005 by Research Fund, Kumoh National Institute of Technology and Electronics and Telecommunications Research Institute. We also thank Dr. Daniel Amyot and the anonymous reviewers for their valuable comments.

References

1. P.R. James, M. Endler, and M.-C. Gaudel, Development of an atomic-broadcast protocol using LOTOS. Software - Practice & Experience, Vol. 29, Issue 8, pp.699–719, John Wiley & Sons, Inc. 1999.
2. P. Amer, A. Sethi, M. Fecko, and M. Uyar, Formal design and testing of army communication protocols based on Estelle. Proc. of the 1st ARL/ATIRP Conference, College Park, pp.107–114, 1997.
3. B. Hatim, M. O. Droma, Telecommunication software development using SDL-92: practical experience. The 2nd IEEE Int'l Conf. on Engineering of Complex Computer Systems (ICECCS'96), pp.273–277, 1996.
4. ITU, Recommendation Z.100, Specification and Description Language (SDL). ITU, Geneva, 1999.
5. Telelogic AB Inc., Telelogic TAU Generation 1 SDL Suite Ver.4.6, 2005. See http://www.telelogic.com.
6. 3GPP, Radio Resource Control (RRC) protocol specification. 3GPP TS 25.331 V.6.5.0, 2005.
7. P.J. Song, M.H. Noh, and D.H. Kim, Design and Implementation of W-CDMA Radio Interface Protocols Using SDL Development Environment. CIC 2002, LNCS 2524, pp.442-452, Sringer, 2003.
8. ETRI, HMm, Technical Specification Radio Access Research Team, 'Radio Control (RC)'. HMm SPC-0310-250.200, 2004.
9. Wind River Systems Inc., Wind River Platform for Network Equipment, VxWorks Edition. See http://www.windriver.com.
10. R.J., Skehill, I. Rics, and S. McGrath, SDL System Development of Distributed UMTS Signalling Layers. 2nd Annual ICT Information Technology and Telecommunications, 2002.
11. J. Colás, J.M.Perez, J.Poncela, and J.T. Entrambasaguas, Implementation of UMTS Protocol Layers for the Radio Access Interface. SAM 2002, LNCS 2599, pp.74-89, Sringer, 2003.

12. V. Morillo-Velarde, J. Colás, J. Poncela, B. Soret, and J.T. Entrambasaguas, UMTS Protocol Development using Formal Languages. Proc. of the IASTED Int'l Conf. on Communication Systems and Networks, pp.274–279, 2004. Entrambasaguas Proceeding IASTED Communication Systems and Networks, Spain, 2004
13. Objective Systems Inc., ASN1C - ASN.1 to C/C++ Compiler, Ver.5.3, 2002. See http://www.obj-sys.com.
14. Object Management Group, The Unified Modelling Language Version 2.0, 2004. See http://www.uml.org.
15. Rick Reed, The chairman's report. The Annual Meeting of the SDL Forum Society, 2005.

Evaluation of Development Tools for Domain-Specific Modeling Languages

Daniel Amyot, Hanna Farah, and Jean-François Roy

SITE, University of Ottawa, Ottawa, Canada
{damyot, hfarah, jroy}@site.uottawa.ca

Abstract. Creating and maintaining tools for domain-specific modeling languages (DSML) demands time and efforts that often discourage potential developers. However, several tools are now available that promise to accelerate the development of DSML environments. In this paper, we evaluate five such tools (GME, Tau G2, RSA, XMF-Mosaic, and Eclipse with GEF and EMF) by observing how well they can be used to create graphical editors for the Goal-oriented Requirement Language (GRL), for which a simplified metamodel is provided. We discuss the evaluation criteria, results, and lessons learned during the creation of GRL editors with these technologies.

1 Introduction

Domain-specific modeling languages (DSML) are high-level languages specific to a particular application or set of tasks. They are closer to the problem domain and concepts than general-purpose programming languages such as Java or modeling languages such as UML. Many companies have such languages developed in-house to satisfy some of their specific modeling, scripting, or testing needs. Improvements in productivity and comprehensibility are often cited as benefits. Still, supporting a development environment for DSML with compilers, (graphical) editors, translators, debuggers and other such tools is often onerous and prevents the rapid adoption and use of DSML.

In the past decade, a strong interest in model-driven engineering has resulted in various theories and technologies that support easier and faster development of DSML environments. The purpose of this paper is to evaluate some of these tool-supported technologies, namely the *Generic Modeling Environment* (GME), *Xactium's XMF-Mosaic*, the combination of the *Eclipse Modeling Framework* (EMF) with the *Graphical Editing Framework* (GEF), and the UML profiling capabilities of *Telelogic Tau G2* and of *Rational Software Architect* (RSA). The general context is one where we want to develop a graphical editor for an evolving graphical modeling language defined by a metamodel. A common case study, based on a simplified version of the Goal-oriented Requirement Language (GRL), is used to assess the maturity of these technologies.

This paper is structured as follows. Section 2 describes our case study and evaluation criteria. Each of the five tools is used in Section 3 to develop simple GRL editors (with lessons learned), and then section 4 summarizes their main strengths and weaknesses. We present our conclusions in section 5.

R. Gotzhein and R. Reed (Eds.): SAM 2006, LNCS 4320, pp. 183–197, 2006.
© Springer-Verlag Berlin Heidelberg 2006

2   Evaluation Context

Our context is one where we are interested in approaches that can help develop new DSML such as those found in ITU-T and OMG, together with early prototypes for modeling environments. Accordingly, a representative metamodel for such a language and a set of evaluation criteria are suggested to enable comparisons between the vari-ous approaches.

2.1   Simplified GRL Metamodel

Part of the proposal for ITU-T's User Requirements Notation [9], the Goal-Oriented Requirement Language (GRL) is used to specify and reason about business or system goals, alternative means of achieving goals, and the rationale for goals and alternatives. The notation is applicable to non-functional as well as functional requirements. GRL has concepts for various intentional elements including goals, softgoals, tasks, and beliefs. Various types of contributions link these elements into AND-OR graphs used to evaluate strategies that best balance the (often conflicting) goals stakeholders have in a system.

For the purpose of our evaluation, we have created a simple metamodel that includes a subset of the language concepts (Figure 1). The classes and associations were structured to cover the most interesting element notations (named nodes, links between nodes, links attached to links) and situations commonly

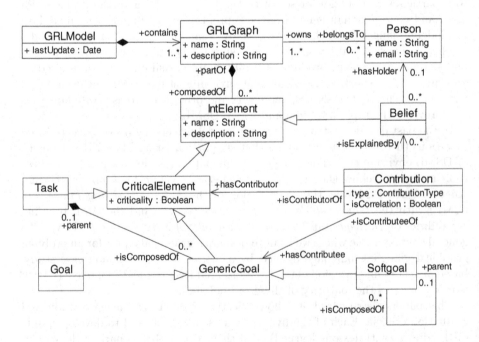

Fig. 1. Simplified GRL metamodel

found in metamodels (e.g., associations, generalizations, aggregations, typed attributes, different multiplicities, and navigation). This metamodel is not meant to be a realistic representation of GRL (this is outside the scope of this study). A more complete discussion of the GRL elements and semantics can be found in [1,15].

In terms of syntactical notation elements in the graphical representation, the symbols corresponding to the metamodel in Figure 1 are summarized in Figure 2.

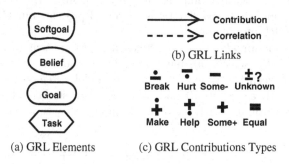

Fig. 2. Graphical symbols for the selected GRL subset

2.2 Evaluation Criteria

Our study puts a particular emphasis on the following evaluation criteria, which are most relevant in our context:

- *Graphical completeness*: Can we represent all the notation elements?
- *Editor usability*: Does the editor generated support undo/redo, load/save, simple manipulation of notation elements and properties, etc.?
- *Effort*: How much time and effort is required to learn the approach and produce DSML tools?
- *Language evolution*: How are older models handled when the language or metamodel evolves?
- *Integration with other languages*: How can we support additional languages (e.g., Use Case Maps in combination with GRL) or integrate with other tools?
- *Analysis capabilities*: Can we easily analyze or transform models produced with the graphical editor?

3 Evaluation of DSML Development Tools

In this section, we study five tools that support the development of DSML environments. Our selection is based on the relative popularity or technical potential of the tools, but many other tools could be studied as well (the DSM Forum discusses some of them [3], including the well-known MetaCase+ [12]).

3.1   Generic Modeling Environment (GME)

The Generic Modeling Environment is a configurable framework developed at Vanderbilt University and used to create domain-specific modeling environments [8]. Version 4.0 was used in our evaluation. Version 5.0 has been released since then but the functionalities we used in our study have essentially remained the same.

In GME, a DSML is described as a paradigm, which is essentially a meta-model. GME comes with a plug-in (actually a DSML) that can be used to describe paradigms with class diagrams. Figure 3 presents our GME paradigm capturing our GRL metamodel.

GME's meta-metamodel offers stereotyped concepts such as *Atom* (elementary object), *Model* (which can have inner parts and structures), *Connection* (relationship between two objects within one model), *Reference, Attribute, Set* (similar to a UML aggregation) and other *FCO* (first-class objects). Most of the classes in our original GRL metamodel map directly to FCOs and Atoms in

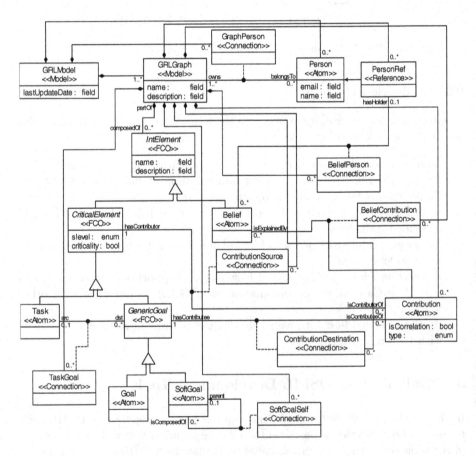

Fig. 3. GRL paradigm (metamodel) in GME

the GME metamodel, but additional Connection classes are also required for the original associations that are meant be manipulated (e.g., TaskGoal). Predefined data types such as *field*, *enum*, and *bool* are also available. An *Aspect* can be used to control the visibility of elements in the editor. OCL constraints can be added to increase the precision of the paradigm and to enable syntactical validation of user models in the target DSML editor.

GME supports the visual drawing of an object with a COM object called *decorator*. This allows one to associate the GRL shapes and symbols of Figure 2 to their respective concept in the paradigm. Simple bitmaps can be used as icons, but in this editor (implemented mainly by Y. Chu [2]) COM objects were programmed in C++, with great efforts, to reproduce the symbols correctly and have them automatically resized according to the length of the labels they contain. GME also offers a higher-level C++ interface called Builder Object Network, which is simpler to use than plain COM decorators but which is more limited.

Once a paradigm is created (and the decorators defined), it can be registered in GME and then used as an editor, as shown in Figure 4. The framework provides many features for free, including loading/saving (binary and XML), multiple undo/redo, drag and drop interface for the creation of model elements, validation against the metamodel multiplicities and OCL constraints, printing,

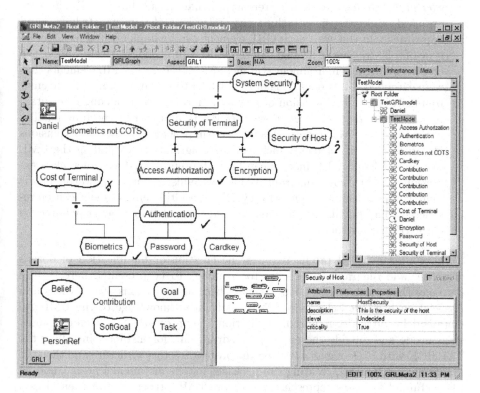

Fig. 4. GRL editor with GME

zooming, overviews, property views, etc. Multiple diagrams from the same model can be viewed and edited at the same time (in different sub-windows). The documentation is very good. However, we have found it difficult to associate decorators to links (e.g., for GRL levels of contributions) and intermediate nodes had to be defined, therefore hurting the usability of the editor. We could not find a way to visualize GRL correlations properly either.

Evolving paradigms can preserve backward compatibility if elements, links and references are added but not renamed or deleted (there is more robustness for attributes). Multiple paradigm versions can be registered, allowing one to open older files. Finally, it is possible to create our own analysis and transformation functions (and interfaces to the model are provided), but at the cost of fairly heavy C++ programming.

3.2   Telelogic Tau G2

Telelogic Tau G2 is a model-driven development environment [14] that supports UML 2.0. It can also be tailored and customized to specific modeling domains such as GRL via UML 2.0 *profiles* [13]. There are two ways of using profiles in this environment:

- *Stereotype Mechanism (SM)*: Stereotypes that extend basic UML elements are used, and extensions include customizations of names, attributes, and appearance. In this way, each GRL element can be implemented as a stereotype of a UML class. Although constructing a profile is relatively simple, the created modeling environment still includes all the basic UML elements that were extended. In essence, this does not lead to a real domain-specific environment, just to the addition of new and more precise modeling elements.
- *Metamodel Extension Mechanism (MEM)*: In addition to the functionality of the previous SM category, this mechanism provides metamodel extensions of non-basic UML element, such as class diagrams, by extending the UML metamodel itself. GRL models can hence be represented as a metaclass extension of UML class diagrams. This mechanism is more powerful but is more complex to implement. However, the resulting environment can be restricted to a domain-specific modeling language, without being polluted by other UML constructs.

Developing a MEM profile requires the creation or modification of dozens of classes and diagrams, which are too complex to be presented here (suffice it to say that most of the GRL concepts became extensions of the Class and Association base metaclasses in UML). Advanced knowledge of the UML 2.0 metamodel itself is also required. In addition, the process demands many manual steps inside and outside the modeling environment, for instance: installing the TAU SDK with FIDebugger, creating the profile directory structure and then the profile project in TAU, creating sub-packages for the metamodel profile, adding the metamodel classes representing the core UML structure and then classes representing the GRL customizations, and finally creating the TCL script that must accompany the profile. The SM approach is more straightforward, yet is it still not trivial; Tau's usability for creating and deploying profiles is still rather weak (but improving with each new version).

Two GRL editors were created with Tau G2 2.4 using both profile approaches (version 2.7 has been released since then). Figure 5 shows a GRL model example created with our metamodel-extended profile.

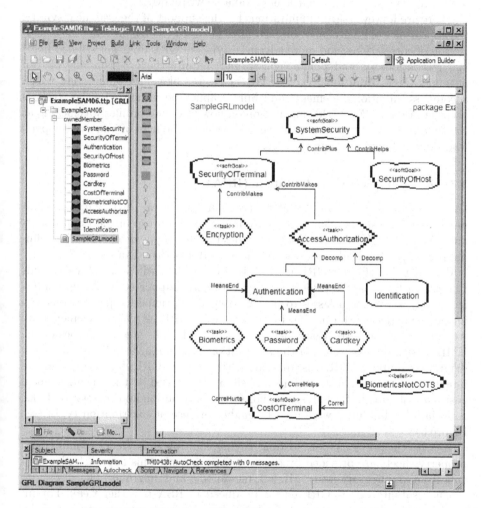

Fig. 5. GRL editor based on a UML 2.0 profile with Tau G2

The MEM approach is superior to the SM approach in many ways. For instance, the former enables one to customize diagram types as well as the user interface itself. Using this mechanism, a custom GRL diagram type was created along with a customized palette and model view, hence preventing one from mixing elements from different notations. This palette can be used to create GRL elements in the model directly, whereas in the SM approach classes need to be created and then their stereotype changed via menus.

Editors implemented with Tau G2's profiles get many functionalities for free, including loading/saving models, printing, multiple undo/redo, zooming, property sheets, and some validation against the UML 2.0 metamodel. But the best benefit is likely the integration to the rest of UML 2.0 models (possibly with other profiles), something that is not available with GME.

There are however several limitations for the support of the graphical syntax: the appearance of links cannot be customized in TAU (which prevents the visualization of correlations, and more advanced types of GRL links not studied here) and restrictions on end points (constraints) require the programming of Tau *agents* in C++. Additionally, other GRL concepts like actor boundaries, which encompass intentional elements and links, cannot be visualized either (this is also the case for GME). Documentation on how to create profiles was lacking at the time this study was done, but we acknowledge the help of Tau's developers, who provided guidance and answers.

3.3   Rational Software Architect (RSA)

IBM's Rational Software Architect (version 6.0) is a UML 2.0 compliant integrated software development environment, built on top of the Eclipse platform [7]. Unlike Tau G2, RSA only provides the stereotype mechanism for defining profiles, which leads to less sophisticated editors than Tau's.

Creating a profile for GRL in RSA is simpler than with Tau. A user needs to create a UML profile project (so this is directly supported at the user interface level), select metaclasses to be stereotyped, (optionally) specify icons and images, and release the profile. In our example, GRL intentional elements are stereotypes of the UML Class metaclass, and GRL links are stereotypes of the UML Association metaclass or the Association Class metaclass. The actual GRL diagram is simply a UML class diagram with the extra GRL stereotypes. For the intentional elements, custom icons and shapes were used, but no such graphical customization exists for link styles. For GRL contribution and correlation links, Association Class links were used to enable the use of contribution types (see Figure 6).

As with the previous tools, loading/saving, multiple undo/redo, zooming, and property sheets are provided by the tool environment. This approach also benefits from an integration to UML 2.0, metamodel and diagrams alike.

The usability of the GRL editor produced in RSA is rather weak. For intentional elements (extensions of Class), the palette provides easy access by clicking on the Stereotyped Class icon and then selecting the desired stereotype from a list. However, for stereotypes that do not extend the UML Class metaclass (such as GRL Correlation, which extended the Association Class metaclass) these stereotypes have to be applied manually using the Properties view.

Other issues similar to the SM approach in Tau have been observed. RSA does not support custom restrictions on the end points of UML links, and custom diagram types cannot be created (and hence class diagram elements can get mixed to the GRL diagram, for instance multiplicities are shown by default, as shown in the dashed circles in Figure 6). The user interface cannot be customized directly via the profile, however RSA allows for customization via its Eclipse-based Java API (but this was beyond the scope of this study).

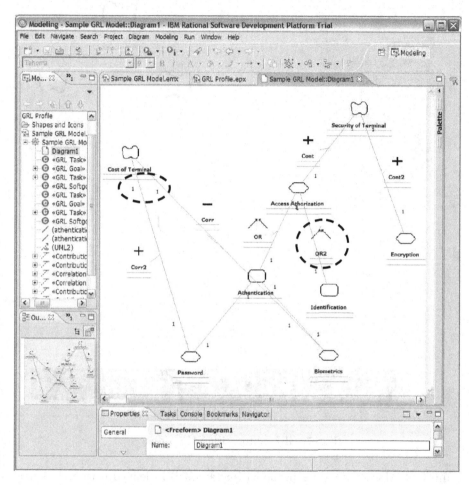

Fig. 6. Example of GRL diagram produced using a UML 2.0 profile with RSA

3.4 XMF-Mosaic

Xactium XMF-Mosaic is an integrated, Eclipse-based, extensible development environment for domain-specific (modeling) languages [16]. Building on standards such as MOF and OCL, it supports the definition of grammars and the generation of parsers. It also supports domain model design with constraints, model transformations, and editor generation by providing the DSML metamodel to the Xtools module. This tool also has a unique feature: concrete textual and graphical syntaxes can easily be provided and supported for the same language.

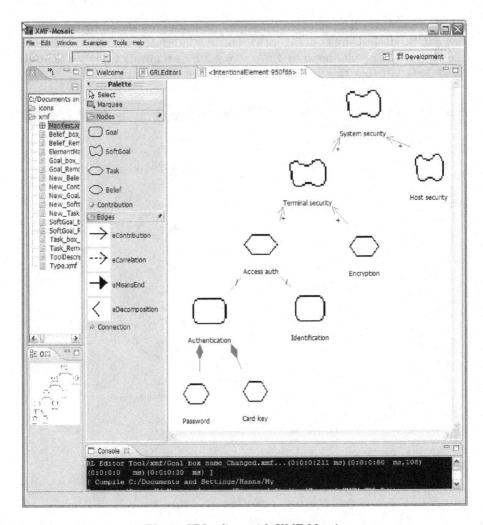

Fig. 7. GRL editor with XMF-Mosaic

In XMF-Mosaic, the domain model (metamodel) is defined with a class diagram in MOF/XCore, and OCL constraints can be added (via menus) to improve its precision. The environment supports the creation of *snapshots*, which are essentially object diagrams allowing one to test the metamodel and its constraints at an early stage. This is useful in our context, where a new language is being developed.

A graphical editor can be generated automatically from the domain model, however this feature still contains many limitations and bugs. For instance, if a superclass has an association with another class, an automatically generated editor supports creating the link for the superclass but not for its subclasses. An additional problem is that this approach generates visual items/nodes for every class in the domain model (including link classes) as the tool has limited understanding of the semantics. Potential solutions include coding the necessary elements manually, or generating the whole code first and deleting the parts corresponding to unnecessary elements (the first option was selected in our editor).

Different icons can be associated to classes in the palette by editing the *type.xmf* file, and the shapes of the GRL elements in the model can also be changed to bitmaps (see the example in Figure 7). For GRL beliefs, connecting a node to an existing link seemed to be impossible and a workaround (involving an invisible node) had to be used. Also, we could not find a way to modify link ends beyond symbols used in class diagrams.

XMF-Mosaic provides good feedback during the development of the domain model and of the editor. Additionally, the building process is incremental and not everything needs to be recompiled upon modifications, which accelerates the development of editors. The text console, which offers a different mode of interaction, was well appreciated.

Although the approach suggested by this tool is very interesting in theory, the early age of XMF-Mosaic (version 0.7 was used in this experiment) results in several weaknesses. For instance, there is no undo/redo in the GRL editor produced, and one cannot load/save models; this prevented us from evaluating how well the evolution of metamodels is supported. Also, the OCL constraints in the domain model are not transferred to the editor generated (and cannot be used for validation). Documentation was severely lacking, but we acknowledge the help of Xactium's support team who answered many questions. We have quickly looked at version 1.0 (released at the end of this study) and, although the editor generation works better with an attempt at supporting the saving of models, most problems cited here still remained.

3.5   Eclipse EMF+GEF

Eclipse is an open source and extensible Java-based platform that provides many useful services for the creation of textual and graphical editors. Versions 3.0 and 3.1 were successively used, and now version 3.2 has been released. For building graphical editors, two Eclipse plug-ins are especially relevant.

The *Eclipse Modeling Framework* (EMF) is a framework and code generation facility for building tools and other applications based on a structured data model [4]. From a metamodel specification described as an XML Schema or as a class diagram in Rational Rose (such as the one in Figure 1), EMF provides tools and runtime support to produce a set of Java classes for the metamodel, a set of adapter classes that enable viewing and command-based editing of the model, and a basic editor. The *Graphical Editing Framework* (GEF) is a framework that allows developers to take an existing application model and quickly create a rich graphical editor for it. It can easily be hooked to EMF metamodels [5].

Based on our experience in creating an Eclipse plug-in editor for the Use Case Map notation called jUCMNav [11], which uses GEF and EMF, we decided to add support for GRL to this tool. The metamodel was created as a class diagram with Rational Rose, and then imported into Eclipse by EMF. This mechanism, which we have found reliable and easy to use, generates EMF classes in Java

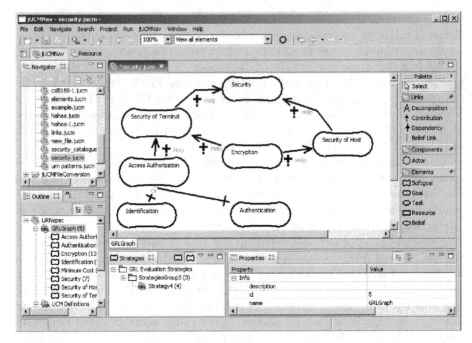

Fig. 8. GRL editor with Eclipse, GEF and EMF

that can be connected to GEF-based GUIs. The only noticeable problem we have observed with this code is that it does not enforce the minimum and maximum multiplicities found in the metamodel. OCL is not supported either.

Much effort is required to learn EMF and GEF and to understand how they are combined. Documentation (including tutorials and books) and useful discussion forums are however available. The quality of the resulting editor is very high, especially from a usability viewpoint. The Eclipse platform, together with EMF and GEF, offers several useful services that can be used with little effort: loading/saving (in XMI), zooming, tool palettes, overviews, exporting to images, offering extension points for other applications to access the models created, and multi-platform support. However, much programming effort is required to implement the various shapes and connectors, multiple undo/redo, label editing, and property sheets. The entire notation can be supported (see Figure 8), although at this time our prototype does not support beliefs attached to contributions (this proved to be difficult, like for all the other tools).

Once a basic editor is in place, adding new functionalities becomes efficient. Also, adapting the editor to changes in the metamodel is fairly simple. If new attributes, class, or associations are added to the metamodel, then the editor can still open files created with the previous version. However, deleting or renaming classes or attributes can lead to backward incompatibility problems.

Finally, it is important to note that such a plug-in enables the integration of the editor with other modeling and programming tools offered for the Eclipse platforms.

4   Comparison Summary

Many items related to the evaluation criteria introduced in section 2.2 were discussed in the section 3, and the current section provides a brief summary with additional insights based on our experience with these tools. Table 1 provides a quick overview of the strengths and weaknesses of each tool.

Table 1. Overview of comparison

	GME	Tau G2	RSA	XMF-Mosaic	Eclipse
Graphical Completeness	Medium	Low	Very Low	Low	High
Editor Usability	Medium	Medium	Low	Low	Very High
Effortlessness	Medium	Low	High	Low	Very Low
Language Evolution	High	?	?	?	Medium
Integration	Low	High	High	Low	High
Analysis / Transformation	Medium	Medium	Low	High	Medium

- *Graphical completeness*: The Eclipse approach is the only one that allowed reproducing the GRL notation with fidelity (including more advanced concepts like actor boundaries). GME did well in general, except for a few restrictions. Both required substantial additional programming. RSA offered the least flexibility for this criterion.
- *Editor usability*: The best usability is offered by the Eclipse editor (by far) in terms of user experience, tool feedback, and overall number of features. All tools except XMF-Mosaic support multiple undo/redo and loading/saving of models. The manipulation of elements is somewhat awkward in RSA.
- *Effort*: All these tools require some effort for learning the technology and for creating a DSML editor. The profile creation and usage mechanism in RSA is likely the easiest one among the five studied here, followed by GME, and Eclipse is definitely the worst.
- *Language evolution*: When the language metamodel evolves, Eclipse and GME share many common characteristics regarding backward compatibility (with files saved using the previous version). The time spent for fixing the editor is small in GME and, again, fairly high in Eclipse (although the modifications are not difficult in our experience). This aspect was not tested in XFM-Mosaic because models could not be saved and reloaded.
- *Integration with other languages*: Tau G2 and RSA both offer a direct integration with UML 2.0 as well as with other profiles. The Eclipse solution offers a different integration via extension points and the simultaneous presence of multiple plug-ins (some of which might be related to other languages). Integration appears to be weak with XMF-Mosaic (although it has some potential, being Eclipse-based) and similarly with GME, more isolated.
- *Analysis capabilities*: This aspect was not thoroughly studied in our experiments. Such capabilities appear to be weak in RSA. Tau G2 supports the concept of agents, which can be programmed (in C++ and possibly TCL) to examine/transform models. GME offers interfaces (in COM/C++) to access

and transform models. Eclipse/EMF provides Java interfaces to easily access models, but transformations are manual. XMF-Mosaic is probably the most promising environment in this category, with specific (and standard) languages for analysis and transformations. Note also that the only environment that generates editors where models are checked against the OCL constraints in the metamodel is GME.

5   Conclusions

This paper compared five different tools for the generation of development environments targeting domain-specific modeling languages. A particular emphasis was put on the generation of graphical editors with a case study involving a simple but representative subset of the Goal-oriented Requirement Language whose abstract syntax is specified with a metamodel. Editors were created with each tool, and our experiments helped us compare the approaches against criteria such as graphical completeness, usability, development effort, handling of language evolution, integration with other languages, and analysis capabilities.

For simple prototyping of modeling language editors, GME offers an interesting balance between metamodel precision and validation, ease of editor generation, and usability of the editor. For serious, industrial-strength editors, Eclipse (with EMF and GEF) appears to be the most viable (and multi-platform) solution among those studied here, and this is in part why GRL tools such as jUCMNav [11] and OpenOME [17] are headed this way. However, the development effort will be proportional to the benefits. If the integration with UML 2.0 is a must, then Tau G2 and its metamodel extension mechanism for profiles has several interesting benefits over RSA, which is currently limited to a stereotype mechanism. XMF-Mosaic brings novel and promising ideas in the DSML area, but at this time it still suffers from a lack of maturity.

To alleviate some of Eclipse's weaknesses in terms of required development efforts, a new plug-in called *Graphical Modeling Framework* (GMF) [6] attempts to provide a generative component and runtime infrastructure for developing graphical editors based on EMF and GEF. We plan to study GMF in the near future. We also plan to continue the integration of GRL and UCM in jUCMNav, and to improve its analysis and transformation features.

Acknowledgments

This research was supported by the Natural Sciences and Engineering Research Council of Canada, through its programs of Strategic Grants and Discovery Grants. The development of editors with GME and RSA/Tau was done respectively by Yi Chu [2] and Nadir Janmohamed [10], whom we thank. We are grateful to IBM, Telelogic, Vanderbilt University, and Xactium for providing their tools and technical support for this study.

References

1. Amyot, D. and Mussbacher, G: URN: Towards a New Standard for the Visual Description of Requirements. In E. Sherratt (Ed.): Telecommunications and beyond: The Broader Applicability of SDL and MSC (SAM 2002). Lecture Notes in Computer Science 2599, Springer 2003, 21–37.
2. Chu, Y.: Tool Support for the Goal-Oriented Requirement Language. M.C.S. project report, University of Ottawa, August 2005.
   http://www.site.uottawa.ca/ damyot/students/YiChuReportAndTool.zip
3. Domain-Specific Modeling Forum, http://www.dsmforum.org
4. Eclipse: Eclipse Modeling Framework (EMF), http://www.eclipse.org/emf/
5. Eclipse: Graphical Editing Framework (GEF), http://www.eclipse.org/gmf/
6. Eclipse: Graphical Modeling Framework (GMF), http://www.eclipse.org/gmf/
7. IBM: Rational Software Architect (RSA), 2005. http://www-306.ibm.com/software/awdtools/architect/swarchitect/
8. Institute for Software Integrated Systems: The Generic Modeling Environment (GME), 2004. http://www.isis.vanderbilt.edu/Projects/gme/
9. ITU-T: Recommendation Z.150, User Requirements Notation (URN) – Language Requirements and Framework. Geneva, Switzerland, 2003.
10. Janmohamed, N: Expressing Goal-oriented Requirement Language in UML 2.0: Examining the functionality of UML Profiles. CSI 4900 project report, University of Ottawa, April 2005. http://www.site.uottawa.ca/damyot/students/NadirRep.zip
11. Kealey, J., Tremblay, E., Daigle, J.-P., McManus, J., Clift-Noël, O., and Amyot, D.: jUCMNav: une nouvelle plateforme ouverte pour l'édition et l'analyse de modèles UCM. 5ième colloque sur les Nouvelles TEchnnologies de la RÉpartition (NOTERE'05), Gatineau, Canada, August 2005, 215–222.
    http://jucmnav.softwareengineering.ca/twiki/bin/view/ProjetSEG/WebHome
12. MetaCase, MetaEdit+, http://www.metacase.com/mep/
13. OMG: Unified Modeling Language (UML), version 2.0, October 2004. http://www.uml.org/#UML2.0
14. Telelogic AB: TAU G2, 2005. http://www.telelogic.com/products/tau/
15. URN Focus Group: Draft Rec. Z.151 – Goal-oriented Requirement Language (GRL). Geneva, Switzerland, Sept. 2003.
16. Xactium: XMF-Mosaic Getting Started Guide, Version 1.0, July 2005. http://www.xactium.com/
17. Yu, E.: OpenOME, an open-source requirements engineering tool, 2005. http://www.cs.toronto.edu/km/openome

Towards Integrated Tool Support for the User Requirements Notation

Jean-François Roy, Jason Kealey, and Daniel Amyot

SITE, University of Ottawa, Canada
{jroy, jkeal036, damyot}@site.uottawa.ca

Abstract. The User Requirements Notation (URN) combines the Goal-oriented Requirement Language (GRL) with the Use Case Map (UCM) scenario notation. Although tools exist in isolation for both views, they are currently not meant to work together, hence preventing one to exploit URN to its fullest extent. This paper presents *jUCMNav*, a new Eclipse-based tool that supports both UCM and GRL in an integrated way. jUCMNav supports links between the two languages that can be exploited during analysis. An overview of the current editing and analysis capabilities is given, with a particular emphasis on the new concept of GRL *strategies*, which simplify the evaluation of GRL models. The extensibility of the tool is also discussed.

1 Introduction

The User Requirement Notation (URN) [1,8] enables the modeling and analysis of user and system requirements at a high level of abstraction. It combines two complementary views: the Goal-oriented Requirement Language (GRL) for modeling goals, (non-functional) requirements, alternatives, and rationales [16], and the Use Case Map (UCM) notation for operational scenarios superimposed onto architectural components [17]. An overview of URN's concrete syntax is given in Appendix A, and a simple URN model is introduced in Section 2.

Tools exist in isolation for each individual view. The UCMNAV tool [12] supports the various applications of the UCM notation via an X11-based graphical editor and transformation procedures to various target languages (including Message Sequence Charts). UCMNAV however suffers from usability and maintainability issues and only the scenario-oriented view of URN is supported, not GRL. For creating and analysing GRL models, the best solution currently available is OpenOME [18]. This visual editor supports multiple goal and agent languages (including GRL, the NFR framework, and i^*) and can be integrated to different development environments (Protégé and Eclipse). However, as it does not cover scenario languages, URN is again only partially supported.

This paper introduces *jUCMNav*, a new open-source tool for editing and analysing URN models. This tool is a plug-in for Eclipse, an extensible Java-based development platform. jUCMNav was first developed to support the UCM notation [9], but GRL was recently added to achieve complete coverage of URN.

R. Gotzhein and R. Reed (Eds.): SAM 2006, LNCS 4320, pp. 198–215, 2006.

This tool enables the creation of links between elements of both views, hence producing an original and highly desirable integration. A particular emphasis was put on producing a usable and maintainable tool to support transformations and explore extensions to the notation.

In this paper, our goal is to provide an overview of jUCMNav and of its capabilities, as this is the first tool that supports the URN notation in its entirety. A simple URN model is first introduced in Section 2. Section 3 gives an overview of jUCMNav's architecture and metamodel while Section 4 presents the editing capabilities of the tool. Section 5 describes analysis capabilities, with a particular emphasis on the new concept of *strategies*, which support multiple evaluations of GRL models in a simple way. In Section 7, we give an overview of the extensibility of the tool, and then we conclude with a discussion of ongoing development work.

2   A Simple URN Model

This section includes a brief example that illustrates part of the URN notation and some of its typical uses. The interested reader can access more comprehensive tutorial material online[1].

The context is the following. Since security has become an important objective in a company that develops Web-based applications, the company is considering improving how to access these applications securely. Different stakeholders may have different concerns related to that new feature. For instance, management is interested in minimal costs, users desire a system that is easy to use, and company shareholders want to see a good return on their investments. Also, alternative means of authentication (e.g., passwords, cardkeys, or biometric information) can lead to different impacts on how well security is achieved, and at what cost.

In GRL, *softgoals* (clouds) are used to express qualitative and non-functional concerns such as security and performance, whereas *goals* (ellipses) are used to denote functional concerns. *Tasks* (hexagons) usually represent element of solutions used to achieve goals. All these types of intentional elements can be decomposed as AND/OR graphs, and they can also *contribute* to each other at various degrees, positively or negatively. An example GRL model capturing some of the aspects of our example is shown in Figure 1.

Stakeholders can be captured as *actors* (dashed circles), which can include intentional elements of interest (see Figure 2). Actors may depend on each other to achieve goals or tasks, or for resources to be produced. One such *dependency* is depicted in our example: shareholders depend on users for a high utilization of the system. The ease of use on one side can hence influence the return on the investment on the other side.

Some aspects of requirements are more operational or architectural in nature and are better represented as scenarios. The UCM view models scenarios as causal sequences of *responsibilities* (crosses on a path). Scenarios evolve from

---

[1] Please see http://jucmnav.softwareengineering.ca/twiki/bin/view/ProjetSEG/ and
  http://www.UseCaseMaps.org for tutorials, tools, and demonstrations.

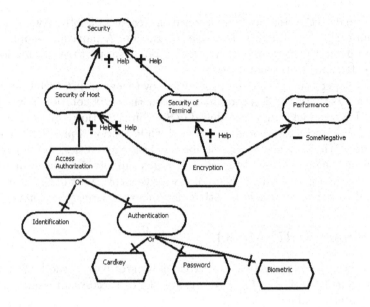

Fig. 1. Simple GRL diagram with decompositions and contributions

start points (filled circles), representing pre-conditions or triggering events, to *end points* (bars), representing post-conditions or resulting events. The various scenario elements can be bound to actors and architectural *components* (rectangles). Paths can be forked and joined using alternatives and concurrency. An AND-Fork is used in Figure 3 to split the path into two concurrent paths. Complex maps can be decomposed in sub-maps. *Stubs* (diamonds) are containers for such sub-maps, called *plug-ins*. Start/end points in the plug-in can be bound to input/output segments of the stubs, hence ensuring continuity of the scenarios across multiple map levels.

URN models can help answer many analysis questions at that level, such as:

- How are the top-level goals affected by a given selection of alternatives? For instance, each of the alternative authentication task could have side-effects (called *correlations* in GRL) on other goals in the system, e.g. cost. The best trade-off can hence be searched by studying multiple combinations, which we will call strategies in Section 5.1.
- How best can we satisfy the goals of the various stakeholders?
- What is the most suitable component architecture to support the scenarios while achieving a good global trade-off?
- If some selected GRL tasks and goals describe operations or activities, are they supported by scenarios in the UCM model?
- Are the scenarios documented the ones stakeholders really want?
- What happens to the scenarios when objectives change, and vice-versa?

However, to answer such questions and help automating the analysis process, the elements of the two views need to be linked explicitly. This is one of the

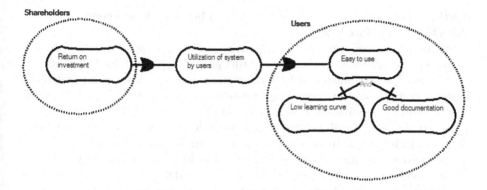

Fig. 2. Simple GRL diagram with actors and dependencies

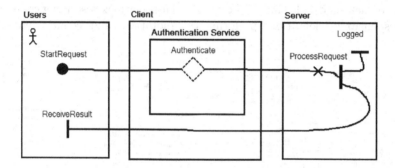

Fig. 3. Simple UCM diagram (map)

main motivations behind the creation of the jUCMNav tool. To enable this
support, we created a metamodel for GRL and linked it to the UCM part. We also
created implementation metamodels to generalize and reuse the implementation
mechanisms already present in jUCMNav's UCM editor. These are explained in
the next section.

3   jUCMNav Architecture and Metamodels

Based on a Model-View-Controller (MVC) architecture, jUCMNav makes extensive use of two complementary Eclipse plug-ins: the Graphical Editing Framework (GEF) [5] and the Eclipse Modeling Framework (EMF) [4]. GEF provides
rich reusable components and a flexible infrastructure for creating graphical editors (MVC's view and controller). EMF handles the model part of MVC with
a set of Java classes generated automatically from a metamodel (e.g. URN's)
commonly expressed with UML class diagrams. EMF also provides the serializa-
tion of models in XMI, hence automating the saving/loading of models. Changes
to the metamodel are automatically replicated in the implementation with minimal coding effort. However, we observed that several types of changes (e.g.,

deleting/renaming an attribute or a class) can break backward compatibility of the XMI files produced [3].

We have developed two distinct metamodels in order to split the core URN concepts from the additions required to capture graphical layout information as well as elements and attributes that have no semantic impact. Thus, we separated the abstract syntax from the internal representation of the concrete graphical syntax.

The abstract metamodel defines the concepts of both URN views. For the GRL sub-notation, the abstract syntax metamodel in Figure 4 defines basic GRL-Graphs, which contain intentional elements (softgoal, goal, resource and task), beliefs, actors, and links (contribution, decomposition and dependency). For the UCM sub-notation (not shown here), the metamodel defines concepts such as UCMmaps, which contain component references, path nodes, and node connections. Different sub-types of path nodes exist, such as start and end points, responsibility references, AND/OR forks and joins, waiting places, and timers. The complete metamodel also includes classes and associations describing component and responsibility definitions, performance annotations, and scenario definitions.

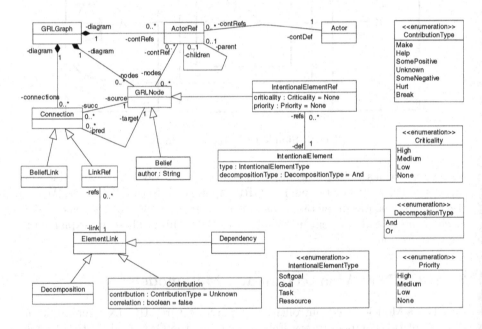

Fig. 4. Main elements of the abstract URN/GRL metamodel

From this abstract syntax metamodel, we developed an *implementation meta-model* and used it to generate Java code via EMF. In jUCMNav, URN's implementation metamodel is composed of nearly 100 classes.

We transformed the abstract syntax metamodel to an implementation metamodel in two steps. First, we created packages for GRL and UCM, and added a URNcore package that defines concepts common to GRL and UCM, including a generic URNmodelElement class, which is a superclass of most of the URN conceptual classes. Also, amongst the most important elements in this package are the *interfaces* that define the common traits between both URN sub-languages, such as diagrams, nodes, connections, containers, and container references. A container is an element that can contain nodes whereas references allow for multiple instances of a container in the same URN model. These generalizations enable the simplification and standardization of the editors for both notations.

The second step of the metamodel refactoring was the addition of (visual) attributes and classes for the implementation of our concrete syntax. Attributes are elements such as position (x, y), size (height, width), color, and informal descriptions. These changes are mainly located in the interfaces of the URNcore package. We also added classes in both of the notations to support link routing in URN diagrams.

Figure 5 shows how the basic GRL notation implements the URN abstract interfaces. For instance, the ActorRef class implements the IURNContainerRef interface. Note that all the classes, attributes, and associations from the abstract syntax metamodel are preserved in this implementation metamodel.

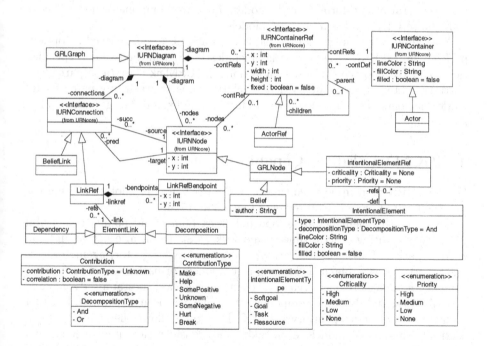

Fig. 5. Main elements of the implementation URN/GRL metamodel

The new LinkRefBendpoint class has been added to support link routing. This class defines the position in a graph where its associated link should be routed. This package also includes the analysis attributes of the GRL model, i.e. evaluations and strategies, which will be further explored in Section 5. The same

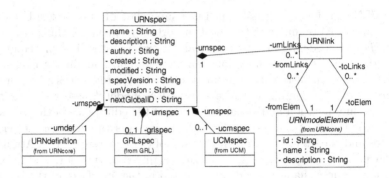

Fig. 6. Links in the URN package of the implementation metamodel

interfaces are reused in GRL and UCM. For instance, GRL nodes and UCM path nodes both implement the IURNNode interface, as they both have a location and can be moved, connected together, and bound to a IURNContainerRef container (i.e., an ActorRef in GRL and a ComponentRef in UCM). Most of the editing operations performed on the nodes, links, and components hence become common to GRL models and UCM models.

To complete the integration of the two notations, we also added a top-level package named URN (Figure 6) that includes URN definitions, GRL specifications, and UCM specifications. In addition, the URNlink class (also part of the abstract syntax) allows one to define relationships between any pair of URN model elements. This important capability will be explored in greater detail in Section 5.3.

4   jUCMNav Editor Capabilities

Our new URN tool supports editing both the Use Case Map notation (Figure 7) and the Goal-Oriented Requirements Language (Figure 8).

The core path elements are supported: start points, end points, responsibilities, stubs, waiting places, timers, and forks/joins (both alternative and concurrent paths). Furthermore, various component types (actor, agent, process, and team) are available, as is binding a component or path element to a parent component. The more unconventional elements, such as timestamps, dynamic responsibilities, and dynamic components have not yet been integrated, but their addition should be straightforward. jUCMNav only allows the creation of syntactically valid UCM models, even taking into consideration implicit loops. Not only is the creation and manipulation more intuitive than other UCM/GRL tools, but the deletion mechanisms are richer, more robust, and less restrictive.

The GRL editor supports most of the constructs defined in the draft standard [16]. The intentional elements supported are goals, softgoals, tasks, and resources. These elements can have multiple references to simplify the creation and visualization of complex model via multiple diagrams. These references can be bound to actors, influencing the result of some analysis features offered in the tool.

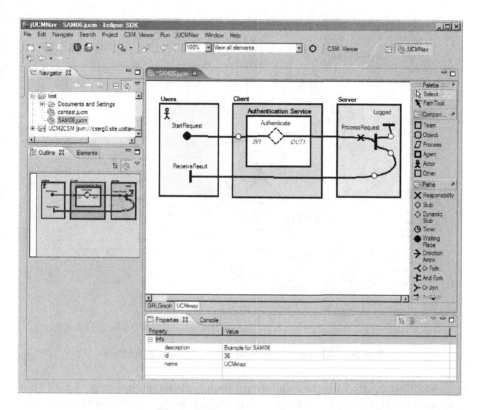

Fig. 7. UCM view in jUCMNav

In contrast with previous GRL tools and for a better integration with its UCM counterpart, the actor's boundary (dashed circle) is not optional and has many commonalities with UCM components in its implementation and behaviour. Beliefs are also available in the application; however they are used mainly to document rationales in the graphical view of the model when linked to intentional elements (without affecting analysis). Finally, the links supported include AND/OR decompositions, contributions, correlations, and dependencies, with their respective attributes, annotations, and graphical representations.

In addition to conventional dropdown and contextual menus, the new editor infrastructure offers a good user experience thanks to drag and drop editing, group manipulation and especially unlimited undos and redos. Furthermore, taking advantage of the standard Eclipse views, jUCMNav features an outline (hierarchical and graphical), a properties view, and a resource view. These views can be moved, closed, or maximized. Both GRL and UCM diagram editors use the same Eclipse-based user interface metaphors. Images can also be exported in various formats.

A new feature in jUCMNav that is available to both notations is an optional auto-layout mechanism, which relies on Graphviz [13] to position the diagram elements. Although imperfect, the presence of this feature is necessary in the

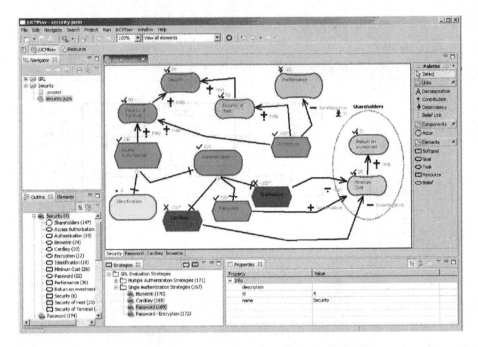

Fig. 8. GRL view with strategy analysis in jUCMNav

context of automated reverse/round-trip requirements engineering. A tool that generates UCM/GRL models from design artifacts such as code, execution traces, requirements, or textual use cases hence does not require manual positioning of the elements.

The auto-layout mechanism is also used in jUCMNav's *catalogues*, which are repositories of reusable GRL models or patterns often used to describe common model elements and relationships related to security, performance, and other non-functional aspects. Using the import/export facilities integrated in Eclipse, this feature allows one to export a model's intentional element definitions and links to an XML file. Modellers can then reuse patterns from such catalogues to kick-start new URN models or add elements to existing ones. The import creates the GRL definitions and links in the new model and builds a new GRL diagram representing the pattern.

5 New Analysis Capabilities for URN Models

5.1 GRL Strategies

By providing access to a complete URN model, jUCMNav can offer novel analysis mechanisms. In order to more easily analyze GRL models and find what selection of alternatives can lead to the best trade-off amongst the often conflicting goals of the stakeholders, we developed the concept of GRL *strategies*, which are user-defined sets of initial evaluations on a GRL graph (Figure 9). These evaluations are satisfaction levels initially assigned to some of the intentional elements in the model (often the leaves of the graph), which are then propagated to the top-level intentional elements through the various links. Evaluations are used to determine how well goals in a model are achieved in a given context.

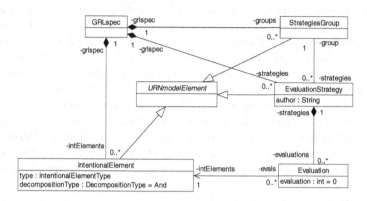

Fig. 9. Evaluation strategies metamodel

In jUCMNav, strategies can be created, grouped, modified, evaluated, and deleted through the Strategies View. Once a strategy is selected (e.g., Password strategy in Figure 8), the user can access and modify the initial satisfaction level of an intentional element by using the Properties View.

In GRL, satisfaction levels for intentional elements are shown graphically using a qualitative scale (satisfied, weakly satisfied, weakly denied, and denied). During jUCMNav's requirement elicitation phase, we realized that some users were interested in having a quantitative interpretation of satisfaction levels in a strategy. We have hence implemented an equivalent but more granular representation using numerical values between -100 (denied) and +100 (satisfied). These values are used to display feedback on the affected intentional elements. Both the numerical value and the corresponding qualitative symbol can be used. In addition, element references are color-coded with shades varying from red (-100) to green (+100).

Once a value is entered in a strategy, the propagation algorithm is applied immediately and the user can see the result on the fly. Users can also change the evaluation value of any node in the model, not only the leaf nodes.

The evaluation algorithm, inspired from [1,7], has been implemented with an automatic conflict resolution mechanism that does not require user involvement. Evaluations depend on the various links (decomposition, contribution, and dependency) between the intentional elements. An evaluation is first calculated from the Decomposition links, as a standard AND/OR graph. For AND and OR decompositions, the results correspond respectively to the minimal and maximal evaluations of the source nodes. In our metamodel (Figure 4), the decomposition type is an attribute of the target IntentionalElement node, which causes a node to be decomposed by only one type of decomposition.

The propagation algorithm then evaluates the Contribution links. For each contribution x of a target element with N input contributions, the satisfaction level of the source element and the contribution level are used as described in Algorithm 1. The contribution level, LEV_x, is given a numerical value between -1 and 1 according to the contribution type on the link (1 for make, 0.5 for help, -1 for break, etc.). The satisfaction level, $NEVAL_x$, is normalized to a value between 0 (denied) and 100 (satisfied). The normalized evaluation is multiplied by the contribution level. The results of each of the contributions are added and normalized to provide the total contribution, $TCON$, between -100 and 100.

The normalized evaluation is calculated using the *Tolerance* attribute, which is set to 0 by default but can be modified by the jUCMNav user. It defines the range of values that are considered satisfied (or denied). For example, with a tolerance of 10, evaluations between 90 and 100 are considered fully satisfied and evaluations between -90 to -100 are considered fully denied. If there are no make/break contributions, then the result is normalized to weakly satisfied or weakly denied $(100 \pm (1 + Tolerance))$ and is added to the decomposition value.

Algorithm 1: Contribution evaluation

$$TCON = \sum_{x=1}^{N} NEVAL_x \times LEV_x$$

if $((TCON \geq (100 - Tolerance))$ **and** $(LEV_{x=1..n} \neq 1))$
then
    $TCON = 100 - (1 + Tolerance)$
else
    if $((TCON \leq (-100 + Tolerance))$ **and** $(LEV_{x=1..n} \neq -1))$
    then
        $TCON = -100 + (1 + Tolerance)$
    endif
endif

When jUCMNav's strategy view is used (see Figure 8), elements with an initial value in the selected strategy are indicated with the * annotation. Figure 10 shows the evaluation of a given strategy on the GRL diagram of Figure 1, and its impact on Security and Performance.

Finally, the Dependency links are evaluated. The minimal value among the dependees is compared with the current evaluation of the source node. The resulting evaluation corresponds to the minimum value of those two evaluations. The rationale is that an intentional element cannot have a higher value than those it depends on. Figure 11 shows a case where an element A depends on two other elements, B and D, which depend on elements C and E respectively. By default, evaluations are set to 0. Element C does not influence the evaluation of B because it is greater than the default evaluation. However, element E is less than the default evaluation of element D, which causes D's evaluation to become -30. This is in turn propagated to element A.

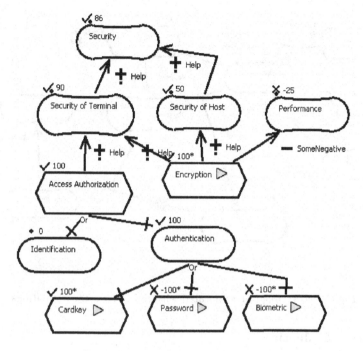

Fig. 10. Evaluation of a GRL model

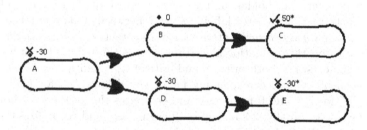

Fig. 11. Dependencies evaluations

The implementation of this algorithm has been done in a generic and open way using the *strategy design pattern* [6] (not to be confused with GRL strategies), which offers the possibility to easily implement other propagation and evaluation algorithms. To implement such an extension, the developer makes use of the provided Eclipse extension point, which includes methods to calculate the evaluations of one node based on its decomposition, dependency, and contribution links, as well as methods to specify how the evaluations should be propagated in the model. This means that several variants of this algorithm, with different tolerances and logic, could be supported by jUCMNav.

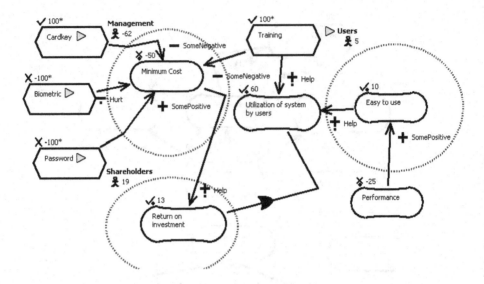

Fig. 12. GRL diagram annotated with links and actor evaluations

5.2   Actor Evaluation

Our tool also offers a novel analysis label for actors in order to help visualize negotiations between stakeholders and assess the global satisfaction level of actors for a given strategy. This actor label is a value between -100 and 100 computed from the *criticality* and *priority* attributes of its intentional elements references. For a given actor, the evaluation algorithm iterates through its list of bound intentional elements. For both priority and criticality, it multiplies the evaluation of each element by the corresponding factor (by default, 1.5 for high, 1.0 for medium, 0.5 for low and 0 for none), and computes the average per bound intentional element. Finally, it sums up both evaluations and normalizes the result between -100 and 100. A simple example is shown in Figure 12, which illustrates part of a more complex model that includes Figure 10 and the strategy discussed in the previous section. The selection of the CardKey alternative that led to a good security now also leads to high costs that will dissatisfy management.

5.3   URN Links

The integration of UCM and GRL views in the same tool allows for the creation of various types of traceability links between elements of both notations, as shown in Figure 6. These links can be used to measure the impact of a modification to any evolving GRL/UCM diagram on the other aspects of the model. They can also improve consistency between the URN views. For instance, links can be defined between GRL intentional elements or actors as source, and UCM responsibilities, components, or maps as target. In this case, when the user selects a strategy, the satisfaction level of the source GRL element is *also* displayed on the target UCM element at the other end of the link (if any). Using this approach, one can evaluate the impact of a goal strategy on the operational and architectural aspects of the model.

The partial URN model in Figure 13 extends the simple scenario of Figure 3 to one that authenticates the user and then processes the request over encrypted channels if the request and the user are valid. This diagram is part of the same URN model as Figure 10 and Figure 12. In this model, URN links were created from the GRL Encryption task to the UCM Encryption and Decryption components, as well as to the UCM Encrypt and Decrypt responsibilities. Other URN links are set between the User actor in GRL and the User component in UCM, as well as between the Authentication tasks (Cardkey, Password, Biometric) and each of the corresponding UCM plug-in maps (bound to the Authenticate stub but not shown here).

The triangles in this figure and the previous ones are not part of the URN notation. They indicate the presence of URN links, and the evaluation results from the corresponding GRL elements are displayed between curly brackets. For instance, the Encryption UCM component shows the degree of satisfaction of the linked Encryption GRL task. Feedback is updated automatically as other strategies are selected.

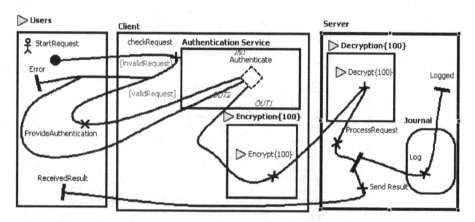

Fig. 13. UCM diagram annotated with links and actor evaluations

6 Extensibility of the Tool

jUCMNav can be extended with new algorithms for evaluating strategies in a GRL graph, as discussed in Section 5.1. Taking advantage of Eclipse's component model, the tool also offers other extension opportunities.

As suggested previously, URN models can be generated from other artefacts. A specific example is the automatic generation of UCM models from textual use cases defined in a structured natural language. Textual use cases are inherently ambiguous, and completeness and consistency are often hard to analyze.

Tools already exist to extract domain models, scenarios, and finite state machines from textual use cases to help facilitate this analysis (e.g., UCEd, a use case editor [15]). We recently demonstrated the usefulness of jUCMNav extension points with a complementary plug-in that generates graphical UCM models (with automatic layout) from validated UCEd project files [11].

jUCMNav's extension points, which provide access to the URN model under design, were also used in a plug-in that enables the import and synchronization of URN models in a requirements management system, namely Telelogic DOORS. jUCMNav can export URN models (i.e., UCM and GRL views) via script files in the DOORS eXtensible Language (DXL). URN elements can be linked to other requirements in DOORS and both views can be kept synchronized as they evolve (e.g., by re-importing the modified URN model) [10]. Figure 14 shows one of the views, corresponding to a UCM diagram, as seen from DOORS.

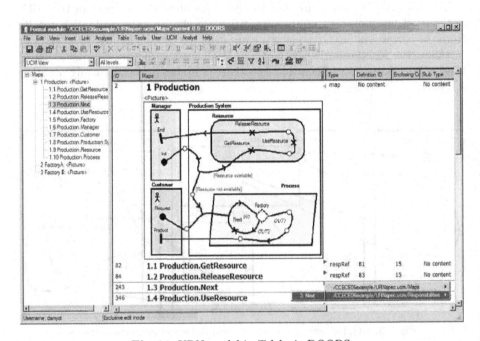

Fig. 14. URN model in Telelogic DOORS

7   Conclusions and Future Work

The development of jUCMNav allowed us to validate many of the existing URN concepts recently expressed with a metamodel. This is the first tool that supports both URN views in a uniform and unified way, thanks in part to the generalization done at the level of the implementation metamodel, which eased the addition of the GRL editor by reusing much of the code developed for the original UCM editor. This open platform also allowed us to prototype and to explore new URN concepts related to GRL strategies, propagation algorithms, and catalogues, as well as various useful links and connections between GRL and UCM. Strategies and links for URN models contribute greatly to answering the types of questions mentioned in Section 2. Extension points were added and exercised for the creation of various functionalities such as use case import, integration with a requirements management system, image export, catalogue export, and support for multiple GRL evaluation algorithms.

In the near future, the missing UCM notation elements will be added. Also, jUCMNav will be extended to support *scenario definitions* enabling dynamic analysis and transformations to MSCs, UML, and test goals [2], as well as an export mechanism to the Core Scenario Model for *performance modelling* [19]. A simple data model compatible with SDL is being added, and UCM scenarios will be defined with a user interface similarly to GRL strategies. We will also add an import filter for the old UCMNAV file format, for backward compatibility.

The integration of GRL and UCM in one tool opens the door to many new possibilities. We plan to add better analysis capabilities in jUCMNav that will measure the impact of strategic decisions on the scenario and architectural aspects of the model. This will be possible by building dynamic views of the UCMs. For example, operational choices for goals, realized through tasks, have an influence on the system architecture. We will modify the UCM views depending of the operational choices made in the GRL strategy. The main contribution of this feature would be to visualize impact of goals and non-functional choices through scenarios. We will also work on further URNlink types and on improving the modeling and analysis process with such links.

Acknowledgments

This research was supported by NSERC, through its programs of Strategic Grants, Discovery Grants, and Postgraduate Scholarships. We are grateful to E. Tremblay, J.-P. Daigle, J. McManus, Y. Kim, J. Sincennes, and G. Mussbacher for various contributions to the tool. We also thank A. Prinz and the anonymous reviewers for their comments on the workshop version of this paper.

References

1. Amyot, D. and Mussbacher, G: URN: Towards a New Standard for the Visual Description of Requirements. In E. Sherratt (Ed.): Telecommunications and beyond: The Broader Applicability of SDL and MSC (SAM 2002). Lecture Notes in Computer Science 2599, Springer 2003, 21–37.
2. Amyot, D., Cho, D.Y., He X., and He, Y.: Generating Scenarios from Use Case Map Specifications. Third International Conference on Quality Software (QSIC'03), Dallas, USA, November 2003, 108-115.
3. Amyot, D., Farah, H., and Roy, J.-F.: Evaluation of Development Tools for Domain-Specific Modeling Languages. Fifth Workshop on System Analysis and Modelling (SAM06), Kaiserslautern, Germany, May 2006. LNCS 4320, Springer, 183-197.
4. Eclipse: Eclipse Modeling Framework (EMF), http://www.eclipse.org/emf/
5. Eclipse: Graphical Editing Framework (GEF), http://www.eclipse.org/gmf/

6. Gamma, E., Helm, R., Johnson, R., and Vlissides, J.M.: Design Patterns: Elements of Reusable Object-Oriented Software. Addison-Wesley, USA, 1995.
7. Giorgini, O., Mylopoulos, J. and Sebastiani, R.: Goal-Oriented Requirements Analysis and Reasoning in the Tropos Methodology. Engineering Applications of Artificial Intelligence, 18(2):159–171, March 2005.
8. ITU-T: Recommendation Z.150, User Requirements Notation (URN) – Language Requirements and Framework. Geneva, Switzerland, 2003.
9. Kealey, J., Tremblay, E., Daigle, J.-P., McManus, J., Clift-Noël, O., and Amyot, D.: jUCMNav: une nouvelle plateforme ouverte pour l'édition et l'analyse de modèles UCM. 5ième colloque sur les Nouvelles TEchnnologies de la RÉpartition (NOTERE'05), Gatineau, Canada, August 2005, 215–222.
   http://jucmnav.softwareengineering.ca/twiki/bin/view/ProjetSEG/WebHome
10. Kealey, J., Kim, Y., Amyot, D., and Mussbacher, G.: Integrating an Eclipse-Based Scenario Modeling Environment with a Requirements Management System. 2006 IEEE Canadian Conf. on Electrical and Computer Engineering (CCECE'06), Ottawa, Canada.
11. Kealey, J. and Amyot, D.: Towards the Automated Conversion of Natural-Language Use Cases to Graphical Use Case Maps. 2006 IEEE Canadian Conf. on Electrical and Computer Engineering (CCECE'06), Ottawa, Canada.
12. Miga, A.: Application of Use Case Maps to System Design with Tool Support. M.Eng. thesis, Dept. of Systems and Computer Engineering, Carleton University, Ottawa. October 1998. http://www.UseCaseMaps.org/tools/ucmnav/
13. North, S., et al.: Graphviz, 2005. http://www.graphviz.org/
14. OMG: Unified Modeling Language (UML), version 2.0, October 2004. http://www.uml.org/#UML2.0
15. Somé, S.: An Environment for Use Cases based Requirements Engineering. Formal demonstration. 12th IEEE Int. Requirements Engineering Conf. (RE04), Japan, September 2004. http://sourceforge.net/projects/uced/
16. URN Focus Group: Draft Rec. Z.151 – Goal-oriented Requirement Language (GRL). Geneva, Switzerland, Sept. 2003.
17. URN Focus Group: Draft Rec. Z.152 – Use Case Map Notation (UCM). Geneva, Switzerland, Sept. 2003.
18. Yu, E.: OpenOME, an open-source requirements engineering tool, 2005. http://www.cs.toronto.edu/km/openome
19. Zeng, Y.X.: Transforming Use Case Maps to the Core Scenario Model Representation. M.Sc. thesis, SITE, University of Ottawa, Canada, June 2005.

Annex A: Overview of the User Requirements Notation

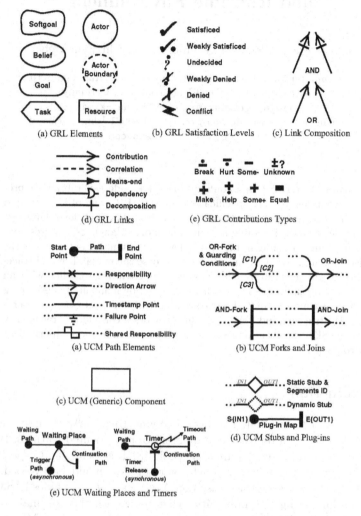

Fig. 15. Summary of the GRL and of (a subset of) the UCM concrete notations

ConTraST - A Configurable SDL Transpiler and Runtime Environment

Ingmar Fliege[1], Rüdiger Grammes[1], and Christian Weber[2]

[1] Computer Science Department, University of Kaiserslautern
Postfach 3049, D-67653 Kaiserslautern, Germany
{fliege, grammes}@informatik.uni-kl.de
[2] Siemens AG, Lise-Meitner-Str. 7/2, D-89081 Ulm, Germany
christian-weber@siemens.com

Abstract. ConTraST is a configurable C++ code generator that provides a mapping of SDL specifications in SDL/PR to an object oriented C++ representation. The transformation from one high level language to another allows the configuration of supported language features, giving the name: a configurable transpiler. The intention is to obtain the object oriented structure and thereby increase the readability and traceability of the generated code. This code is compiled together with an SDL runtime environment, which was derived by manually transforming the formal semantics of SDL-2000 standard Z.100 F.3 into C++ preserving both structure and behavior. This provides a continuous traceability from the SDL specification to the executing system including its runtime environment.

1 Introduction

Over the past 30 years, SDL has been evolving to a fairly complex description language offering a multitude of different object oriented features. But not all features are necessarily required to specify SDL systems, and especially in embedded systems, the resulting waste of resources should be avoided. With SDL-2000 [1] a formal semantics based on Abstract State Machines (ASM) was introduced, eliminating the ambiguities that come with the informal language definition. Additionally, the precise mathematical formalisms of ASMs, which are used to describe the formal semantics, provide a rigorous basis for compilers and runtime environments.

In this paper, we present a runtime environment derived from the formal semantics of SDL-2000. We have defined language profiles to divide SDL into a core language and a set of language modules to augment this core with welldefined language features. Thus, we have defined a subset of the SDL-2000 language representing the language coverage of SDL-96. The transformation of ASM into C++ was performed manually.

SDL is supported by several commercial tools. We use the generated SDL/PR to transpile it to C++ with our developed tool ConTraST. This transformation retains the specified system structure and generates understandable code that

R. Gotzhein and R. Reed (Eds.): SAM 2006, LNCS 4320, pp. 216–228, 2006.

is similar to the SDL/PR syntax. This, together with the runtime environment, provides a continuous traceability from the SDL specification to the executing system including its runtime environment.

In Section 2, we introduce the transpiler ConTraST, which generates C++ code from given SDL specifications. Section 3 describes the developed SDL runtime environment derived from the formal semantics of SDL-2000. A short introduction to ASMs is given, and the accomplished mapping to C++ is explained. In Section 4, we address some related work and finally draw conclusions in Section 5.

2   The SDL Transpiler

ConTraST [3] (**Con**figurable **Tra**nspiler for **S**DL to C++ **T**ranslation) is based on the SDL-96 grammar provided by ITU recommendation Z.100 [2], complemented by some required variations for compatibility and conflict avoidance. The decision for SDL-96 was taken due to leak of tool support for SDL-2000.

SDL-96 is a powerful and comprehensive language, which offers a large variety of different features. In most SDL systems, the majority of them are not required, especially if the executing platform has resource limitations. For this, we have divided SDL-96 into four coherent language profiles (see [4]):

- **Core:** The minimum language coverage to provide communicating Mealy machines. This contains primarily systems, blocks, processes, channels, signals and simple transitions.
- **Static$_1$:** Extension with common language features within processes covering, e.g., timers, decisions, tasks, and basic data types.
- **Static$_2$:** Language extension with services, inheritance and all other transition triggers, e.g. priority input and enabling conditions.
- **Dynamic:** Covers those language features which make use of dynamic memory or extension to the state tree during runtime, e.g. procedures, creation of instances, and complex data types.

ConTraST supports the configuration of an entire language profile as well as the usage of individual language features and warns the user when an illegal construct is used. The defined language coverage is used during code generation, but also allows the definition of SDL language profiles, which can be used to systematically derive an individual runtime environment from the formal SDL semantics [4].

The transformation of an SDL specification into a C++ representation is done in six steps:

- **Step 1:** A syntax analysis of the specification in SDL/PR is performed using the established gnu tools flex and bison. From the derived information, an object oriented syntax tree is generated, which builds the base for the following steps.
- **Step 2:** The syntax tree is transformed by e.g. removing references and transforming processes into process types and instances. This step implements the static analysis and transformation described in the Z.100 F2.

- **Step 3:** All SDL expressions are transformed to an object oriented format by changing the order of tokens (e.g. length(str) → str.length())
- **Step 4:** An analysis is performed to determine potential for possible optimizations or further transformations.
- **Step 5:** The resulting syntax tree is used for the code generation. Separate files are generated for each system and package.
- **Step 6:** A system file (main) and a makefile for compilation on different platforms is generated.

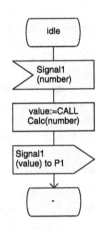

The challenge in transformation is to exploit and retain the given object oriented structure of SDL/PR allowing a successive traceability from an SDL specification to its C++ representation. This is achieved by inheritance of C++ classes, each representing one specific SDL-96 object. Most of these objects such as plain data types or signals can be described by simple classes with parameters, while processes with corresponding types are represented by the use of template classes. Thereby, a complete SDL system specification can be transformed to an object oriented C++ representation. A hierarchical composition of classes is used to implement the visibility of definitions and variables, which also allows the application of identifiers with scope information.

Fig. 1. A transition

```
1   void ::SAM06::b::Demo::Transition1::fire(SDLInstance* owner, SignalInst* signal)
2   {
3       Demo* VAR = (Demo*)context;
4       switch (offset) {
5       case 0:
6           LeaveStateNode(1);
7           break;
8       case 1:
9           VAR->number = ((::SAM06::b::Signal::Signal1*)signal)->Param1;
10          delete signal;
11          VAR->value = ::SAM06::b::Demo::Calc(owner, VAR->number).Call();
12          Output( (new ::SAM06::b::Signal::Signal1(VAR->value))->To("P1") );
13          NextState(DASH);
14          break;
15      default: break;
16      }
17  };
```

Listing 1. Transformation of transition with ConTraST

The generated code of ConTraST in Listing 1 shows the transformation of the given transition of Figure 1. In C++, this transition is represented by a method

Transition1::*fire*() within the given context, where *Demo*, *b* and *SAM06* are the surrounding process, block and system. The prefix of the method *fire*() represents the scope and the first parameter of the method gives a pointer to the surrounding owner (in this case the process *Demo*) in order to access local variables during execution. The second parameter represents the SDL signal triggering the transition. The execution of transitions can be interrupted as shown in line 7 to execute required actions of the Z.100 F3, in this case the LEAVESTATENODE macro. The usage of switch/case constructs (line 4) permits the continuation of transition execution. The used variable *offset* is a private variable of the class *transition*. This mechanism enables the interruption of transitions after every behavior primitive and the continuation at any other position within the agent's program. If required, the transpiler adds information during code generation to set the variable *offset* in order to indicate the next behavior primitive for the runtime environment. It therefore replaces the continue label of the Z.100 F3 and enables e.g. the usage of connectors.

Line 9 shows the assignment of signal parameters to local variables, followed by deallocation of the signal memory. In line 11, a new instance of the procedure *Calc* with its parameter *number* is allocated. The procedure call is performed by the execution of the method *Call*(). According to Z.100 F.3 the procedure call requires the extension of the state graph, which is achieved in several steps (call of the macro CREATEPROCEDURE). These required steps are controlled by the runtime environment, the execution of the procedure with possible states and the termination with an optional return value. Therefore, the procedure call must be implemented as an intermediate execution, while all other agents can still be executed.

Line 12 represents the OUTPUT of a signal *Signal1* with the parameter *value*. The optional constraints to the signal (Via and To) are assigned by the call of corresponding methods. The next line completes the transition with a NEXTSTATE() call, which instructs the runtime environment to enter the new state by the call of the EVALENTERSTATENODE macro.

```
case 1:
9     yAssF_SDL_Integer(yVarP->z002_number, ((yPDef_z02_Signal1 *)ySVarP)->
          Param1, XASS_AR_ASS_FR);

11    ALLOC_PROCEDURE(z000_Calc, yPrdN_z000_Calc, sizeof(yVDef_z000_Calc))
      PROCEDURE_ALLOC_ERROR
      yAssF_SDL_Integer(((yVDef_z000_Calc *)PROC_DATA_PTR)->z0000_x,
          yVarP->z002_number, XASS_MR_ASS_NF);
      ((yVDef_z000_Calc *)PROC_DATA_PTR)->z0001_y =
          &yVarP->xPrdCallRes1_SDL_Integer;
      CALL_PROCEDURE(z000_Calc, yPrdN_z000_Calc, 0, 2)
      PROCEDURE_ALLOC_ERROR_END
      XAFTER_VALUE_RET_PRDCALL(2)

      yAssF_SDL_Integer(yVarP->z003_value, yVarP->xPrdCallRes1_SDL_Integer,
          XASS_MR_ASS_FR);
```

```
12     ALLOC_SIGNAL_PAR(Signal1, ySigN_z02_Signal1,
           TO_PROCESS(P1, yPrsN_z01_P1), yPDef_z02_Signal1)
       SIGNAL_ALLOC_ERROR
       yAssF_SDL_Integer((((yPDef_z02_Signal1 *)OUTSIGNAL_DATA_PTR)->
           Param1, yVarP->z003_value, XASS_MR_ASS_NF);
       SDL_2OUTPUT(xDefaultPrioSignal, (xIdNode *)0, Signal1, ySigN_z02_Signal1,
           TO_PROCESS(P1, yPrsN_z01_P1), sizeof(yPDef_z02_Signal1), "Signal1")
       SIGNAL_ALLOC_ERROR_END

13     SDL_DASH_NEXTSTATE
```

Listing 2. Transformation of transition with Telelogic Cadvanced

Listing 2 shows the generated C code of Tau 4.6 [10] for the transition from
Figure 1 with line numbers corresponding to Listing 1 (code for debugging has
been removed). The generated macros in principle allow the developer to influence the behavior (tight integration). But with automatically numbered variables
and already applied optimizations, the code is difficult to understand and differs
significantly from the original SDL specification.

3   SDL Runtime Environment

3.1   Abstract State Machines

Abstract State Machines are based on many-sorted first-order structures, called
states. A state consists of a signature containing sorts (also called domains),
function names and relational names, together with an interpretation of those
names. A state can be viewed as a memory that maps locations to values.

Rules describe the dynamic behavior of Abstract State Machines, by updating
locations in the memory. An important feature of ASMs is the parallel execution
of rules. Based on the current state, an update set, that is a set of memory
locations including the new values for these locations, is computed from these
rules. The new state is obtained from the previous state by applying all updates
in the update set at the same time. In order to execute rules sequentially, agent
modes are defined in the state of the ASM. Rule fragments can be guarded so
that hey only apply in their respective agent modes.

3.2   Mapping ASM to C++

The most widely used programming language in the telecommunications domain
is C, and therefore, it is not surprising that most tool chains for SDL generate C
code. In 1992, object oriented features were included in SDL, and with the latest
recommendation (SDL-2000), this development continued. As a consequence, we
have chosen C++ as the object oriented implementation language for SDL.

The focus for the development of an SDL runtime environment was the dynamic semantics of SDL, which is described in the Z.100 Annex F3. Other parts
such as the data semantics, necessary transformation, or ASN.1 coder were added

as considered necessary. For a systematic transformation from ASM to C++, we have applied the following rules.

Domains. In ASM describe types of elements, which are mapped to C++ classes. This also allows the definition of derived domains by the use of inheritance of classes. The following example points out this procedure.

$$\text{SIGNALINST} =_{def} \text{PLAINSIGNALINST} \cup \text{TIMERINST}$$

is represented in C++ as:

```
class PlainSignalInst : public SignalInst {
    ...
};
class TimerInst : public SignalInst {
    ...
};
```

The resulting behavior in C++ corresponds to the definition in ASM, since an element of SIGNALINST may be an element of a PLAINSIGNALINST or TIMERINST and all functions or macros defined on SIGNALINST can also be applied to the inherited classes.

Controlled functions. In ASM are represented by member variables of classes. Again the definition on multiple domains as shown in the following example can be expressed by inheritance of classes in C++.

controlled *owner*: AGENT ∪ STATENODE ∪ LINK → [*AGENT*]

In C++, the classes AGENT, STATENODE and LINK inherit from one class which contains *owner* as a member variable. All variables can store the special value *undefined*, which can be used as keyword in the ASM. It is also used to express an optional value, as in this example the optional return value from the domain AGENT.

All ASM **macros** are transformed to methods of classes. This assignment of methods to classes is possible, since either it is implicitly given by the description, or one of the macro parameters is an object on which an operation is performed. The following example FORWARDSIGNAL shows this transformation in line 5 of Listing 3. The macro DELETE is only defined on the domain GATE. Therefore, the method is implemented within the class Gate, and the second parameter *g* is redundant and can be removed.

The described transformations were performed manually to a subset of Z.100 F3. This subset is a language profile, which covers all language features of SDL-2000 that are necessary to support the execution of SDL-96 specifications. Currently, we are working on an automatic transformation of Z.100 F.3 or any language profile to this C++ representation.

The following example shows an excerpt from the ITU Recommendation Z.100 F.3 (2.1.1.3), the macro FORWARDSIGNAL, which is used to transport signals through an SDL system:

```
1   FORWARDSIGNAL ≡
2     if Self.from.queue ≠ empty then
3       let si = Self.from.queue.head in
4         if Applicable(si.signalType,si.toArg,si.viaArg,Self.from,Self) then
5           DELETE(si,Self.from)
6           INSERT(si,now+Self.delay,Self.to)
7           si.viaArg := si.viaArg \
8           { Self.from.gateAS1.nodeAS1ToId,
9             Self.channelAS1.nodeAS1ToId }
10        endif
11      endlet
12    endif
```

Listing 3. Excerpt from the Z.100 F.3 - Forward Signal

The resulting transformation to C++ retains the given structure by mapping all ASM macro calls onto corresponding C++ method calls. By the definition of more keywords, e.g., empty or self, it is possible to build an even more alike representation. However, this has been avoided to preserve the readability for C++ developers.

```
1   bool Link::ForwardSignal(void) {
2     if ( this->from->queue()->empty()==false ) {
3       SignalInst* si = this->from->queue()->head();
4       if(Applicable(si->signalType(),si->toArg,si->viaArg,this->from,this)) {
5         this->from->Delete(si);
6         this->to->Insert(si,this->delay);
7         si->viaArg.erase(this->from->Gate_name);
8         si->viaArg.erase(this->Agent_name);
9         return true;
10      }
11    }
12    return false;
13  }
```

Listing 4. Forward Signal transformed into C++

This example illustrates the straight transformation of an excerpt from the SDL recommendation to a C++ implementation. Most differences are simple rewrite rules from the ASM syntax to the C++ notation. Some operations as shown in line 7-9 were modified to achieve a higher performance, since the construction of a tuple for removal requires a memory allocation, which can be avoided by fragmentation of these operations into two calls. Because the name of links are given by the channel name, in line 8 the name of the link can be used for simplification.

Another important difference is the return value, which is added to this method in order to support an optimized execution of agents. The macro FORWARDSIGNAL is part of the program of a link agent, which forwards signals from one gate to another, if a signal is available. The return value of the method indicates whether the agent was able to perform the desired action. In case there is no signal, FORWARDSIGNAL returns false to inform the scheduler that no reasonable action can be performed until the state of the from-queue has changed. This optional optimization has been implemented, but will not be presented in this paper.

Figure 2 shows an excerpt from the ConTraST SDL runtime environment in C++ as an UML diagram. ASMRuntime controls the execution of all AGENTs within a given system by executing their program. Without any optimizations, the execution is performed in a sequential order. The three active components in SDL, SDLAGENT, SDLAGENTSET, and LINK, specialize the class AGENT and implement the virtual method *program()* in order to execute their assigned program.

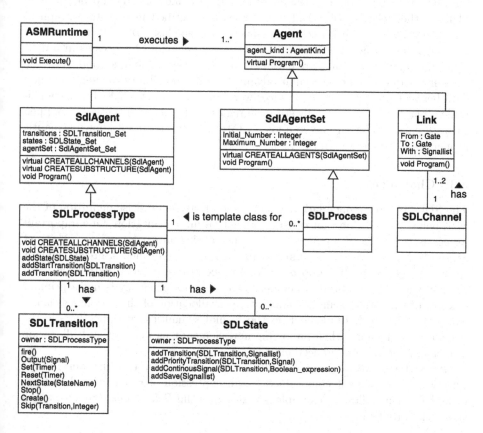

Fig. 2. Architecture of the ConTraST runtime environment and the abstract syntax

SDLAGENT defines the two virtual functions CREATEALLCHANNELS and CREATESUBSTRUCTURE, which are completed by inheritance of ConTraST to define the architecture of a given system. These methods are used during the recursive initialization of an SDL system within the macro INITAGENT.

The classes inheriting from SDLAGENT, SDLAGENTSET, and LINK define an abstract syntax, which is used by the transpiler to generate the code for a given SDL specification. In Figure 2, SDLProcess and SDLProcessType are shown as placeholders for systems, blocks and processes of SDL-96.

The combination of a given SDL-96 system transformed by ConTraST with runtime environment is given in the next step. The behavior of any process in SDL-96 is described by SDLProcessType. All instances of a given process type are managed by an SDL process, which represents a container of instances with a constraint to the actual number of instances. Therefore, SDLProcess inherits its functionality from SDLAGENTSET, whose role in SDL-2000 is a container managing all instances of SDLAGENTs within its scope. SDLAGENT and SDLA-GENTSET both contain state graphs describing the behavior of an SDL system, but since SDLAGENTSET is the surrounding container and has no behavior in SDL-96, the behavior of SDL-96 processes is described in the state graph of SDLAGENT. Thus, SDLProcessType specializes the class SDLAGENT.

In SDL-96, services are used to partition the behavior of processes into multiple state machines, which are executed in an interleaved manner and share the same input queue. One particular advantage is the possibility to share common data between state machines. Services were removed in SDL-2000, but a comparable replacement was given by state aggregation. Therefore services are mapped to state partitions with one composite state, which reflects all known semantic properties from services in SDL-96.

3.3 Challenges

The SDL-2000 recommendation Z.100 Annex F gives a precise definition of the SDL behavior, but does not consider an actual implementation. One important aspect is the memory management of the mathematical formalism. Abstract State Machines have access to an unlimited *reserve* of elements. Fresh elements from the reserve can be imported with the **extend**-statement, extending a domain of the Abstract State Machine. However, since efficiency is not a primary concern of the formal semantics definition, deallocation of these elements is not explicitly described. Implementing the formal semantics, we must handle the allocation of memory when importing new elements, as well as the deallocation of memory for all unreferenced elements.

ASMs offer powerful constructs such as **choose** and **take**, which permits the selection of an element constrained by an expression of propositional or first-order logic. The following example is taken from the *DeliverSignal* macro, which shows the problem:

choose sa: $sa \in$ SDLAGENT $\wedge$ $sa.owner = Self \wedge sa.self = si.toArg$

Here, an element from the domain SDLAGENT has to be chosen, which is the addressed receiver of the given signal si and whose owner (the surrounding agent) is the current executing agent. The main problem for imperative programming languages is to select an element of the given type SDLAGENT without having a reference to this object. Our solution for this example is shown below:

```
sa = agents.choose(si−>toArg);
if (sa != undefined) {  ...
```

Each agent keeps track of the elements within its scope. This is the same mechanism that AsmL [9] implements to allow the usage of e.g. choose.

In this example, we must examine the list *agents* in order to find objects of the domain SDLAGENT. This also assures the second constraint that the owning agent is *Self*. The last term concerning the receiver is then handled by the operation choose() to filter all elements according to the given expression. Additionally, the returned value must be checked, since the following rules must only be evaluated if the choose has returned an element.

Another specific characteristic of the ASM is the parallel execution of rules leading to a new state. The transformation of this into a sequential programming language must therefore analyze all rules for any dependencies. So far, dependencies have only been found in very few cases.

The definition of the dynamic behavior of SDL is based on the elementary data types such as sets and sequences with their corresponding operations as described in [5]. The foundation for the development of an SDL runtime environment therefore was the implementation of template classes describing the required data types and operations. Other data types used by the runtime environment, e.g., DURATION or PID, were also implemented as classes with a mapping to plain data types.

3.4   Execution

ConTraST generates, from a given SDL system specification, all required C++ source files and a makefile with references to the runtime environment. The source files already include a main function and the runtime environment contains a scheduler to execute all instantiated agents, which is by default in a sequential order. This execution may be influenced by numerous optional parameters to the compiler. For instance, an uninterrupted execution of a transition can be set (e.g., for debug purposes) or an optimized scheduling for agents without signals in their queues can be performed.

The complete execution is performed within one single thread, which guarantees the best portability among platforms, especially in case of embedded systems and micro controllers. The code may be compiled by various programs (e.g. Visual C++, Borland Compilers, gcc), and the executables were tested on Windows and Linux platforms. The execution has a deterministic behavior, except when using an *ANY* construct or when a real time clock is used for *Now*(), because all non-deterministic operations in the ASM (e.g. **choose**) always return the same result. Thus, one of all possible traces of an SDL system is actually executed.

If required, an SDLAGENT representing the SDL environment is automatically generated to allow the interaction with the environment (e.g. hardware drivers). The implementation of the environment interface has been modelled on the Telelogic environment functions [10]. Figure 3 shows an SDL description of the implemented behavior of the environment agent which calls the function *InitEnv*() to provide an opportunity for the environment to initialize its resources. For every signal from the SDL system, the function *OutEnv*() is executed with the signal as parameter. Sending of signals to the SDL system is achieved by the use of a continuous signal that calls the environment function *InEnv*().

The compatibility with Telelogic Tau allows the reuse of the already existing *SDL Environment Framework* [6], which provides access to several hardware drivers, communication technolgies, and operating system functions. This enabled us to specify systems with SDL, simulate the behavior within SDL, generate MSCs, but also build a target executable for various platforms with access to hardware. This executable may be also debugged by the use of a textual output displaying all required information. This covers the executing agent, the current state, fired transition, any behavior primitives, but also actions within the ASM program. Another possibility is to connect the executable to the MSC editor of Telelogic [10] and generate an MSC diagram of an actual execution. An additional benefit can

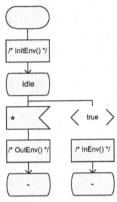

Fig. 3. SdlAgent for the environment

be taken by *ns*+SDL[7], a network simulator usable with ConTraST. This enables us to use SDL design specifications as basis for the simulation of multi-hop networks, and assures the same code base as for the production code.

4   Related Work

For SDL code generation, exist already some mostly commercial tools. Most of them generate plain C code, as the code generators *Cadvanced* and *Cmicro* of Telelogic tau [10]. Cinderella offers with Slipper [11] a code generator for C and also provides with SITE an implementation in C++. Other tools assign a special subject such as the Pragmadev Real Time Developer Studio [12], which covers real time subjects. All of them combine the aspect that the runtime environment is an adapted realisation of the SDL behavior.

Another interesting approach for SDL is the development of a compiler [8] producing a program that is then executed by the use of AsmL [9]. This solution enables automatic translation of the formal definition.

In our experience, that debugging of implemented SDL system is a fundamental part and parcel of our work with SDL. In recent years, we have identified various errors in runtime environments and ASN.1 code generators of commercial tools, but also had to handle different problems with the connection to the computer hardware. Therefore, a continuous traceability from a specified SDL system to the generated code and the implemented runtime environment gives the opportunity to fully understand the execution of SDL and improves the ability to locate errors in the implementation.

5 Conclusions

Development of ConTraST began in March 2005. The transpiler ConTraST and the associated runtime environment were tested in an educational context at the end of 2005. At this time, still major problems during code generation were detected, which have been corrected in the current version.

Additionally, some discrepancies between the formal and the concrete semantics of SDL have been identified during development of the runtime environment. For instance, during initialization of SDL systems, the loss of signals has been observed, which was corrected in coordination with the developers of the SDL formal semantics. Other major problems occurred during the implementation of the procedure calls, where return values and recursive calls of procedures pointed out new errors in the formal semantics. Thus, the development of ConTraST has provided valuable feedback.

The transformation of SDL/PR to C++ always attempts to obtain all object oriented features, by mapping them to corresponding constructs of the target language, e.g. in case of scope information, visibility of variables and the usage of templates to implement parameterized SDLAGENTSET. But the most interesting object oriented features of SDL, such as inheritance of objects, are still work in progress. While the implementation of virtual transitions is a rather simple venture, the realization of inheritance of e.g. processes will require more effort, since here static transformations of transitions are involved.

Today, ConTraST is used as an alternative to commercial tools in our group. Selected projects such as AdaI[1] and several student projects are used to examine the language coverage and to identify possible errors. Since all major issues for practical usage such as the implementation of data types and a BER encoding have been done, ConTraST and its runtime environment show an increasing usage.

As soon as usable graphical editors for the specification of SDL-2000 systems are available, the runtime environment may be extended by the use of language profiles to provide the execution of SDL-2000 systems. At this time, the automatic implementation of a C++ runtime environment, according to given language profiles, is a further research topic. This will pave the way for validation or prove of the correctness of the runtime environment.

In addition to the extension of the language coverage, studies about the execution performance have been done. With some applied optimizations, ConTraST did not show serious differences in execution time compared to the commercial tools. However, there still remain further possibilities to optimize the generated code. Another interesting objective is the multi-threaded implementation and the parallel execution of SDL systems by the usage of multiple CPUs. Here, the synchronization of the signal queues must be guaranteed.

---

[1] Thanks to Alexander Geraldy to support the development of ConTraST by his examples and tests.

References

1. ITU-T Recommendation Z.100 (11/00) - Specification and Description Language (SDL), International Telecommunication Union (ITU), (11/00)
2. ITU-T Recommendation Z.100 (10/96) - Specification and Description Language (SDL), International Telecommunication Union (ITU), (03/93) + (10/96)
3. C. Weber, Design And Implementation of a configurable SDL transpiler for a C++ runtime environment (in german), Diploma-Thesis, December 2005, TU Kaiserslautern, Germany
4. Grammes, R., Formal Operations for SDL Language Profiles, SAM06, 2006
5. Glässer, U., Gotzhein, R., Prinz, A., An introduction to abstract state machines, Technical Report 326/03, University of Kaiserslautern, 2003
6. Fliege, I., Geraldy, A., Konzept und Struktur des SDL Environment Frameworks (SEnF) (in german), Technical Report 341/05, University of Kaiserslautern, 2005
7. Kuhn, T., Geraldy, A., Gotzhein, R., Rothländer, F., ns+SDL - The Network Simulator for SDL Systems, in: A. Prinz, R. Reed, J.Reed (Eds.), SDL 2005 - Model Driven, Lecture Notes in Computer Science 3530, Springer, 2005, pp. 103-116
8. Prinz, A., von Löwis, M.: Generating a Compiler for SDL from the Formal Language Definition. In Reed, R., Reed, J., eds.: SDL 2003: System Design. Volume 2708 of LNCS., Springer (2003) pp. 150 - 165
9. Microsoft Research. AsmL. http://research.microsoft.com/fse/AsmL/
10. Telelogic Tau 4.6, http://www.telelogic.com/corp/products/tau/sdl/
11. Rauchwerger, Y., Kristoffersen, F., Lahav, Y.: Cinderella SLIPPER: An SDL to C-Code Generator. SDL Forum 2005: 210-223
12. Pragmadev Real Time Developer Studio, http://www.pragmadev.com/

Author Index

Lecture Notes in Computer Science

For information about Vols. 1–4244

please contact your bookseller or Springer

Vol. 4283: Y.Q. Shi, B. Jeon (Eds.), Digital Watermarking. XII, 474 pages. 2006.

Vol. 4282: Z. Pan, A. Cheok, M. Haller, R.W.H. Lau, H. Saito, R. Liang (Eds.), Advances in Artificial Reality and Tele-Existence. XXIII, 1347 pages. 2006.

Vol. 4281: K. Barkaoui, A. Cavalcanti, A. Cerone (Eds.), Theoretical Aspects of Computing - ICTAC 2006. XV, 371 pages. 2006.

Vol. 4280: A.K. Datta, M. Gradinariu (Eds.), Stabilization, Safety, and Security of Distributed Systems. XVII, 590 pages. 2006.

Vol. 4279: N. Kobayashi (Ed.), Programming Languages and Systems. XI, 423 pages. 2006.

Vol. 4278: R. Meersman, Z. Tari, P. Herrero (Eds.), On the Move to Meaningful Internet Systems 2006: OTM 2006 Workshops, Part II. XLV, 1004 pages. 2006.

Vol. 4277: R. Meersman, Z. Tari, P. Herrero (Eds.), On the Move to Meaningful Internet Systems 2006: OTM 2006 Workshops, Part I. XLV, 1009 pages. 2006.

Vol. 4276: R. Meersman, Z. Tari (Eds.), On the Move to Meaningful Internet Systems 2006: CoopIS, DOA, GADA, and ODBASE, Part II. XXXII, 752 pages. 2006.

Vol. 4275: R. Meersman, Z. Tari (Eds.), On the Move to Meaningful Internet Systems 2006: CoopIS, DOA, GADA, and ODBASE, Part I. XXXI, 1115 pages. 2006.

Vol. 4274: Q. Huo, B. Ma, E.-S. Chng, H. Li (Eds.), Chinese Spoken Language Processing. XXIV, 805 pages. 2006. (Sublibrary LNAI).

Vol. 4273: I. Cruz, S. Decker, D. Allemang, C. Preist, D. Schwabe, P. Mika, M. Uschold, L. Aroyo (Eds.), The Semantic Web - ISWC 2006. XXIV, 1001 pages. 2006.

Vol. 4272: P. Havinga, M. Lijding, N. Meratnia, M. Wegdam (Eds.), Smart Sensing and Context. XI, 267 pages. 2006.

Vol. 4271: F.V. Fomin (Ed.), Graph-Theoretic Concepts in Computer Science. XIII, 358 pages. 2006.

Vol. 4270: H. Zha, Z. Pan, H. Thwaites, A.C. Addison, M. Forte (Eds.), Interactive Technologies and Sociotechnical Systems. XVI, 547 pages. 2006.

Vol. 4269: R. State, S. van der Meer, D. O'Sullivan, T. Pfeifer (Eds.), Large Scale Management of Distributed Systems. XIII, 282 pages. 2006.

Vol. 4268: G. Parr, D. Malone, M. Ó Foghlú (Eds.), Autonomic Principles of IP Operations and Management. XIII, 237 pages. 2006.

Vol. 4267: A. Helmy, B. Jennings, L. Murphy, T. Pfeifer (Eds.), Autonomic Management of Mobile Multimedia Services. XIII, 257 pages. 2006.

Vol. 4266: H. Yoshiura, K. Sakurai, K. Rannenberg, Y. Murayama, S. Kawamura (Eds.), Advances in Information and Computer Security. XIII, 438 pages. 2006.

Vol. 4265: L. Todorovski, N. Lavrač, K.P. Jantke (Eds.), Discovery Science. XIV, 384 pages. 2006. (Sublibrary LNAI).

Vol. 4264: J.L. Balcázar, P.M. Long, F. Stephan (Eds.), Algorithmic Learning Theory. XIII, 393 pages. 2006. (Sublibrary LNAI).

Vol. 4263: A. Levi, E. Savaş, H. Yenigün, S. Balcısoy, Y. Saygın (Eds.), Computer and Information Sciences – ISCIS 2006. XXIII, 1084 pages. 2006.

Vol. 4262: K. Havelund, M. Núñez, B. Wolff. G. Roşu (Eds.), Formal Approaches to Software Testing and Runtime Verification. VIII, 255 pages. 2006.

Vol. 4261: Y. Zhuang, S. Yang, Y. Rui, Q. He (Eds.), Advances in Multimedia Information Processing - PCM 2006. XXII, 1040 pages. 2006.

Vol. 4260: Z. Liu, J. He (Eds.), Formal Methods and Software Engineering. XII, 778 pages. 2006.

Vol. 4259: S. Greco, Y. Hata, S. Hirano, M. Inuiguchi, S. Miyamoto, H.S. Nguyen, R. Słowiński (Eds.), Rough Sets and Current Trends in Computing. XXII, 951 pages. 2006. (Sublibrary LNAI).

Vol. 4257: I. Richardson, P. Runeson, R. Messnarz (Eds.), Software Process Improvement. XI, 219 pages. 2006.

Vol. 4256: L. Feng, G. Wang, C. Zeng, R. Huang (Eds.), Web Information Systems – WISE 2006 Workshops. XIV, 320 pages. 2006.

Vol. 4255: K. Aberer, Z. Peng, E.A. Rundensteiner, Y. Zhang, X. Li (Eds.), Web Information Systems – WISE 2006. XIV, 563 pages. 2006.

Vol. 4254: T. Grust, H. Höpfner, A. Illarramendi, S. Jablonski, M. Mesiti, S. Müller, P.-L. Patranjan, K.-U. Sattler, M. Spiliopoulou, J. Wijsen (Eds.), Current Trends in Database Technology – EDBT 2006. XXXI, 932 pages. 2006.

Vol. 4253: B. Gabrys, R.J. Howlett, L.C. Jain (Eds.), Knowledge-Based Intelligent Information and Engineering Systems, Part III. XXXII, 1301 pages. 2006. (Sublibrary LNAI).

Vol. 4252: B. Gabrys, R.J. Howlett, L.C. Jain (Eds.), Knowledge-Based Intelligent Information and Engineering Systems, Part II. XXXIII, 1335 pages. 2006. (Sublibrary LNAI).

Vol. 4251: B. Gabrys, R.J. Howlett, L.C. Jain (Eds.), Knowledge-Based Intelligent Information and Engineering Systems, Part I. LXVI, 1297 pages. 2006. (Sublibrary LNAI).

Vol. 4250: H.J. van den Herik, S.-C. Hsu, T.-s. Hsu, H.H.L.M. Donkers (Eds.), Advances in Computer Games. XIV, 273 pages. 2006.

Vol. 4249: L. Goubin, M. Matsui (Eds.), Cryptographic Hardware and Embedded Systems - CHES 2006. XII, 462 pages. 2006.

Vol. 4248: S. Staab, V. Svátek (Eds.), Managing Knowledge in a World of Networks. XIV, 400 pages. 2006. (Sublibrary LNAI).

Vol. 4247: T.-D. Wang, X. Li, S.-H. Chen, X. Wang, H. Abbass, H. Iba, G. Chen, X. Yao (Eds.), Simulated Evolution and Learning. XXI, 940 pages. 2006.

Vol. 4246: M. Hermann, A. Voronkov (Eds.), Logic for Programming, Artificial Intelligence, and Reasoning. XIII, 588 pages. 2006. (Sublibrary LNAI).

Vol. 4245: A. Kuba, L.G. Nyúl, K. Palágyi (Eds.), Discrete Geometry for Computer Imagery. XIII, 688 pages. 2006.